LIABILITY ISSUES IN COMMUNITY-BASED PROGRAMS

LIABILITY ISSUES IN COMMUNITY-BASED PROGRAMS
LEGAL PRINCIPLES, PROBLEM AREAS, AND RECOMMENDATIONS

by

Alan VanBiervliet, Ph.D.
Lecturer
Clinical and Special Services Unit
Department of Education
University of Otago
Dunedin, New Zealand
and
Department of Human Development and Family Life
and Bureau of Child Research
University of Kansas

and

Jan Sheldon-Wildgen, Ph.D., J.D.
Assistant Professor
Department of Human Development and Family Life
and
Research Associate
Bureau of Child Research
University of Kansas

·P·A·U·L·H·
BROOKES
PUBLISHING CO

Baltimore • London

Paul H. Brookes Publishing Co.
Post Office Box 10624
Baltimore, Maryland 21204

Typeset by Brushwood Graphics, Baltimore, Maryland.
Manufactured in the United States of America by
Universal Lithographers, Inc., Cockeysville, Maryland.

The information and recommendations contained in this publication were
derived from the most current and authoritative sources known to the authors
and publisher at the time this book went to press. In no way should the recommendations presented here be regarded as a substitute for knowledgeable
legal counsel. The reader seeking legal advice or expert interpretation of the
law is urged to consult with an attorney or other professional advocate well
versed in the subject matter of concern.

Library of Congress Cataloging in Publication Data
VanBiervliet, Alan, 1953–
    Liability issues in community-based programs.

    Bibliography: p.
    Includes index.
    1. Tort liability of social service agencies—United States.
I. Sheldon-Wildgen, Jan, 1949–   joint author. II. Title.
KF1311.V36   346.7303'3   81-245
ISBN 0-933716-08-7   AACR1

CONTENTS

PREFACE

This book is a guide to legal liability issues facing persons who are developing, operating, or monitoring community-based residential or day training agencies that serve physically or mentally impaired persons, or juveniles. As a result of a lack of understanding about negligence and about their legal responsibilities, service agency administrators often make unnecessary mistakes that jeopardize their clients' well-being and that unwittingly expose the agency and themselves to lawsuits. This book provides a practical approach to the legal principles surrounding negligence and other liability issues as they apply to community-based service agencies. In addition, this book provides recommendations for helping persons in community-based agencies conduct their operations in ways that will help them minimize injuries, avoid destructive lawsuits, and conduct positive programs that enable the clients to cope with personal and environmental demands. By conducting community agencies in this way, pitfalls that might otherwise occur may be avoided. *Acquiring an accurate understanding of the legal issues involved in community-based services is both a professional and an ethical requirement.*

There are many liability issues common to a majority of community-based agencies. Some minor differences may exist between the principles of law presented here and those adhered to in your state or locality. Different jurisdictions and administrative officials also vary in their interpretations of the laws at any given time. In addition, the laws governing agencies serving persons in need are changing so rapidly that it is difficult for administrators to keep abreast of the changes. We urge administrators and developers of community-based agencies to seek the advice and assistance of a local attorney with a special interest in and knowledge of laws concerning the center's clients. In no way is this book intended to serve as a substitute for knowledgeable legal counsel.

The information and the recommendations in this book were derived from the most current and accurate sources known to the authors. There is no guarantee that following the recommendations in this book will completely protect an agency against lawsuits, or that all injuries to clients, staff, or others will be averted. If, however, an agency adopts the recommendations discussed here, that agency should be well on its way toward developing a safe, effective program.

Only general recommendations are made because persons served by community centers are heterogeneous with widely differing abilities and needs. Care must be taken to ensure that the community center's safety precautions adequately meet the needs of the clients, staff, and agency. Thus, the recommendations made in this book may need considerable modification before they will meet the needs of a particular community center. In addition, some of the liability questions facing certain community centers may not have been adequately answered in this book, either because the issues have not been clearly addressed by the courts or legislatures or because conflicts currently exist between jurisdictions. It is our hope, however, that the general principles that we have discussed will help agencies to deal appropriately with these situations.

Although this book is primarily intended to serve as a guide for persons directly involved with the operation of community-based services, it is also intended to serve as a reference source for lawyers, insurance company representatives, and other professionals concerned with community-based agencies or disability law. In addition, due to the burgeoning interest in rehabilitating debilitated elderly citizens, the issues discussed in this book are important for developers and administrators of geriatric services. The content of this book also makes it useful as a reference source or supplementary text for college and university courses in administration, community health services, law, personnel management, rehabilitation, social and applied psychology, social welfare, special education, and other courses concerned with planning and providing community-based service programs.

ACKNOWLEDGMENTS

No book is ever written without the help of numerous people, many of whom often go unrecognized, yet all of whom are appreciated. Although it is impossible to list all those who, in one way or another, made this book possible, we would like to acknowledge the following people. The faculty, staff, and students of the Department of Human Development and Family Life and the Bureau of Child Research at the University of Kansas continually supported the authors during the preparation of this manuscript; their patience and encouragement have been highly valued. Several people, including Flora Thompson, Kelly Cox, Marcie Cumpton, Joy Hatfield, Julia Saenz, and Margaret Laube, patiently and persistently typed and retyped various forms of the manuscript; a very special thanks goes to each of them. We would also like to thank Bob Hoyt who was instrumental in helping us pursue publication of the book. We are especially grateful to Melissa Behm, who gently prodded us along and who polished the manuscript with her excellent editorial skills, and to Paul Brookes, who saw the need for this book and who stayed with it in spite of numerous setbacks. The authors also appreciate the contributions made by the staff at Concerned Care, Inc., in Kansas City, Missouri, and at Achievement Place at the University of Kansas. Finally, we will remain indebted to our colleagues, Jim Sherman, Joe Spradlin, Paula VanBiervliet, Karl Morris, Barbara Griggs, Randy Kindred, John Anthony, and Peter Griggs whose input is reflected throughout the book.

A Note on Style

Several points regarding this book are called to the reader's attention:

1. Throughout the book, all residential agencies (e.g., group homes, half-way houses, and boarding homes), day training agencies (e.g., educational, vocational, and sheltered work programs), and any combination of such programs that are intended to habilitate or rehabilitate small numbers of physically or mentally disabled persons, or juveniles, in a community setting are referred to with the general term of *community center.*
2. The term *client* is used to refer to the primary consumer of a community center's services. If the point being made refers specifically to a particular type of client, then a more precise descriptor is used.
3. Many of the cases that are mentioned in this book are still subject to revision by the courts as the cases are appealed and new decisions are reached. Those readers who wish to use the facts and/or conclusions of a particular case should determine the current status of the case before doing so.
4. In discussing the legal principles and explaining legal terminology, the authors have attempted to be as thorough as possible without unduly burdening the reader. For an explanation of some of the finer nuances concerning these legal principles, the reader is encouraged to refer to a hornbook on the subject of torts.

To my father and mother, to my wife, Paula, and to my friend and adviser, Joe Spradlin, for their encouragement, assistance, and constant support.

A.VB.

To my parents, whose love and support throughout the years taught me that nothing was impossible, and to Jim, C., and B., whose patience and encouragement helped me to pursue what often seemed like the impossible.

J.S.-W.

To all the clients with whom we have worked and who, unknowingly, provided the impetus to write this book.

A.VB. & J.S.-W.

Liability Issues in
Community-Based Programs

1

INTRODUCTION

"I'm gonna sue you!" This statement was directed at one of the authors by a mentally retarded youth with whom the author was working. When the youth was questioned by the author, it became apparent that the youth did not understand what the statement meant. Such a statement does, however, indicate a current trend in the mental health field. As a means of redressing the wrongs or presumed wrongs committed upon clients by mental health and social service agencies and their employees, clients and their representatives have turned to the judicial system. In fact, the movement toward the utilization of the least restrictive environment for habilitation[1] has accelerated as a result of well known lawsuits, such as *Lake v. Cameron,*[2] *Wyatt v. Stickney,*[3] and *Halderman v. Pennhurst State School and Hospital.*[4]

Repp (1977) has pointed out an increasing tendency in the last decade to hold mental health personnel accountable for the services they are paid to provide. The public is now scrutinizing all aspects of the service delivery systems within institutions and the full spectrum of activities within the community at large (Friedman, 1976). This examination often results in lawsuits. Melcher (1976) has predicted that lawsuits against schools, educators, support personnel, and administrators will continue to increase over the next 10 years. In the 1973 version of "Case Law and the Education of the Handicapped," Collings and Singletary reported 39 cases of existing litigation involving exceptional children. In the 1977 update, the authors reported over 100 cases, many of which were still in process. This is a dramatic increase in lawsuits involving handicapped individuals. Rothblatt and Leroy (1973) reported a boom in both the frequency of psychiatric malpractice lawsuits and in the dollar amount of settlements. They reported almost a threefold increase in the number of psychiatric malpractice cases between 1951 and 1960, compared to the period of 1961–1971. These lawsuits often result in devastating judgments of hundreds of thousands of dollars against agencies and professionals. As an example, in 1964 a court in New Jersey awarded a young man over $1,000,000 for crippling injuries he suffered in a physical education class.[5] This sum represented a substantial part of the annual district outlay for the education of the 21,000 students in the school district.

Over the past 20 years, there has been a growing movement in the health and social services fields toward the creation of community-based alternatives to institutional care. Community placement has affected the treatment of mentally and physically disabled persons and juveniles by both governmental and private service agencies. Several federal legislative acts, such as the Mental Retardation Facilities and Community Mental Health Centers Construction Act of 1963[6] and the Developmental Disabilities Services and Facilities Construction Amendments of 1970,[7] have been passed in order to encourage and provide support for the establishment of community programs. Various types of programs have already been established and many more will be established intending to meet the unique needs of disabled persons and juveniles.

Potentially dangerous situations exist for community centers because they may be held legally responsible for any injury that results from the center staff's failure to use reasonable care in their conduct toward clients, staff, or the general public. This danger is increasing due partially to the following factors: 1) increased public scrutiny of the activities of service agencies, 2) the current general propensity to sue, 3) community agencies' attempts to provide their clients with the least restrictive environment for habilitation, and 4) more severely and profoundly disabled individuals being served by community centers. In addition, problems have occurred with community centers, such as inappropriate evaluation and selection of clients, as a result of the rapid, and sometimes hurried, manner in which some community centers have developed. In community centers, individuals who had been secluded from the rest of society most of their lives are now being expected to cope with the same daily hazards faced by most citizens. For example, previously institutionalized individuals must now face danger from vehicular traffic and the danger of burns or lacerations incurred during food preparation. Some accidents are bound to occur, despite all measures taken to prevent them. Therefore, in addition to accident prevention, an agency must be prepared to reduce the degree of damage caused by accidents. In attempting to prevent accidents and to lessen the degree of damage, however, community centers must not lose sight of the objective of providing the kinds of services for disabled individuals that will help them achieve their fullest potential.

One of the most important considerations in the development of group homes, boarding houses, sheltered workshops, or any other community center for disabled individuals or juveniles is the protection of the health and well-being of the clients, the staff, and the public from undue risk of harm without overprotecting the clients. If a community center adopts highly restrictive and protective policies, their clients may have no more opportunity to develop independence and autonomy in the community than they would in an institution. Nevertheless, the large settlements and the adverse publicity resulting from lawsuits can essentially ruin a community center that becomes liable for an accident. For protection against lawsuits, the administrators of community centers and others involved in establishing community centers should inform themselves about the basic legal principles concerning liability lawsuits, and they should develop safeguards to help prevent injuries. The following chapters present basic legal principles related to negligence (the primary basis for liability lawsuits) and examples of lawsuits resulting from "accidents." In addition, a series of recommendations is presented concerning ways a community center can develop an effective habilitation or rehabilitation program while protecting the clients, the staff, and the general public from undue risk of harm without unnecessarily overprotecting clients and hindering their progress toward self-actualization and independence. In cases where it seems appropriate, the actions of the courts have been related to potentially dangerous situations in a variety of community centers and ways have been highlighted in which community center personnel and administrators can recognize hazards and prevent accidents that may lead to legal action.

REFERENCES

Appenzeller, H. *From the gym to the jury.* Charlotteville, VA: The Michie Co., 1970.

Collings, G.D., & Singletary, E.E. Case law and education of the handicapped. *Florida Education Research and Development Council Research Bulletin,* 1973, *8*(3).

Friedman, P.R. *The rights of mentally retarded persons.* New York: Avon Books, 1976.

Melcher, J.W. Law, litigation, and handicapped children. *Exceptional Children,* 1976, *43,* 126–130.

Repp, A.C. An accountability system in behavioral programs for the severely and profoundly handicapped. In B. Wilcox, F. Kohl, & T. Vogelsberg (eds.), *The severely and profoundly handicapped child: Proceedings from the 1977 Statewide Institute for Educators of the Severely and Profoundly Handicapped.* Illinois State Board of Education, 1977.

Rothblatt, H.B., & Leroy, D.H. Avoiding psychiatric malpractice. *California Western Law Review,* 1973, *9,* 260–272.

Singletary, E.E., & Collings, G.D. *Case law and the education of the handicapped—Update one.* Gainesville, FL: Florida Educational Research and Development Council, Inc., 1977.

ENDNOTES

[1]"[H]abilitation—the process by which the staff of the institution [or community center] assists the resident to acquire and maintain these life skills which enable him to cope more effectively with the demands of his own person and of his environment and to raise the level of his physical, mental, and social efficiency." *Wyatt v. Stickney,* 344 F. Supp. 387, 395 (M.D. Ala. 1972).

[2]364 F. 2d 657 (D.C. C. 1967).

[3]344 F. Supp. 387 (M.D. Ala. 1972).

[4]446 F. Supp. 1295 (E.D. Pa. 1977).

⁵Miller v. Cloidt and the Board of Education of the Borough of Chatham, Docket No. L. 7241–62 (N.J. Sup. Ct. 1964). Reported in Appenzeller (1970).

⁶P.L. 88–164; 77 Stat. 282.

⁷P.L. 89–105; 79 Stat. 427.

2

LEGAL ISSUES CONCERNING NEGLIGENCE

"Today the commonplace charge leveled at all professionals is negligence" (Dooley, 1977, Vol. 2, p. 454). A large percentage of the lawsuits involving injury-causing "accidents" fall into the category of negligence. *Negligence* is legal shorthand for the failure of a person to act as a reasonable, prudent, and careful person would act under similar circumstances to avoid exposing others to unreasonable risk of injury (Gifis, 1975). If the injury is alleged to have resulted from an action or an inaction of a professional, such as a teacher or a doctor, in the performance of his or her duties, then the term *malpractice* rather than negligence applies. Acts of negligence and malpractice are non-criminal civil wrongs called *torts*.[1] In a tort case, the court has the authority to require the defendant[2] to remedy the situation caused by the negligent act. Usually this remedy is in the form of a cash award paid to the plaintiff[3] by the defendant.

The underlying principle of negligence is that an injured party is entitled to collect damages from those who cause the injury. In order for the court to award a settlement to the plaintiff, the plaintiff must prove four elements by a preponderance of the evidence.[4] These elements are: 1) the defendant owed the plaintiff a duty[5] to conform to a particular standard of conduct that would not have subjected the plaintiff to an unreasonable risk of injury, 2) the defendant breached that duty to the plaintiff, 3) the plaintiff suffered an actual injury, and 4) the act of the defendant was the direct or proximate cause of the injury (Dooley, 1977, Vol. 1). It should be noted that once a court renders a verdict against a defendant and damages are awarded, the plaintiff has a right to levy an attachment on certain real estate, bank accounts, and other assets of the defendant in order to recover payment.

THE DUTY

Both the community center staff and teachers have a relationship with clients or students that involves a certain degree of trust and confidence. This relationship helps to establish the staff's legally enforceable duty to each client. Often, a large part of the staff's responsibilities in a community-based program is to act as teachers, thus providing educational experiences. These educational experiences may involve anything from basic self-help skills training to teaching acceptable forms of sexual behaviors. Thus, in many ways the staff-client relationship is similar to the teacher-student relationship. The courts have ruled that teachers and their school boards have a duty to protect persons under their supervision from an unreasonable risk of harm.[6] The Pennsylvania Superior Court in *Bottorf v. Waltz*[7] stated that, due to the teacher-student relationship, teachers owe students three basic duties:

1. To provide adequate supervision
2. To exercise good judgment
3. To provide proper instruction, particularly when potentially hazardous conditions exist

The contracts a community center makes with funding agencies may also state that the community center and its personnel have a duty to protect clients from unreasonable harm. Additionally, it would appear likely that clients would occupy the legal status of "business visitor".[8] As "business visitors," a duty is owed to warn the clients adequately about the dangers that are present and to make the premises reasonably free from dangerous conditions or activities (Prosser, 1971). A more obvious duty would exist in residential programs where the clients and staff live together and where clients may be somewhat dependent on the staff for certain essential needs and may trust that the staff will not allow them to encounter unnecessary dangers. With these issues in mind, it is clear that community centers and their staffs have a legally enforceable duty to protect each individual from an unreasonable risk of harm.

ESTABLISHING A STANDARD OF CARE AND ITS BREACH

In general, the standard of care to which courts have held an individual responsible has been to act as a reasonable, prudent, and careful person. Regarding physically and mentally handicapped clients, an even greater degree of care is required to take into account the client's limitations (Dooley, 1977, Vol. 1). The courts have said that where a reasonable, prudent, and careful person would anticipate danger or an accident under the existing circumstances, it is negligent to permit those circumstances to continue without taking remedial action.[9] The key to determining what comprises reasonably prudent and careful action is the foreseeability of the potential danger and the probability that an injury will occur. If the conduct that caused the injury was not intended to cause an injury, and if the occurrence of an injury could not have been foreseen or prevented by the use of reasonable precautions, then the court would consider the injury to be the result of an unavoidable accident. Typically, the court would not hold a defendant responsible for injuries resulting from such an unavoidable accident (Leibee, 1965). For example, in *West v. Board of Education of the City of New York*,[10] a teacher had requested that a child pick up a paper bag on the school grounds. The child was cut by a piece of broken glass that was concealed in the bag. The court ruled that the teacher and the school board were not negligent because the latent danger could not have been reasonably foreseen. Even if harm is not intended, however, if the injury is *foreseeable,* liability may be imposed.

In most negligence cases, determining the standard of conduct is the responsibility of the jury or judge. Factors such as age, maturity, intelligence, previous behavior of the plaintiff, and the social value of the action in question may bear on the degree of care the defendant should have exercised. In particular cases, the courts may even look to statutes and administrative regulations for the standard of care expected. For example, in *Peter W. v. San Francisco Unified School District,*[11] a court in California examined provisions of the California Education Code for a standard to judge the teachers and the school district in a case concerning the appropriateness of the plaintiff's educational experiences.

In cases concerning the *professional treatment* of a client, a judge or lay jury would presumably lack the necessary knowledge and expertise to determine the appropriate standard of conduct. The judge's or jury's decision in these cases is guided by the testimony of witnesses with special or expert qualifications. An academic degree per se does not automatically justify a professional's testimony for acceptance as expert evidence; rather, it is the person's unique qualifications, including education, training, work experiences, publications, and other accomplishments in the specialty area, that are weighed and considered by the court (Woody, 1974). A greater amount of latitude in answering questions is given to expert witnesses as compared to lay witnesses. Lay witnesses are limited to testifying about actual events that they have seen or heard, whereas expert witnesses are allowed to give opinions about hypothetical events or occurrences with which they have had no direct contact. The court normally believes that expert witnesses are qualified to give this type of testimony because of their expertise in the area being questioned. Both the plaintiff and the defendants may present expert witnesses, who may give conflicting testimony. In such a situation, the judge or jury must exercise personal discretion in utilizing the testimony. (For further information concerning expert witnesses, the reader can refer to Allen, Ferster, and Rubin (1968), Brodsky and Robey (1972), and Pacht, Kuehn, Basset, and Nash (1973).) In addition to qualified professionals providing expert testimony, information from books may also be introduced into evidence as expert testimony. The Federal Rules of Evidence[12] permit an attorney in a federal case to take statements from books, written by individuals who have been demonstrated to be reliable authorities on the topic in question, and enter these statements into the court record as expert testimony. Several states have adopted the Federal Rules of Evidence, so that "book testimony" is available in several state courts as well.

In a negligence case concerning the conduct of a community center or its employees, the court would probably rely upon the testimony of experts (e.g., other administrators of community centers or professional workers in the field) in order to determine the appropriate standard of conduct. Historically, the standard established by expert testimony has been the standard of the community in which the injury occurred (Dooley, 1977, Vol. 1). More recently, the courts have required professionals to abide by statewide or nationwide professional standards, particularly if the local standards expose the client to an unreasonable risk of harm. A basic postulate to remember concerning community standards is that no amount of adherence to an inadequate community standard can absolve anyone from negligence simply because he or she adhered to the community standard (Gottlieb, 1972).

One exception to the general rule that expert testimony is required to establish the standard of conduct in a malpractice lawsuit occurs in cases where the matter under investigation is so simple and the lack of professional care is so obvious as to be within the range of experience and comprehension of a lay jury (Dooley, 1977, Vol. 2). In *Hammer v. Rosen,*[13] the New York Court of Appeals held that expert testimony was not necessary to establish negligence because the treatment in question was a form of aggressive psychoanalytic therapy that involved striking the client whenever the psychiatrist decided such blows were appropriate. The client later filed suit claiming that the therapy constituted negligent treatment. A lower court ruled in favor of the psychiatrist because the plaintiff failed to produce expert testimony to show that the mode of therapy did not conform to the professional standard of conduct. The court of appeals reversed the decision stating that expert testimony was not necessary in this case because laypersons could determine that the treatment constituted negligence. Subsequently, the psychiatrist was held liable for the injuries to this client.

A second exception to the expert testimony requirement involves the doctrine of *res ipsa loquitur*, "the thing speaks for itself." This doctrine is permitted to be invoked when:

1. An injury occurs that would not have occurred unless someone had been negligent
2. The conduct or mechanism that caused the injury was within the exclusive control of the defendant
3. The plaintiff must not have done anything that could in any way have contributed to the injury (Prosser, 1971)

If the plaintiff presents satisfactory evidence that these three elements exist, then the defendant will be found negligent unless the defendant can prove otherwise.

This discussion of the legal standard of care should not unduly alarm professionals or paraprofessionals working in community programs. The courts will not hold an individual liable for an injury that results from a mere error in judgment if that judgment is made in accordance with acceptable procedures. In a well known case, the California Supreme Court stated that a therapist is free to exercise his or her own best judgment, within the broad range of reasonable practice and treatment in which professional opinion and judgment may differ, without fear of liability.[14] Hindsight evidence that an individual acted wrongly is insufficient evidence to establish negligence. The level of skill, training, diligence, and care the law requires of an individual is that possessed by an average member in good standing of the profession or occupation. The court, in *Pike v. Honsinger*,[15] in discussing the obligations doctors owe to their patients, stated that "[t]he rule requiring [the doctor] to use [the doctor's] best judgment does not hold [the doctor] liable for a mere error in judgment, provided [the doctor] does what [the doctor] thinks is best after careful examination. . . . [The doctor] does not guarantee a good result, but does promise . . . to exercise reasonable care and to exert [the doctor's] best judgment in an effort to bring about a good result" (p. 762).

A similar obligation is owed to the clients of community centers. An example of the court's unwillingness to find professionals guilty of negligence for a sincere error in professional judgment can be found in *Eanes v. U.S.*[16] In this case a V.A. patient, while on a 15-day trial home visit, attacked and seriously injured his wife. The wife filed suit against the Veterans Administration and its staff claiming that they were negligent for allowing her husband to leave the hospital. A trial court decided, and the U.S. Court of Appeals affirmed the decision, that there was no actionable negligence on the part of the V.A. or its staff, since they could not have reasonably foreseen the patient's violent actions in light of his preceding good behavior which had earned him the home visit privilege. Furthermore, the Court of Appeals recognized that an "open door" or reintegration treatment policy entails a certain degree of risk of harm to the patient and to others. Nevertheless, the court felt that taking such risks was justified when the risks are balanced against the value these enlightened policies have for mentally ill persons.

Once the standard of care is established in a negligence trial, it is then necessary to show that the defendant had not adhered to that standard in the injury-causing event. An expert witness is usually not needed to furnish this information. Any admissible testimony or evidence that illustrates how the defendant actually behaved toward the plaintiff can be used for this purpose.

PROOF OF AN INJURY

The third element that must be proved by a preponderance of the evidence is that the plaintiff has indeed suffered an injury. This is typically limited to injuries to the physical person or to tangible property. In addition, the plaintiff may seek compensation for related injuries, such as:

1. Physical harm resulting from fright or shock or other similar or immediate emotional disturbances caused by the injury or the negligent conduct.
2. For additional bodily harm resulting from acts done by third persons in rendering aid irrespective of whether such acts are done in a proper or a negligent manner.
3. Any disease which is contracted because of a lowered vitality resulting from the injury caused by the negligent conduct.
4. Harm sustained in a subsequent accident which would not have occurred had the person's bodily efficiency not been impaired by the original negligence (National Education Association Research Division, 1963, p. 15).

More recently, a majority of jurisdictions have allowed recovery, under certain circumstances, for negligently induced mental distress or psychological disorder in the absence of actual physical impact or injury to the plaintiff (Dooley, 1977, Vol. 1). The plaintiff may also request compensation for the loss of earnings and for the loss of future earning power. Expert testimony, such as the testimony of a doctor or psychiatrist, is usually required to support the plaintiff's claim of an injury.

THE CAUSATION

Once the duty, the deviation from the standard of care, and the existence of an injury are established, the plaintiff must prove that the defendant's departure from the proper practice was the direct or proximate cause of the injuries or that it precipitated or aggravated the plaintiff's condition. Expert testimony is usually required to prove causation except when the situation involved is readily apparent or within the common knowledge of the layman, or when the previously discussed doctrine of *res ipsa loquitur* can be applied.

In most negligence cases in the United States, the "but-for" test has been an adequate criterion of causation. The "but-for" test involves determining whether or not the injury would have occurred but-for the defendant's actions. If the injury would not have occurred but-for the defendant's actions, then the defendant's actions have a causal relationship with the injury (Leibee, 1965). In order for the defendant's act to be declared negligent, this causal relationship must involve a natural and continuous sequence, unbroken except for events that result from the defendant's action (Dooley, 1977, Vol. 1). An example of a break in this causal chain can be found in *Harris v. State of Ohio*.[17] In this case, the Ohio Court of Claims ruled that the state was not liable for injuries sustained by the victim of an assault by a man who had been released from a state mental hospital 2 years before the assault occurred. The plaintiff contended that had it not been for the man's release, he could not have assaulted the plaintiff with a revolver and shot him seven times. The court concluded that the assault could not have been reasonably foreseen and that the patient's actions were not the natural and probable consequences of the release, considering the variety of events that occurred in the 2-year period between the release and the assault.

RESPONDEAT SUPERIOR[18]

Another legal principle involved in negligence concerns the responsibilities of an employer. An employer can be held legally responsible for injuries caused by an employee that occur within the scope of employment. For example, in *Kent v. Whitaker,*[19] the Supreme Court of Washington found the superintendent of a county hospital personally liable in the amount of $10,000 for the suicide of a patient. Even though the superintendent did not personally direct the care of the patient, he was required by statute to perform the administrative services of the hospital, including hiring and supervising the direct care staff. The court held that the superintendent was legally responsible for the negligence of the hospital staff. The doctrine of employer responsibility has been called *respondeat superior,* vicarious liability, and imputed liability.

Common law and statutes impose various duties upon employers. Some of an employer's obligations are:

1. To make frequent and adequate inspections of work areas, machinery and appliances used in the business
2. To repair, within a reasonable amount of time, any latent defects
3. To promulgate, implement, and enforce reasonable safety rules and regulations
4. To hire reasonable careful, competent employees
5. To dismiss employees, who through their actions, present a threat of harm to other employees or clients (Mirabel and Levy, 1962)

An employer must fulfill these obligations to the same degree as would a reasonably prudent and careful person under similar circumstances. If an injury occurs as a result of the employer's failure to perform these duties adequately, the employer may be held legally responsible for any resulting injury. Obviously, there are situations in which an employee would not be responsible for an employee's actions such as instances in which the employee wantonly disregards clearly specified policies, procedures, or instructions or engages in some non–job-related activity.

LEGAL DEFENSES AGAINST NEGLIGENCE

Even though the defendant's actions appear to be the proximate cause of the injury, there are several types of mitigating circumstances. Three of these are:

1. When an uncontrollable and unforeseeable intervening act has occurred.
2. When the plaintiff has assumed the risk involved prior to engaging in the activity in question.
3. When the plaintiff contributes to the injury by failing to act as a reasonably careful and prudent person.

If any of these events has occurred, the defendant may be exempted or partially exempted from the liability resulting from the negligent act.

Intervening Event

In order for an intervening event to exempt the defendant from liability it must satisfy four criteria. There criteria are:

1. The intervening event cannot be reasonably foreseen by the defendant
2. The event altered the outcome of the defendant's original act from the outcome that would have occurred in the absence of the event
3. The intervening event occurs independent of the defendant's action
4. The defendant's action alone would not have resulted in an injury (Leibee, 1965)

In other words, if an event is the normal outcome of the situation caused by the defendant or if the defendant should have foreseen the occurrence of the event, the event would not be considered as the superseding cause of the injury. An illustration of an intervening cause that relieved the defendant of liability can be found in *Meyer v. Board of Education, Middletown Township.*[20] While a student was cleaning a jigsaw, a second student turned the machine on. The student's finger was caught and injured in the unguarded belt-drive mechanism of the jigsaw. The school board was subsequently accused of negligence for failing to provide the mechanism with a safety guard. During the trial, it was established that the shop teacher had conducted and maintained an adequate safety program and that turning on the machine without proper warning was clearly in violation of known safety regulations. The court ruled that the second student's act of turning on the machine was an unforeseeable independent intervening act and that the school's failure to equip the machine with a guard was not the proximate cause of the accident.

Another example of the intervening event defense can be found in *Fagan v. Summers.*[21] In this case, the Supreme Court of Wyoming affirmed a lower court's ruling in favor of the defendants. The lawsuit was brought by the parents of a 7-year-old boy who was partially blinded by a small rock. The rock, which had been thrown by a fellow student, was deflected by a larger rock on the ground and struck the boy's eye. The teacher's aide in charge of the noon recess had walked by the group of boys approximately 30 seconds before the accident occurred and observed nothing out of the ordinary. The court found that the aide had not acted improperly in her supervision of the youths, and that even if the court were to assume that the school district was negligent for having the rocks in the playground, the injury was caused by the intervening act of the rock throwing and that neither the school district nor the aide was liable.

Assumption of Risk

In situations where the plaintiff has ventured into the injury-causing relationship or situation voluntarily and with an understanding of the foreseeable hazards, the defendant may be relieved of the legal responsibility for any resulting injuries (Dooley, 1977, Vol. 1). This defense was used in *Timmins v. State*[22] where the plaintiff claimed that the erroneous professional judgment of a mental hospital and its staff resulted in the wrongful death of her daughter. The young girl was killed by the plaintiff's husband (the young girl's father) while he was on a temporary visit from a state mental hospital. When the hospital's psychiatrists granted permission for the visit, they had stipulated that the patient was to stay with his brother. He was not to be allowed to visit his wife or children, who lived in another city, for fear that he might cause them harm. The patient's family had agreed to those terms at the onset of the visit. Later, however, the terms of the visit were modified by the patient's family, without notifying the hospital, and a meeting was arranged between the patient and his daughter. This meeting resulted in the daughter's death. The court ruled that in modifying the terms of the visit without the hospital's authorization, the patient's family was assuming the inherent risk of harm and, therefore, neither the hospital nor its staff was liable for the girl's unfortunate death.

The demonstration that prior to the injury the injured party voluntarily consented to relieve the defendant from the duty to protect the injured party from unreasonable risks of injury is critical to the assumption of risk defense (Leibee, 1965). The existence of the consent can be shown by an agreement between the individuals involved, or consent can be implied by the court from the conduct of the injured person. Consent is a voluntary, conscious act involving observation, analysis, and deliberation of the available information. Some mentally handicapped persons and minors have a limited capacity for determining the reasonableness of a particular situation. Due to these limitations, a court may decide that such a person is not able to assume a given risk. In deciding whether an individual could assume a given risk, the court determines whether someone similar in age, experience, mental abilities, and physical capacities is capable of assuming the risk involved. This determination is made by the judge or jury, but it is typically guided by the testimony of expert witnesses.

Contributory and Comparative Negligence

Contributory negligence is the legal term used when an injured person fails to use due care in protecting himself or herself and that failure is a legally contributing cause in producing the injury (Giffis, 1975). In some states, if the defendant can prove contributory negligence, the court may prevent the plaintiff from recovering any damage. An example of this contributory negligence defense can be found in *Petras v. Kellas.*[23] A woman fell and injured herself while attempting to descend a stairway. On the side of the stairway she used, there was no handrail and the steps were rounded, wet, and slippery. There was a handrail, however, on the opposite side of the stairway. The West Virginia court ruled that the woman was guilty of contributory negligence in not using the handrail, and the defendant was not held responsible for the woman's injuries. It is important to remember that the plaintiff's own contributorily negligent act will not always automatically relieve the defendant of liability. As with the intervening cause defense, if the defendant's act alone would have been sufficient to bring about the injury, this act may be considered the legal cause of harm regardless of other causes.

In the assumption of risk defense, the judge or jury determines the standard of conduct to which the injured person should have adhered. Persons of different ages and abilities are not expected to follow the same standard of conduct. Also, in order for individuals to be contributorily negligent, they must have had complete freedom and choice over their actions (Knaak, 1969). The courts have held that if an individual, particularly a student, contributes to his or her injury while following the instructions of a teacher or supervisor, that individual is not guilty of contributory negligence. This is illustrated in *Feuerstein v. Board of Education of the City of New York.*[24] A noticeably frail 95-pound, 14-year-old boy was required to carry heavy packages and books as part of his supply room monitor duties. He continued to carry heavy loads around the building as directed, even though he experienced heart pains. His father sued the board of education, contending that his son's work as a supply monitor resulted in his present heart ailment. The court ruled that the boy was not guilty of contributory negligence for failing to stop the work when he experienced pain because he was acting as his teacher had directed. The school board was held negligent, through its employees, for improperly supervising the boy and requiring him to do such work.

The assumption of risk and contributory negligence defenses are often used together, as in the case of *Schuyler v. Board of Education of Union Free School District No. 7.*[25] This case concerns a 12-year-old boy who fell off a fence on school property. The boy testified that he was aware of the school's admonitory directive which banned walking on the fence. There was no testimony that indicated the fence itself was inherently dangerous. The court ruled that the school district was not liable for the injury because the boy had assumed the risk of using the fence in that way, and he was, therefore, guilty of contributory negligence. In some jurisdictions, the defense of assumption of risk has been abolished and subsumed under the doctrine of contributory negligence or it has been considered when the court determines the duty owed by the defendant (Prosser, 1971).

There is an increasing dissatisfaction within the courts with the all-or-nothing aspect of the contributory negligence defense. In cases where the court decides that the negligence of the injured party contributed to the degree of harm suffered, the court may rely upon the doctrine of *comparative negligence* in determining the amount of damages to be awarded. The doctrine of comparative negligence allows the court to proportionally share the compensation for the injuries between the plaintiff and the defendant based upon the relative fault of each (Prosser, 1971). The plaintiff does not recover full compensation for the damages suffered when the court relies upon the comparative negligence doctrine. *Scott v. Independent School District No.*

709, Duluth,[26] a lawsuit arising from a serious eye injury sustained by a junior high school student, represents an example of comparative negligence. The plaintiff alleged that the school district was negligent because the state statute requiring students to wear protective safety goggles in industrial arts classes had not been properly enforced. While the student was working with a drill in an industrial arts class, the drill bit broke and a piece of the broken bit struck his unprotected left eye. The Minnesota Supreme Court found that the school board was not totally responsible for the injury and that the student was partially responsible for his injuries because he failed to follow the clearly specified safety regulations. The court stated that if the consideration of negligence on the part of the student were not allowed, teachers would be potentially liable for pupil injuries resulting whenever students defied instructions, regardless of how the instructions were announced. The student was found to have contributed 10% of the negligence and the school board to have contributed 90% of the negligence. Many of the states that have adopted the comparative negligence doctrine have also established the rule that the plaintiff can only recover when he or she is found to be less than 50% at fault (Alton, 1977).

ADDITIONAL DEFENSES

In addition to the existence of an intervening cause, the assumption of risk, and contributory negligence on the part of the injured person, three other circumstances may bar recovery from a defendant who otherwise appears to be negligent and liable. These situations are:

1. When statutes declare that the defendant is immune from liability
2. When the plaintiff does not follow proper procedures in filing the claim
3. When the plaintiff brings suit after the statutory time limit has expired

Immunity

There are some cases where defendants, because of their status or position, may avoid tort liability under a doctrine labeled *immunity* (Prosser, 1971). The most common immunity that would be applicable for community centers would be *governmental immunity.* The origin of this theory was based on the fact that the king could essentially do no wrong, and therefore, to allow the king to be sued would be a contradiction (Prosser, 1971). The doctrine has been applied to federal, state, and municipal governments under several theories, one of which is that the government is the people and the people cannot sue themselves. Exceptions have been made to this, especially when the government, by statute, consents to being sued. Under the Federal Tort Claims Act, the government has allowed itself to be sued for the negligent or wrongful acts of federal employees who are acting within the scope of their employment. There are many exceptions provided by the act, and an individual or center concerned about immunity from liability would need to specifically examine the Federal Tort Claims Act. Generally, however, at the federal level, immunity exists for "discretionary functions or duties" but not for "operational activities." Discretionary acts involve planning, decision, and policymaking activities; operational activities involve carrying out the duties. Thus, one might state that it would be discretionary to admit a person to a community program (and if the administrators were wrong in their decision to do so, there would be a higher probability of no liability being imposed), but it would not be discretionary to treat the person in a negligent manner once the person was in the program (that would be an operational act and, thus, liability could exist).

Governmental immunity exists at the state level also, but, in most states, procedures exist that allow the state either to be sued in certain situations or to establish special courts of claims which can award monetary damages to individuals injured by state employees or by state activities. The immunity given to the states has been extended to various state hospitals and institutions, although the legislation creating these facilities often appears to allow the facility to be subject to liability. Each state may differ, and, thus, one interested in this area should check the particular state's statutes and case law on the subject.

Municipalities are normally provided with a somewhat limited type of governmental immunity. Because of the dual character of municipalities (being both a governmental subdivision of the state and a corporate body similar to many private corporations), full governmental immunity is not given to them. Normally, a distinction exists between "governmental" and "proprietary" functions. Those activities that are governmental in nature (i.e., activities only carried out by the government, for example, police and fire protection) are generally immune from liability, while activities that are proprietary in nature (i.e., activities that could be carried out by private enterprise, for example, airport or public market) usually enjoy no immunity (Prosser, 1971).

The doctrine of governmental immunity is often complicated and difficult to understand and, at the same time, is changing constantly. Unfortunately, it has been utilized in the past in a manner in which an individual has been unjustly forced to bear the entire burden of an injury. In *Picard v. Greisinger*,[27] injuries were sustained by a student who was struck in the head by a basketball thrown at him intentionally and forcibly by a gym teacher. In addition, the teacher refused to allow the student to seek medical treatment and required the boy to remain in the gym class in spite of his injuries. The plaintiff claimed that the school board was negligent for retaining in employment an instructor they knew, or should have known, had a violent temper and who was likely to harm the students when angered. The school district merely claimed that they were immune under the doctrine of governmental immunity and the case was dismissed.

The doctrine of governmental immunity has been eroded by the courts in many states. Although there still may exist situations in which immunity from liability has prevented the plaintiff from recovering damages from a negligent governmental employee or facility, the trend is rapidly changing. It is clear that some governmental immunity must remain, especially for legislative and judicial functions, but for the most part, the general governmental immunity is being rapidly diminished. State tort claims acts, modeled after the federal act, are becoming a more prevalent method of addressing the issue of governmental immunity. Thus, operations that in the past have been shielded by their governmental activities or ties may no longer enjoy such protection.

Claims Procedures

In order to help ensure fairness and to promote the speedy resolution of disputes, statutes have been enacted that specify the form that must be followed in making a claim for damages and the time period within which a claim must be filed (McCarthy, 1978). The failure to follow such procedures properly may preclude the recovery for damages. This occurred in *Horowitz v. Board of Education, Town of Hempstead, Union Free School District No. 3.*[28] The notice of claim was sent by regular mail to the "Board of Education." State statutes, however, required that the notice must be delivered by hand or registered mail to a member of the board of education, to any trustee, or the clerk thereof. The court dismissed the case because the claim was served improperly.

Statute of Limitations

Every state has a statute setting a time limit for making a legal claim for damages (Holder, 1975). Ordinarily once this time limit expires, an injured individual can be barred from making a claim for damages. This time limit, called the statute of limitations, varies from as little as 1 year in some states to as long as 6 years in others. There are basically three ways that states determine when the time limit begins to run. One technique that is used by many states involves the time limit beginning when the alleged negligent act occurred. In a second method for determining the onset of this period (one used primarily for treatment cases), the time period begins following the last treatment in the course of care that resulted in the injury. In other states, the time period begins when the injured person discovers or should have discovered that the negligent act occurred. If the injured person is a minor or if the injured person is mentally disabled, the time period usually begins at the age of majority or after the disability no longer exists (Holder, 1975).

An example of a court barring an injured person from making a claim for damages due to the expiration of the time limit can be found in *McGill v. Board of Education Union Free School District No. 3, Town of Hempstead.*[29] This case involved a 12-year-old girl who fractured her leg when she was required to perform a physical dexterity test by springing over a "buck" in the school gymnasium. The accident occurred in 1968. According to New York state law, the girl had 1 year and 90 days from the time when she reached the age of majority in which to file a claim. She reached the age of majority on September 1, 1974. The girl, however, did not file a notice of the claim until August, 1976. Since she failed to file notice of the claim within the specified period of time, the appeals court barred her from recovering any damages.

The court has the authority to extend the time limitation if it deems that the particular circumstances of the case warrant such action. An appeals court in New York utilized this authority in *Matey v. Bethlehem Central School District, Delmar.*[30] This case concerned a student who injured her back while participating in a trampoline exercise in a physical education class. The court found it apparent from the records that neither the girl nor her parents were aware of the statutory requirements for filing a notice of claim against a school district. Furthermore, once the plaintiff did seek the advice of a lawyer, they promptly filed a notice of claim. The appeals court extended the time limit in this situation and allowed the claim to be processed.

In addition, states usually have a separate statute of limitations for claims alleging wrongful death.[31] This time period is typically less than the period applicable to other negligent actions. Knowledge of the state's statute of limitations is important for a community center so that the administrators can formulate informed policies concerning how long treatment and other records should be preserved. These records are critical if there is ever a need to demonstrate in court the appropriateness of the services a client received.

POINTS TO REMEMBER

1. Community center personnel are accountable for the services they are paid to provide, and they are normally accountable for any injuries that may result.
2. Negligence refers to the failure of a person to act as a reasonable, prudent, and careful person would act under similar circumstances to avoid exposing others to unreasonable risk of injury.
3. In order for the court to award settlement to a plaintiff, the plaintiff must prove that: 1) the defendant owed the plaintiff a duty to conform to a standard of conduct, 2) the defendant breached that duty, 3) the plaintiff suffered an injury, and 4) the defendant's action was the direct or proximate cause of the injury.
4. Community center personnel have a legally enforceable duty to act as a reasonable, prudent, and careful person would act under similar circumstances. This includes both the duty to provide adequate supervision and the duty to instruct the clients properly.
5. Community center personnel are liable if they are aware, or should be aware, that dangerous conditions exist and they take no action to remedy the problem.

6. Adherence to an inadequate or inappropriate community standard or established practice will not absolve anyone from liability for resulting injuries.

7. Unusual therapy or treatment that results in injury to a client can be cause for legal action.

8. Community center personnel must keep abreast of the advances in treatment techniques.

9. Community center personnel do not guarantee positive results, but they must exercise reasonable care to exert their best judgment in an effort to bring about a good result.

10. Community center personnel may be held liable for the direct and indirect physical or mental harm resulting from a negligent act.

11. An employer may be held liable for the negligent acts of his or her employee.

12. An employer is legally responsible for conducting safety inspections, repairing defects, developing and enforcing proper rules and regulations, hiring competent staff, and dismissing incompetent staff.

13. Three mitigating circumstances that may bar recovery by an injured person include: 1) when an uncontrollable and unforeseeable intervening act occurred, 2) when the plaintiff had assumed the risk involved prior to engaging in the activity, and 3) when the plaintiff contributes to the injury by failing to act as a reasonably careful and prudent person.

14. When an accident occurs, information should be promptly gathered regarding the injured person's behavior and regarding the events occurring immediately before and during the accident.

15. Community center administrators should be knowledgeable about their state's statutes of limitations in order to establish policies concerning the storing of records.

REFERENCES

Allen, R.C., Ferster, E.Z., & Rubin, J.G. (eds.). *Readings in law and psychiatry.* Baltimore: The Johns Hopkins Press, 1968.

Alton, A.R. *Medical malpractice law.* Boston: Little, Brown, & Co., 1977.

Anderson, W.S. (ed.). *Ballentine's law dictionary* (3rd ed.). Rochester, NY: The Lawyers Co-Operative Publishing Co., 1969.

Black, H.C. *Black's law dictionary* (rev. 4th ed.). St. Paul, MN: West Publishing Co., 1968.

Brodsky, S.L., & Robey, A. On becoming an expert witness: Issues of orientation and effectiveness. *Professional Psychology,* 1972, *3,* 173–176.

Dooley, J.A. *Modern tort law* (Vols. 1 & 2). Chicago: Callaghan & Company, 1977.

Gifis, S.H. *Law dictionary.* Woodbury, NY: Barron's Educational Series, Inc., 1975.

Gottlieb, I.M. Recent changes in the so-called locality rule involving expert testimony in medical malpractice cases. In C.H. Wecht (ed.), *Exploring the medical malpractice dilemma.* Mount Kisco, NY: Futura Publishing Co., 1972.

Holder, A.R. *Medical malpractice law.* New York: John Wiley & Sons, 1975.

Knaak, W.C. *School district tort liability in the 70's.* St. Paul, MN: Marric Publishing Co., 1969.

Leibee, H. *Tort liability for injuries to pupils.* Ann Arbor, MI: Campus Publishers, 1965.

McCarthy, M.M. Tort liability. In P.K. Piele (ed.). *The yearbook of school law 1978.* Topeka, KS: National Organization on Legal Problems of Education, 1978.

Mirabel, J.T., & Levy, H.A. *The law of negligence.* Amityville, NY: Acme Book Co., 1962.

National Education Association Research Division. *Who is liable for pupil negligence?* Washington, DC: National Education Association, 1963.

Pacht, A.R., Kuehn, J.K., Basset, H.T., & Nash, M.M. The current status of the psychologist as an expert witness. *Professional Psychology,* 1973, *4,* 409–413.

Prosser, W.L. *Handbook of the law of torts* (4th ed.). St. Paul, MN: West Publishing Co., 1971.

Rosenfeld, H.N. *Liability for school accidents: A manual for educational administrators and teachers.* New York: Harper & Brothers Pub., 1941.

Tancredi, L.R., Leib, J., & Slaby, A.E. *Legal issues in psychiatric care.* Hagerstown, MD: Harper & Row Publishers, 1975.

Woody, R.H. *Legal aspects of mental retardation: A search for reliability.* Springfield, IL: Charles C Thomas, 1974.

ENDNOTES

[1]A tort is a private or civil wrong committed upon a person or property other than those wrongs committed under a contract. "It may be either 1) a direct invasion of some legal right of the individual; 2) the infraction of some public duty by which special damage accrues to the individual; 3) the violation of some private obligation·by which like damage accrues to the individual" (Black, 1968, p. 1660).

[2]A defendant is "[t]he person defending or denying; the party against whom relief or recovery is sought in an action or suit" (Black, 1968, p. 507).

[3]A plaintiff is "[a] person who brings an action; the party who complains or sues in a personal action and is so named on the record" (Black, 1968, p. 1309).

[4]Preponderance of the evidence refers to "[t]he weight, credit, and value of aggregate evidence on either side; the greater weight of the evidence; the greater weight of the credible evidence. In the last analysis, the probability of truth; evidence more convincing as worthy of belief than that which is offered in opposition thereto" (Anderson, 1969, p. 980).

[5]"Whoever the professional may be, Judge Cooley well expressed his duty: 'In all those employments where peculiar skill is requisite, if one offers his services, he is understood as holding himself out to the public as possessing the degree of skill commonly possessed by others in the same employment, and if his pretentions are unfounded, he commits a species of fraud upon every man who employs him in reliance on his public profession. But no man, whether skilled or unskilled undertakes the task that he assumes shall be performed successfully, and without fault or error; he undertakes for good faith and integrity, but not for infallibility, and he is liable to his employer for negligence, bad faith, or dishonesty but not to losses consequent upon mere errors in judgement.' " 3 Cooley Torts 335 (4th ed. 1932). "Probably this is as succinct and correct as can be made of the obligation of the professional person to his client." (Dooley, 1977, Vol. 2, pp. 454–455).

[6]Friedman v. Bd. of Education of City of New York, 186 N.E. 865 (N.Y. Ct. App. 1933).

[7]369 A. 2d 332 (Pa. Super. 1976).

[8]"A business visitor is [one] who is invited or permitted to enter or remain upon the premises of another for a purpose directly or indirectly connected with the business dealings between them" (Black, 1968, p. 250).

[9]Drum v. Miller, 47 S.E. 421 (N.C. Sup. Ct. 1904).

[10]187 N.Y.S. 2d 88 (N.Y. Sup. Ct. 1959).

[11]131 Cal. Rptr. 854 (Ct. App., First Dist. 1976). This case involved a dyslexic high school graduate who filed suit against his high school because of his reduced learning capacity. He was only able to read at a lower than 5th grade level. The suit accused the high school and its representatives of negligence and misrepresentation in regard to their past treatment of the plaintiff. The plaintiff alleged that: 1) when his parents had inquired about his school performance the school represented to them that he was doing well and that he had no special problem, 2) the school negligently failed to take notice of his reading disabilities despite school records noting his difficulties, 3) the school district knowingly assigned him to classes unfitted to his reading skills, and 4) the school district negligently passed him from grade to grade and graduated him from high school when its officials knew or should have known he was not qualified. In order to determine how the school district should have behaved in regard to their treatment of the dyslexic student, the court examined the standards and guidelines presented in the California Education Code.

[12]Fed. R. Evid. 803 (18).

[13]165 N.E. 2d 756 (N.Y. Ct. App. 1960).

[14]Tarasoff v. Regents of the University of California, 551 P. 2d 334 (Cal. Sup. Ct. 1976). The general ruling in this case was that when a therapist determines, or should determine, that a client presents a serious danger of harm to another, the therapist has a legally enforceable obligation to protect the intended victim.

[15]49 N.E. 760, 762 (N.Y. Ct. App. 1898).

[16]407 F. 2d 823 (4th Cir. 1969).

[17]358 N.E. 2d 639 (Ohio Ct. Cl. 1976).

[18]Under the doctrine of *respondeat superior* the "master [employer] is responsible for want of care on servant's [employee's] part toward those to whom master [employer] owes duty to use care, provided failure of servant [employee] to use such care occurred in course of his employment" (Black, 1968, p. 1475).

[19]364 P. 2d 556 (Wash. Sup. Ct. 1961).

[20]86 A. 2d 761 (1952).

[21]498 P. 2d 1227 (Wyo. Sup. Ct. 1972).

[22]296 N.Y.S. 2d 429 (N.Y. Ct. Cl. 1968).

[23]122 S.E. 2d 177 (W.Va. Sup. Ct. App. 1961).

[24]202 N.Y.S. 2d 524 (N.Y. Sup. Ct. 1960).

[25]239 N.Y.S. 2d 769 (N.Y. Sup. Ct., App. Div. 1963).

[26]256 N.W. 2d 485 (Minn. Sup. Ct. 1977).

[27]138 N.W. 2d 508 (Mich. Ct. App. 1965).

[28]210 N.Y.S. 2d 600 (N.Y. Sup. Ct. 1960).

[29]399 N.Y.S. 2d 41 (Sup. Ct., App. Div., Second Dept. 1977).

[30]391 N.Y.S. 2d 357 (Sup. Ct. 1977).

[31]A wrongful death is "[a] cause of action asserted by the next of kin of a deceased [client] for the pecuniary loss incurred as a result of the negligent treatment that killed the [client]. Wrongful death is a cause of action created by statute, and it permits compensation only for pecuniary loss to the next of kin as the result of the death (that is, loss of income). It does not include any right to recover for the pain and suffering of the deceased or the anguish of the next of kin. A cause of action for the pain and suffering of the deceased patient can be alleged separately. A cause of action for wrongful death has its own statute of limitations" (Alton, 1977, p. 224).

3

ADDITIONAL LIABILITY ISSUES

The vast majority of lawsuit-producing situations that a community center may encounter would be classified under the rubric of negligence. Not all lawsuits arising from injury-producing situations, however, are based on claims of negligence. There are several other types of lawsuits, arising from issues such as libel, assault, and false imprisonment, that a community center or its staff may find it necessary to address. In order to help avoid such lawsuits, community center personnel must become informed about the legal principles surrounding these issues. Rather than attempt a cursory discussion of the many legal issues that could potentially have been presented in this chapter, more in-depth coverage is devoted to those concerns that appear to be most pertinent to the development and operation of community centers.

ATTRACTIVE NUISANCE

When an injury occurs on the premises of a community center there are many issues to be considered, one of which is whether the injured person had a right to be there (e.g., was the person trespassing or was the person there for a legitimate purpose). A second concern is why the injured person was on the premises (e.g., was the person there on business or was the person there as a guest). Generally, a property owner has a duty to exercise varying degrees of care in keeping the premises safe for trespassers, guests, and business visitors with the highest degree of care being shown for business visitors. A trespasser, on the other hand, cannot normally expect or demand that the premises be safe since the trespasser has no right to be there. Trespassers, by reason of being wrongfully on the property, usually must assume all risks that they may find (Prosser, 1971).

There are obviously exceptions to this general rule regarding trespassers, and the most important for community center personnel is the exception for trespassing children or persons with child-like judgment. Courts have allowed children to recover for injuries sustained while trespassing on another's property when the court rules that the child had been enticed onto the property by a dangerous object or situation. This enticing hazard has been referred to as an *attractive nuisance*. The doctrine allowing recovery in these types of situations is based on the theory that individuals and agencies should exhibit special care toward those persons who, because of immaturity or lack of judgment, may be attracted to the premises by an enticing object (e.g., a swimming pool or a discarded refrigerator) and yet lack the needed judgment to avoid the dangerous situation. For example, a property owner normally has the duty to erect a fence around a swimming pool and to remove or secure the door of a discarded refrigerator because it is foreseeable that a person with child-like judgment could easily be enticed onto the land to explore these things without comprehending the danger that could be involved.

The same issues, such as foreseeability of the danger and the proximate cause of the injury, that apply to other negligence lawsuits also apply to an attractive nuisance suit. The plaintiff in *Hunter v. Evergreen Presbyterian Vocational School*[1] alleged that the unfenced pond in which a mentally retarded youth drowned was an attractive nuisance. The pond provided recreation in the form of fishing and beauty on the 50-acre school campus. At the time of the incident, the student was working with a yard maintenance crew around the pond. The youth entered the pond apparently to retrieve a yard tool and drowned. The youth had attended the school for 3½ years and during that time he had given no indication that he needed constant supervision. He and other students walked by and worked by the pond daily for years without incident prior to the drowning. The school's policy to allow its students a certain amount of freedom consistent with their abilities was viewed by the court to be reasonable and necessary for the accomplishment of the school's habilitative purpose. In addition, the court found that considering the importance of the pond to the school program and the fact that no previous incidents had occurred, the unguarded pond did not present an unreasonable and foreseeable hazard to the school's students. In view of these findings the court did not hold the school liable for the youth's death. Nonetheless, community centers that have attractive and dangerous objects or situations on their premises should exert special care to protect those with child-like judgment.

ABANDONMENT

Another type of negligence issue that community center personnel should be aware of is called *abandonment*. Although abandonment can refer to many different things depending on the situation, for the purposes of this book, the term is used to refer to the termination of a therapist-client relationship while the client is still in need of treatment, without the consent of the client, and without giving the client adequate notice and opportunity to seek assistance from another therapist. Chayet (1969) has presented several elements that should be present in order for a claim of abandonment to be successful. The elements that relate to community centers include proving the following: 1) a treatment relationship has been established between the community center and the client, 2) the relationship has been terminated by the community center without mutual consent of both parties and without giving the client adequate time in which to secure alternative services, 3) the client has had a continuing need of the services provided by the community center, and 4) the abandonment appears to have caused the injury.

A community center can normally terminate a treatment relationship with a client without fear of legal repercussion under the following circumstances: 1) the client consents to the termination, 2) the client has been given sufficient notice in order to obtain alternative services, or 3) the client no longer requires the kinds of services or treatment provided by the community center (Holder, 1975). In addition, termination of the treatment relationship might be justified if the client is totally uncooperative and refuses to accept the plan of treatment that is proposed (Tancredi, Lieb, & Slaby, 1975). Before a termination decision is reached under these conditions, however, substantial efforts should be made to formulate a treatment plan that is acceptable to the parties involved and the client should be allowed an opportunity to contest the community center's decision. In order to avoid problems related to termination decisions, these decisions should be clearly supported by an objective assessment of the client's current condition, careful professional judgment, and written records. When the client chooses to terminate treatment, this decision and the circumstances surrounding it should be carefully recorded so that the community center can avoid liability on the basis of abandonment. In addition, one must remember that many clients have a limited capacity for providing valid consent due to a mental disability or their age. Therefore, consent to terminate treatment should be sought from the client's guardian before the community center considers a termination agreement to be valid.

LIBEL AND SLANDER

Community centers owe a duty to their clients, staff, and others not only to protect their persons and property from harm but also to protect their reputations or good names. If the actions of a community center defame someone, the center may be sued for libel or slander. Defamation refers to the act of communicating to a third person information that tends to harm the reputation of another so as to lower that person in the estimation of the community or that tends to deter persons from associating or dealing with the defamed person (Prosser, 1971). If the communication is made by word of mouth or gestures, the community center may be faced with the tort of *slander*.

For example, if a community center administrator knowingly makes a false accusation about an employee at a public meeting, that administrator may be sued for slander. If the communication is made in writing, printing, or pictures, the community center may be faced with the tort of *libel*. For example, if an administrator makes a knowingly false statement about a client's poor work habits in a letter of reference to a potential employer, the client could sue the administrator and the community center for libel. The defamatory communication must be made to a third party, i.e., someone other than the person about whom the negative statement is made, in order for the communication to constitute libel or slander. In order for a court to award settlement to a plaintiff in a libel or slander lawsuit the plaintiff must prove certain elements. These elements include: 1) the fact that the defendant communicated to a third person a false statement about the plaintiff, 2) the fact that the statement brought hatred, disgrace, ridicule, or contempt upon the plaintiff, and 3) the fact that the plaintiff suffered an injury as a result of the communication (Alexander, Corns, & McCann, 1969). Someone who repeats or republishes a defamatory statement may be liable for the resulting injuries even if the source of the statements is disclosed.

The primary defense against libel or slander is simply truth. If the statements that are made are true, no matter how much damage the statements may cause, they would not be grounds for a libel or slander settlement. The closer the statements are to facts that are based on actual first-hand contact or observation, the more likely a court is to accept the statements as being true (Clear, 1978). Statements that are based simply on hearsay (i.e., not actually observed but rather based on the statements of others) or on opinion may be very difficult to prove as true in court.

The second basic defense against libel or slander involves the protection by privilege or immunity. A privilege against lawsuits is allowed in certain instances where the speaker is acting in "some interest of social importance" such that courts have held that the person's conduct should be protected, even at the expense of "uncompensated harm" to another's reputation (Prosser, 1971). The immunity or privilege given to an individual may be either absolute or conditional (qualified). If an absolute privilege exists, even if untruthful, malicious, and devastating statements are made, the individual would be immune from lawsuit. Only a limited number of federal and state officers (e.g., judges) are afforded an absolute privilege with regard to the pursuit of their official duties. Some minor government officials, such as school board members, may be afforded a conditional privilege that can be abrogated if malicious or intentional defamatory communications occur. Conditional or qualified privileges are sometimes held to exist when making statements to a potential future employer (e.g., in a letter of reference) or to a supervisor (e.g., in a sheltered workshop or treatment program), but the speaker must ensure that nothing more is said than what is actually necessary and that the statements were not made maliciously. No set rules exist in this area; thus, one must be careful of statements made concerning another's work or treatment performance. Statements should be limited to what the speaker has seen or actually heard and should, in the speaker's opinion, be an honest appraisal of the person's performance. More latitude may be given when administrators *within* an organization are discussing an individual's work performance or treatment progress. Nonetheless, the statements must not be made maliciously. Most likely, community center personnel (with the exception of the qualified privilege regarding a person's work performance or progress in a program) would enjoy neither an absolute nor a conditional privilege regarding their communications.

In the past, libel or slander lawsuits involving institutions for disabled persons or educational systems have occurred relatively infrequently. Legally actionable problems seem most likely to occur when staff members make statements at public meetings and when inaccurate statements are made in letters of reference or in personnel or client records. Clear (1978) points out that, in the future, libel and slander lawsuits will probably become more frequent as a result of greater competition for jobs, greater access to personnel and client records, greater demand for due process procedures, and greater demand for accountability and public scrutiny of community centers. This does not mean that community center personnel must refrain from making negative statements about a person; it does mean, however, that community center personnel must be sure that their written and oral statements concerning others are based on adequate factual knowledge.

ASSAULT AND BATTERY

Unlike negligent acts, assault and battery refer to *intentional* acts that cause harm to another individual. Therefore, in addition to being civil wrongs, assault and battery are also criminal offenses. *Battery* is defined as any offensive touching usually involving the unlawful and intentional use of force and violence upon another person or upon anything that is customarily closely attached or associated with a person's body, such as clothing, a cane, or the car the person is riding in or driving. The two basic elements of battery are contact of an offensive nature and the intent to unlawfully contact the person. *Assault* is the act of intentionally placing another person in reasonable fear of bodily harm. For example, both threatening to shoot someone with a gun and shooting at someone would be considered assaults. These instances constitute an assault because there was an intentional threat of harm but no actual contact was made. Not only must there have been an offer to use unlawful force, but the ability and opportunity to carry out the threat immediately must be apparent in order for an actionable assault to have occurred (Prosser, 1971). Making a threat of violence that could not be carried through would generally not be viewed as an assault (e.g., a small child threatening to break an adult's neck). The terms *assault* and *battery* are associated in common usage so frequently that they are generally used together or improperly used synonymously.

A clear case of wanton assault and battery was made against a private school teacher in *Baike v. Luther High School South.* [2] This case concerns an incident that happened before classes in a school corridor. A number of students were gathered near a set of lockers talking to a teacher. There was some conversation and laughter, but the students were not being noisy or causing a commotion. One of the female students dropped her books and the teacher spoke to the group in a teasing manner about the boys not helping her pick up the books. The teacher then left the group. Shortly thereafter, the defendant teacher approached the group of students and without warning seized one of the students by the collar and pushed him into a locker. The youth had said nothing disrespectful, but the defendant claimed that the student was disrespectful to him and had laughed behind his back. The defendant teacher stated he had never met the plaintiff before the incident; nevertheless, he assumed the youth was a student at the time. In view of these facts, an Illinois appeals court affirmed a circuit court's ruling that the teacher was guilty of wanton assault and battery and upheld the judgment of $25,000 against the defendant.

The concept of battery has also been extended to cases involving treatment. A fundamental principle of free government is that each individual has the right to make major decisions concerning his or her mind and body. [3] Several legislative and judicial bodies have interpreted this principle to mean that clients and patients have a legally enforceable right to informed consent prior to treatment. Informed consent refers to "a voluntary agreement by a person in possession and exercise of sufficient mentality [and information] to make an intelligent choice to do something proposed by another" (*Gray v. Grunnagle,* p. 664). [4] This voluntary agreement may be expressed verbally, it may be implied from one's actions, or it may be written, the latter being by far the safest means of obtaining consent. In general, in order to obtain informed consent, the agency representative must explain to the client, in a noncoercive understandable manner, the diagnosis, the proposed treatment procedure, the risks involved, the prospects of success, the likely outcomes if the treatment procedure is not undertaken, alternative methods of treatment, and the freedom the client has to discontinue the treatment at any time (Fraser & Chadsey, 1970).

If a community center fails to secure the client's informed consent before beginning a treatment procedure that invades a person's mind or body (especially one that presents a foreseeable risk of harm to the client or others), or before beginning a treatment procedure that is considered experimental, the community center may be held legally responsible for any injuries that occur. This type of unlawful contact is frequently called *technical battery.* The courts may consider a particular treatment approach experimental if it is still under scientific investigation or if it is not widely reported or accepted in the professional literature (Martin, 1975). Liability may be imposed for non-consensual treatment of a client even if the treatment significantly improved the client's condition; the question of the existence of informed consent may be examined by the court separately from that of the quality of the procedure. If any information necessary to form the basis of an informed consent by the client is withheld or misrepresented, the court may view the consent as worthless and liability may be imposed.

The case of *Rogers v. Lumberman's Mutual Casualty Company*[5] involved the injuries resulting from unauthorized surgery. During a simple appendectomy, the surgeons discovered that the woman patient had diseased reproductive organs and they proceeded to remove them. At the time, no emergency existed which required the removal of the organs and the woman had not consented to have such an operation. The woman's husband was at the hospital before and during the operation, yet the surgeons involved never made any attempt to secure his consent for the additional surgery. The Louisiana Appeals Court found that neither the patient, nor anyone authorized on her behalf, consented to the removal of her reproductive organs and that the surgeons and the hospital were liable for the damages she sustained.

INVASION OF PRIVACY

In addition to requiring a client's informed consent before beginning a risky or experimental treatment procedure, the center should require that the client give his or her consent before any photographs, videotapes, or films are taken of the client and before any information concerning the client is given to the press or any nonauthorized persons. If a therapist or center does take pictures of a client or release information about the client to nonauthorized persons without the client's consent, the therapist and the center may be held liable for damages if the client's interests are harmed (Health Law Center, 1974). Legal actions resulting from such damages are usually in the form of a lawsuit for the defamation of the client's reputation (i.e., libel) or for the violation of the client's right to privacy.

Barber v. Time, Inc.[6] concerns the publication of a picture and an article without the client's consent. A woman entered a hospital for treatment of her unusual eating behavior. A news magazine published a closeup of the woman in a hospital bed, with the headings, "Insatiable-eater Barber" and "she eats for ten." The accompanying article, which described the woman's eating behavior, appeared in a column devoted to medical news. The woman sued the magazine for the unauthorized publication on the basis that it was a violation of her right to privacy and that it was libelous. A jury rendered a judgment in favor of the woman and awarded her compensatory payment. In an appeal the Missouri Supreme Court agreed with the jury's decision. In *Doe v. Roe,*[7] a New York state court ruled that a psychiatrist's verbatim publication of his patients' disclosures made during psychoanalysis violated the patients' right of privacy. The plaintiff and her late, former husband had been patients of the defendant for many years. Eight years after the treatment had terminated, the psychiatrist published an extensive verbatim report of the patients' thoughts, fantasies, intimate personal relationships, and biographies along with a diagnosis of the illnesses purportedly suffered by the patients. At one point in the trial, the psychiatrist claimed that the patient had consented to this publication. During this time, however, the plaintiff was still undergoing treatment by a psychiatrist. In addition, the defendant failed to obtain the consent in writing. The court ruled that the consent was not valid of indeed it ever existed. The plaintiff requested compensation for the injuries she suffered, which included acute embarrassment, threats to her livelihood, and insomnia requiring medical attention. The court awarded the plaintiff $20,000 in compensatory damages and barred the further sale and publication of the book.

Bazemore v. Savannah Hospital[8] concerned the distribution and sale of an unauthorized photograph. A child was born severely deformed and died during a subsequent operation. The hospital allowed a photographer to photograph the infant. The photographer later sold several copies of the photograph. The child's parents subsequently sued the hospital and the photographer. The court held that the photographer and the hospital violated the parents' right of privacy and the court allowed the parents to recover $20,000 in damages.

FALSE IMPRISONMENT

Another type of intentional tort, which is also a criminal offense, is false imprisonment. Basically, *false imprisonment* refers to the unlawful restraint of an individual's personal liberty or freedom of movement. If an improper restraint is imposed by a legal authority and an arrest follows, the action may be called a false arrest. Physical force does not need to be involved as long as the victim reasonably believes that he or she is being restrained against her or his will (Gifis, 1975). Prosser (1971) has pointed out that there can be no imprisonment unless the victim is aware of it at the time, arguing that until the victim is aware of restraint there is no real interference with the right of freedom to go where the victim pleases. In addition, there normally would be no actionable false imprisonment unless the defendant proposefully intended to confine the plaintiff. No malice is required, however, and thus people may be sued for false imprisonment even though they were confining someone for "one's own good." There is no specified minimum or maximum time period in which the restraint must have occurred in order to constitute false imprisonment. For example, both improperly restraining someone in a straitjacket for 10 minutes and improperly confining someone to a locked psychiatric hospital ward for 30 days may be viewed as false imprisonment.

The only injury that the plaintiff must prove is that the confinement occurred. As a result of the unique form of psychological injury resulting from improper confinement, the plaintiff may be entitled to compensation for mental suffering and humiliation in addition to compensation for loss of time, for physical discomfort or inconvenience, and for any resulting physical injury or illness. Particular considerations involving treatment techniques, such as timeout, that involve various forms of restraint are discussed in Chapters 7 and 8.

An example of both false imprisonment and assault and battery can be found in *Stowers v. Wolodzko*.[9] This suit involved allegations that a psychiatrist treated a woman against her will and held her incommunicado. At the time, the woman was temporarily hospitalized as mentally ill pursuant to a court order pending a hearing on her sanity. She was held at the hospital for 23 days and the psychiatrist ordered that she be given considerable quantities of medication. In addition, the psychiatrist ordered the hospital staff to ignore the woman's protests against being given the debilitating medication. At times when she refused medication, she had to be held by three nurses and injected. The state law allowed her to be treated against her will only if it was necessary to keep her on the premises or in order to prevent her from injuring herself or others. None of these conditions was present when the psychiatrist gave the medication orders. The psychiatrist also refused to allow her to call her relatives or an attorney, and he prevented her from writing or receiving letters. The state law clearly granted persons who were temporarily committed to mental hospitals the right to freely contact and communicate with an attorney and/or relatives in order to obtain release. The Michigan Supreme Court upheld a ruling that holding the woman incommunicado was a restraint of her freedom constituting false imprisonment, and that treating her without first obtaining her consent constituted asault and battery. The judgment against the psychiatrist was $40,000 for the harm suffered by the woman.

CONSTITUTIONAL TORT

Most of the tort cases discussed above are civil in nature and were initiated in state courts. There is a class of tort lawsuits, however, called *constitutional torts*, that originate in federal courts. These litigations are initiated in order to recover monetary damages for injuries resulting from an infringement of constitutional or statutory rights. Over the last 20 years, there has been a growing recognition that minors and disabled persons also enjoy the rights and protections that are guaranteed in the constitution and statutes, such as freedom from cruel or unusual punishment, right to due process, and right to education. As a result, more constitutional tort cases, that are initiated by or on the behalf of disabled persons and minors, are beginning to appear in the legal literature. In 1975, the Supreme Court affirmed students' right to sue for damages when school authorities cause them injury by deliberately disregarding established constitutional rights (e.g., by searching students without sufficient cause), when such actions cannot reasonably be characterized as being in good faith.[10]

Many of these cases concerning the abridgment of rights have been grounded on section 1983 of Title 42 of the United States Code enacted in 1871. This section provides that

> Every person who, under color of any statute, ordinance, regulation, custom or usage, of any State or Territory, subjects or causes to be subjected, any citizen of the United States or other person within the jurisdiction thereof to the deprivation of any rights, privileges, or immunities secured by the Constitution and laws, shall be liable to the party injured in an action at law, suit in equity, or other proper proceeding for redress.

If a community center receives monies from local, state, or federal governmental agencies, as most centers do, then it would probably be considered a governmental agent under section 1983. Therefore, the community center must take care not to abrogate individual constitutional or statutory rights without providing the necessary due process. In later chapters of this book, specific due process procedures and requirements are discussed. If a violation of section 1983 is alleged, a lawsuit would be filed against the officials of the community center rather than the community center itself. In addition to a violation of clients' established rights, the administrators may be held liable for violating the constitutional or statutory rights of staff members particularly regarding hiring, promotion, disciplinary, and discharge decisions.

An example of a constitutional tort lawsuit initiated by an employee that was based on 42 U.S.C. § 1983 can be found in *Aumiller v. University of Delaware*.[11] This lawsuit concerns a lecturer who alleged that University of Delaware officials violated the First Amendment rights of free expression and association. The university officials refused to renew the lecturer's contract because of a statement that he made on the subject of homosexuality which appeared in three newspaper articles. The district court found that the university officials had violated the lecturer's right to freedom of expression by failing to rehire him as a result of the newspaper articles. The court also stated that the lecturer was entitled to be rehired and to back pay, that the university officials were liable to the lecturer for his emotional stress, embarrassment, and humiliation, and they were ordered to pay the lecturer $10,000 in compensatory damages. Also, since the university president demonstrated a malicious or wanton disregard for the lecturer's constitutional rights, he was ordered to pay $5,000 in punitive damages[12] to the lecturer.

BREACH OF CONTRACT

Like other persons and entities in our society, community centers and their staff members are legally accountable for contracts that they make with others. Basically, a contract is a transaction involving two or more individuals whereby each becomes obligated to the other, with reciprocal rights to demand performance of what is promised by each individual respectively.[31] Contracts can be made orally or in writing. Except for minors and those persons who are mentally incompetent, the law can impose a monetary penalty upon those who fail to act as they had agreed to act in the contract. This failure to comply with the contract is called *breach of contract*. Contractual disputes can involve almost any area including the sale of property, the rendition of work, labor, or services, and the ownership of property. Of course, a community center and its staff are typically at liberty to contract for a particular result with whomever they wish. For example, the community center can agree to perform a vocational evaluation on a prospective client for a fee, and the center can agree to pay a roofing company to repair a leaking roof. Extreme caution, however, must be used before making any oral or written guarantee of a particular treatment result because failure to obtain that result would constitute a breach of contract. If prior to providing services to a new client, the community center prepares a clear written and oral statement that tactfully explains to the client and/or the client's guardian the services the center will provide, the community center will be in a far better position to defend itself if a difficulty develops.

POINTS TO REMEMBER

1. If a community center maintains on its premises an unreasonable and foreseeable hazard to children or others with child-like judgment, the center can be held responsible for any resulting injuries.
2. A community center may be held responsible for any injury resulting from the termination of its service relationship with a client without the client's consent, if the client is still in need of the center's services and if the client was not given adequate notice and opportunity to seek assistance from another therapist or center.
3. The community center can be held liable for false, damaging communications that are made about clients, staff, or others. Staff members must make sure that their written and oral statements concerning others are based on adequate factual knowledge.
4. Intentional use of injury-producing force against another and the threat thereof constitute the torts of battery and assault, respectively, and the perpetrator can be held responsible for the injuries.
5. A community center must obtain the client's valid consent before beginning a treatment procedure that presents a foreseeable risk of harm and before beginning an experimental procedure. Failure to do so may constitute legally actionable assault and battery.
6. A community center must obtain the client's valid consent before information about or pictures of the client are released to the press or to any unauthorized persons.

7. If a community center lawfully infringes upon a client's personal liberty or freedom of movement, the center may be held responsible for any mental or physical suffering that occurs.

8. Community centers must be careful not to disregard or violate the constitutional and statutory rights and privileges of clients, staff, or others without providing the necessary due process.

9. Community centers and their staff members are legally accountable for contracts that they make with clients or others. Thus, they must be wary of making any oral or written guarantees (contracts) concerning treatment outcomes.

REFERENCES

Alexander, K., Corns, R., & McCann, W. *Public school law: Cases and materials.* St. Paul, MN: West Publishing Co., 1969.

Chayet, N.L. *Legal implications of emergency care.* New York: Meredith Corporation, 1969.

Clear, D.K. Negative statements in letters of recommendation: From defamation to defense. In M.A. McGhehey (ed.), *School law update—1977.* Topeka, KS: National Organization on Legal Problems of Education, 1978.

Fraser, G.H., & Chadsey, P.D. Informed consent in malpractice cases. *Williamette Law Journal,* 1970, 6(2), 183–191.

Gifis, S.H. *Law dictionary.* Woodbury, NY: Barron's Educational Series, Inc., 1975.

Health Law Center. *Problems in hospital law* (2nd ed.). Rockville, MD: Aspen Systems Corporation, 1974.

Holder, A.R. *Medical malpractice law.* New York: John Wiley & Sons, 1975.

Martin, R. *Legal challenges to behavior modification.* Champaign, IL: Research Press, 1975.

Prosser, W.L. *Handbook of the law of torts* (4th ed.). St. Paul, MN: West Publishing Co., 1971.

Tancredi, L.R., Lieb, J., & Slaby, A.E. *Legal issues in psychiatric care.* Hagerstown, MD: Harper & Row Publishers, 1975.

ENDNOTES

[1]388 So. 2d 164 (La. Ct. App., Second Cir. 1976).

[2]366 N.E. 2d 542 (Ill. App. Ct., First Dist., First Div. 1977).

[3]Kaimowitz v. Department of Mental Health, 42 U.S.L.W. 2063 (Mich. Cir. Ct. 1973).

[4]223 A. 2d 663 (Pa. Sup. Ct. 1966).

[5]119 So. 2d 649 (La. Ct. App. 1960).

[6]159 S.W. 2d 291 (Mo. Sup. Ct. 1942).

[7]400 N.Y.S. 2d 668 (N.Y. Sup. Ct. 1977).

[8]155 S.E. 194 (Ga. Sup. Ct. 1930).

[9]191 N.W. 2d 335 (Mich. Sup. Ct. 1971).

[10]Wood v. Strickland, 420 U.S. 308 (1975).

[11]Aumiller v. University of Delaware, 434 F. Supp. 1273 (D. Del. 1977).

[12]"Punitive (exemplary) damages are compensation in excess of the actual damages. It is awarded as a form of punishment for the wrongdoer and an excess

enhancement to the injured party. Actual damages must exist before punitive (exemplary) damages will be found and will be awarded only in circumstances of malicious and willful misconduct" (Gifis, 1975).

[13]Gardner v. City of Englewood, 282 P. 2d 1094 (Col. Sup. Ct. 1955).

4

POTENTIAL
PROBLEM AREAS IN THE
ADMINISTRATION OF A PROGRAM

In addition to a basic understanding of the general legal principles of negligence and other tort issues, an awareness of some specific problem areas that may give rise to a lawsuit should help an agency or therapist minimize risks. In this chapter, the reader will find some circumstances in which courts have found agencies or therapists negligent in their performance of administrative duties. The issues represent both negligent failure to perform a duty and performance of a duty in a negligent manner. Illustrative tort cases related to this type of negligence are also mentioned.

The cases that are discussed in this chapter involve defendants who are primarily doctors, hospitals, state and federal institutions, psychiatrists, school boards, and teachers. Although very few negligence or other tort lawsuits involving community centers have been reported in the literature, the lawsuits presented here are analogous to the problems a community center might face. The paucity of lawsuits against community centers may be attributable to: 1) the fact that until the last 10 years community centers were almost nonexistent and the clients and their guardians viewed placement in such programs as a charitable act rather than as a right, 2) the number of persons served by community programs is quite small and the frequency of "accidents" is correspondingly low, 3) community centers' staffs may have considerable behavioral and counseling expertise and they may be particularly adept at dissuading dissatisfied consumers from bringing legal action against the center, and 4) the client and/or the client's family may not wish to publicize the client's condition. Whatever the reason for the relatively small number of lawsuits involving community centers, considering the current sociopolitical emphasis on normalization (Wolfensberger, 1972) and the growth of community centers (O'Connor, 1976), the likelihood of "accidents" and lawsuits will increase.

FAILURE TO SUPERVISE PROPERLY

The failure to supervise employees and students (clients) properly is the most frequently claimed cause in negligence cases involving schools and psychiatric hospitals (Knaak, 1969). The courts clearly recognize that schools and psychiatric hospitals have a duty to supervise and protect students, clients, and employees properly from an unreasonable risk of harm. People involved in conducting community programs for disabled individuals or juveniles also owe their clients a duty to supervise the clients and staff properly so as to prevent the occurrence of unnecessary, foreseeable harm. Improper supervision can result in a client's self-injury (e.g., suicide) or the client injuring another person (e.g., arson). A community center, however, should not be viewed as an insurer of the clients' safety. Some accidents will occur in any program despite the utmost care taken to prevent bodily harm. In these instances, a reasonable court would not impose liability upon the agency or staff. The courts have recognized that in dealing with a person's behavior there is a certain amount of unpredictability.[1] If, on the other hand, the injury can be proved to have been foreseeable and to have resulted from improper supervision, the court can and will impose liability.

In *Milton v. State (Health & Soc. & Rehab. Serv. Admin.)*,[2] the court found the state of Louisiana responsible for the death of a patient at a state-operated psychiatric hospital. The patient was found dead on the hospital grounds apparently as a result of his exposure to the natural elements. The patient had a history of wandering off due to his mental disorder and hospital staff members were aware of this disorder. Nevertheless, the hospital staff did not closely supervise the patient. The court found that it was apparent that the patient should have been kept in quarters that were locked when the patients were not under close staff supervision. Once the patient was discovered missing, the security chief was notified and a search was organized which lasted only one day. Outside help from individuals trained in searching for missing persons was never requested. Subsequently, the patient's body was found on the hospital grounds approximately 3 weeks after his disappearance. The court stated that the circumstances surrounding the patient's elopement and subsequent death led to the conclusion that the defendant's failure to supervise the patient properly caused his death. The court awarded $12,000 to his widow and $5,000 to each of his 14 children.

A New York institution was found to be negligent and held liable for failing to supervise a mental patient properly who subsequently committed suicide. The decedent patient had previously attempted suicide three times and had asked to be put in a locked ward because he was depressed and wanted to harm himself. Three days after making this request, while still in a depressed state, the patient was permitted to leave the hospital grounds unaccompanied. Subsequently, he jumped in front of a subway train and was killed. The court found that the hospital personnel knew of the patient's suicidal tendencies and failed to provide proper supervision in restraining him and in allowing him to leave.[3]

In another case, a father was awarded $35,000 from the state of Louisiana because of the failure of a state school to supervise the man's retarded son properly. Roy Daniels was a resident of Pinecrest State School and was returning some records to a storage area following a dance at Pinecrest one night. Although Roy had been instructed not to walk in the middle of the street, the staff knew that he had a tendency to do so, especially when pulling his wagon as he was on the night of the accident. When returning the records, Roy walked in the street and was struck and killed by a car. The court found that it would have been quite easy for a supervisor to have accompanied Roy to the storage area. Because of this and the fact that the staff knew of Roy's tendency to walk in the street, the court found that the state had breached its obligation to supervise Roy properly.[4]

In *Lilienthal v. San Leandro Unified School District of Alameda County*,[5] a teacher and a school district were held liable for their failure to provide adequate supervision to students. While a metal class was being held outdoors, a student was playing with a knife by repeatedly throwing it into the ground. On one throw, the knife struck another student's drawing board and the knife was deflected into a third student's eye. At the time of the incident, the students were sitting in a semi-circle around the teacher reviewing a safety test. A lower court ruled that neither the school nor the school district nor the teacher were liable for the injury. An appellate court, however, reversed the lower court's decision, stating that there was adequate evidence to find the school district and the teacher guilty of negligence because of failure to supervise the students properly and to stop the knife throwing.

Many of the cases involving failure to supervise clients properly, especially mentally ill and mentally retarded clients, focus on the foreseeability of harm to the client. Usually, if the court finds that it was foreseeable that the client could harm himself or herself or others, or could be harmed in some way, the court will impose strict standards of supervision on the staff. If it is determined that it is foreseeable that a client could be harmed, the court will then determine if the staff's supervision fell below an acceptable standard of care, i.e., whether staff members were negligent in their supervision.[6]

Supervision problems can arise as a result of understaffing. For example, *Silverman v. City of New York*[7] involved injuries that resulted when one teacher had supervisory responsibilities for more than 200 students on a playground. Among the students on the playground were several youths who were known to be troublesome and violent. It was the practice of the school to separate these "difficult" students from well-behaved students in classes other than gym class. While one of the students was walking toward the locker room he was accosted and brutally assaulted by three other students. Two of the attackers were nonclass members with known histories of violence. The injured 14-year-old boy did nothing to provoke his attackers. At the time of the assault, the teacher was in the locker room with several other students. The court found the school district negligent in their failure to supervise the students properly, primarily as a result of understaffing, and the court awarded damages to the youth and his mother.

The courts have recognized that excessive supervision and restraint to prevent injury will not necessarily benefit clients and, instead, may even worsen clients' conditions (*Baker v. U.S.*).[8] Clients should be given a degree of supervision and restraint commensurate with the client's abilities and the amount of risk facing the client. The decision concerning the degree of supervision a client requires is to be based on available information and on professional judgment. Courts have recognized that a wrong decision can occur honestly and often in such cases will not impose liability for the resulting injuries. An example of a situation in which a court did not hold a defendant liable for injuries resulting from an error in judgment can be found in *Torres v. State*.[6] This lawsuit involved a claim against the state of New York alleging negligent supervision based upon the escape and death of a mental patient from a psychiatric hospital. The patient left the hospital grounds one day and died after apparently either falling or jumping off a bridge and being struck by several cars. During his stay at the hospital, the patient never exhibited violent or suicidal tendencies. He was granted progressively greater privileges only upon his favorable response to treatment. At the time of his death, he had earned an honor card which allowed him to leave the ward during daylight hours and move about the minimally supervised hospital grounds. Nothing in the patient's records indicated that the treatment he received was other than medically sound and proper. Accordingly, the court found that the possibility of his committing suicide as a result of his increased freedom was not a foreseeable risk for which the state could be held liable.

If those responsible for supervision have or should have knowledge of a client's propensity to harm himself or herself or others and they fail to take reasonable precautions, however, they may be held liable for resulting injuries. For example, in *Hilscher v. State*,[10] a mentally retarded adolescent, who was a resident of a state school for the mentally retarded, set fire to a summer house. Even though the authorities of the institution had been warned of the adolescent's fire-setting tendencies (he had started several other fires), they failed to take the proper precautions. The court found that the state employees were guilty of negligence for their failure to supervise the resident properly, and the court noted that liability probably would not have been imposed if the act had been unrelated to the adolescent's previous behavior.

The absence for a few minutes of the person responsible for supervision, such as a shop manager or teacher, will often not be interpreted by the court as a negligent lack of supervision, particularly if the absence is job related. If, however, the absence occurs under hazardous circumstances or in a hazardous location, such as a swimming pool, or if the absence lasts an extended period of time, the courts might impose liability for any resulting injuries. An example of such a case can be found in *Christofides v. Hellenic Eastern Orthodox Christian Church of N.Y.,*[11] which involved a teacher who had been absent from a classroom for approximately 25 minutes. During the absence, one of the students was wielding a knife for 5 to 10 minutes before stabbing a classmate. The court decided that if the teacher had not been away from the class for such a long time the stabbing would not have occurred. Subsequently, the court found the teacher and the school negligent for failing to provide proper supervision. Thus, the more dangerous the situation, the more careful the supervision must be.

One test of liability that has been used by some courts involves determining whether the incident would have occurred had a supervisor been present and performing the supervisory duties (Reutter & Hamilton, 1976). If the incident could have occurred with the supervisor present, neither the supervisor nor the employer would be held liable. For example, in *Albers v. Independent Sch. Dist. No. 302 of Lewis Co.,*[12] the Supreme Court of Idaho found that proper supervision would not have prevented the occurrence of a particular injury. While school was closed for Christmas break, six high school youths persuaded a school custodian to disregard school policy and allow the students to enter the gymnasium and play basketball. After the custodian unlocked the doors, he left the youths and went about his business. While two youths went after a loose ball, one youth seriously injured his spine when he hit his head on the other youth's hip. The injured youth was a member of the basketball team and an accomplished athlete. Testimony indicated that the youths were playing a "real clean game" of basketball at the time of the accident. The court did not find any evidence indicating that the presence of a coach or a teacher would have prevented the collision of the youths chasing the rebounding basketball. The court held neither the custodian nor the school district liable.

A second test of liability involves determining whether under the circumstances the possibility of an injury when the supervisor is absent is reasonably foreseeable (Reutter & Hamilton, 1976). If a general danger is foreseeable and if proper supervision likely would have prevented the accident, the supervisor and/or the supervisor's employer may be held liable. In *Sheehan v. St. Peter's Catholic School,*[13] the Minnesota Supreme Court found the school liable for the injuries to a student's eye. During the morning recess an eighth grade teacher took her female students out to the athletic field and instructed them to stay there until she returned. The teacher then went into the building. A group of eighth grade boys, who were playing baseball nearby, began throwing stones at the girls. Approximately 10 minutes after the teacher left, a pebble struck and blinded one of the girls. In their ruling in favor of the plaintiff, the court emphasized that it was necessary only to prove that a general danger was foreseeable and that supervision would have prevented the accident; it was not necessary to prove that the particular accident which occurred was foreseeable. This ruling should be contrasted with a case presented in Chapter 2 where a boy was partially blinded by a small rock on a school playground. The court, in that case, found the teacher's aide was not negligent in her supervision of youths because she had walked by the group of boys approximately 30 seconds before the accident. Although the two cases are factually similar, liability was not imposed in the latter instance because the teacher's aide had engaged in what the court felt was proper supervision of the youths.

If reasonable precautions are taken and an unforeseen act causes an injury, the absent supervisor would usually not be held liable. For example, in *Swaitkowski v. Board of Ed. of City of Buffalo,*[14] neither the school board nor the teacher was found liable for injuries sustained by a student. The injury occurred when the student sat on a pencil point placed upon his chair by another student. At the time of the incident the teacher was absent from the room assisting a fellow teacher locate books. The book room was 10½ feet away from the class and both doors were open. The court viewed the placing of the pencil point as an unforeseeable event.

FAILURE TO PLACE OR DISCHARGE CLIENTS PROPERLY

Community centers should be designed in such a way so as to allow clients to move in a continuum of steps toward a greater degree of self-care and self-fulfillment. Good sense, as well as scientific theory and practice, dictates that in order to achieve these goals clients need proper stepwise instruction, appropriate feedback, and opportunities under controlled conditions for testing out new abilities. Realistically, a community center is not capable of providing these kinds of specialized services for all potential clients. For example, some potential clients may need a greater degree of restraint or supervision than the community center can provide, or they may need less supervision and more normalizing experiences than the center can provide. Care must be exercised, however, not to discriminate against a client simply because of a disability that requires only reasonable modifications in the center's program or facilities. For example, an otherwise appropriate sheltered workshop must not exclude a person confined to a wheelchair simply because the workshop needs a ramp at the entrance. Rather, the ramp should be constructed. If a community center accepts a client for placement in a program that presents a reasonably foreseeable harm to the client or others, the center may be held liable for resulting injuries. In addition, the client's condition must be periodically evaluated in order to determine whether the placement remains appropriate.

A clear-cut example of an improper placement decision and the subsequent failure to evaluate the placement can be found in *Hoffman v. Board of Education of City of New York*.[15] This case concerned an attempt to recover damages resulting from the placement of the plaintiff, who had normal intelligence, in classes for children with retarded mental development for a period of 11 years. Several years before the plaintiff began school, he was given a primarily nonverbal intelligence test and scored a 94, well within the normal range of intelligence. It was apparent, however, that the boy had a serious speech deficit. Shortly after he entered school, he was given a verbally based intelligence test and his intelligence quotient tested to be 74. Since, pursuant to state law, "75" was the cutoff point, he was assigned to "special" classes. These classes typically moved much more slowly through curricula than did regular classes. After 11 years in "special" classes, he entered an Occupational Training Center for retarded persons. After 1 year, he was given an adult intelligence test and scored well within the normal range. He was never retested during the 12-year period although the school psychologist recommended that he be retested within 2 years of his first placement in the special classes. Since he was no longer labeled retarded, he was dismissed from the Occupational Training Center. He was also denied Social Security benefits even though he had a disabling speech deficit and he could not complete a job application. The lower court held that the school board was liable to the plaintiff for damages resulting from the negligence of school employees who failed to retest the boy and, thus, kept him in special classes. As a result of the injuries sustained by the plaintiff, the lower court found that he was entitled to recover $500,000 from the school board.

Another example of injuries resulting from improper placement can be found in *Eldredge v. Kamp Kachess Youth Services, Inc.*[16] Kamp Kachess was a private, nonprofit group child care facility that accepted private referrals and that contracted with the Department of Social and Health Services for care of dependent children. Shortly after Kamp Kachess accepted two youths referred from the juvenile court, the youths escaped only to be promptly apprehended by the police for car theft and burglary. Kamp Kachess had no physical restraints, such as fences or guards, to deter elopements and maximum supervision was rarely used. Nevertheless, Kamp Kachess accepted the youths back and reassigned them to the same nonsecure facility. A few days later, the juveniles again escaped and they stole and wrecked the plaintiff's car. The court decided that in light of the minimal security at the facility and the lack of any increased supervision of the boys when they were reassigned, the harm was foreseeable. Kamp Kachess was found responsible for the damages to the woman's car.

The courts have rather consistently imposed liability where placement and discharge decisions contradicted or ignored significant information. In addition, the courts have indicated that such decisions are to be supported by clinical data of sufficient detail to enable a judge or jury, if necessary, to evaluate the propriety of the decision (Roby, 1976). These data may include the client's test scores, records of the client's previous behaviors and experiences, the client's performances in the present and previous programs, the client's health status and medical history, and the community's and center's resources. The courts have recognized that professionals and paraprofessionals are not infallible and that honest errors in judgment can occur. If, however, the error results from the blatant failure to use due care in gathering and reviewing relevant information and if such an error causes an injury, the courts can hold the center and its staff liable for the injuries.

In *Kleber v. Stevens,*[17] the plaintiff brought suit against two physicians for negligently committing her to a state mental hospital. Testimony in the trial indicated that the certificate of commitment was based primarily on hearsay of an allegedly vindictive husband rather than on good medical practice and examination. Expert testimony demonstrated that the decision should have been made only after consulting with the patient and after gathering a first-hand detailed history. The court ruled that the physicians made the certificate without proper ordinary care and prudence, and without due examination, inquiry, and evidence of the plaintiff's mental condition. The court found the defendants guilty of negligence and awarded the woman $20,000 in damages.

As with placement decisions, injuries to clients or others can be caused by improperly arrived at discharge decisions. Community centers must, however, have the freedom to discharge from their care those persons who have recovered from the disability that led to the placement, those who have knowingly consented to terminate treatment, and those who cannot benefit from further treatment from the center and who are able to arrange for alternative care without injury to themselves or others (Mathiason, 1963). Discharge decisions must be based on sound professional judgment following a thorough examination of adequate first-hand information or the center may be held responsible for any resulting injuries.

For example, in *Cohen v. State,* [18] the defendant was held responsible for the suicide of a psychiatric patient who had been erroneously discharged. The decedent, a medical student at the time, had voluntarily entered a psychiatric ward of a hospital for help with his debilitating mental condition. It was apparent from his medical records that the doctors and nurses at the hospital were well aware of the patient's suicidal tendencies. The doctor who was treating him was only in the first year of the several year long residency needed for psychiatric certification. At this point in his training, the doctor did not possess the requisite skill or trained judgment to provide treatment to patients without the supervision of a certified psychiatrist. Records indicated, however, that a certified psychiatrist had never examined the patient and had not actively supervised the treating physician's recommendation. On the day of his discharge, the patient committed suicide. The court found the unsupervised treatment and discharge of the patient constituted negligence on the part of the defendants and that this negligence was the proximate cause of the death; his widow was awarded $35,000.

An example of the court's unwillingness to find a defendant liable for an honest error in professional judgment can be found in *St. George v. State.*[19] Five days after a young man was discharged from a state hospital for the criminally insane, he ran down a street and without provocation stabbed seven persons; four of his victims died. The plaintiff claimed that the hospital's employees negligently made an erroneous diagnosis of the youth's problem, and that the release decision was made on inadequate observation and information. The youth's records disclosed, however, that a great deal of attention had been given the youth. He had been personally interviewed and examined by the superintendent about 10 times during the youth's 14-month hospital stay. Voluminous reports by attendants and doctors recording even minor incidents had been presented at staff meetings, and his case had also been discussed at considerable length at several staff meetings. Although the youth's discharge resulted in tragic deaths and injuries, the court found that the diagnosis of mental illness is not an absolute science; therefore, the defendants could not be held responsible for an honest error in professional judgment.

FAILURE TO ADOPT OR FOLLOW
PRUDENT POLICIES AND REGULATIONS

An employer is responsible for promulgating, implementing, and enforcing reasonable treatment policies and regulations protecting both clients and employees. Failure to perform these duties adequately may make the employer legally responsible for any injuries that may result.

Two similar cases in which school authorities were held responsible for injuries resulting from their failure to adopt proper safety regulations are *Taylor v. Oakland Scavenger Co.*[20] and *Satariano v. Sleight,*[21] which both occurred in the early 1940s. Both cases concern injuries sustained by high school students who were struck by vehicles while they were on their way from a gymnasium to an athletic field for a scheduled class. The *Taylor* case involved a 15-year-old girl who had been struck by a garbage truck coming around a blind corner on the school grounds. At the time of the accident, the girl was running from the gymnasium to the athletic field. Evidence presented at the trial indicated that the principal had known for 7 years of the practice of physical education students running to the field. Nevertheless, the school authorities did not establish regulations prohibiting this running. In addition, the school permitted 18 trucks to drive on the school grounds without subjecting the trucks to any safety requirements other than the general provisions of the California Vehicle Code. The Supreme Court of California affirmed a lower court's decision that the failure of the school authorities to establish such regulations warranted a finding that the school district was negligent. In *Satariano*, an 18-year-old boy was struck by an automobile while crossing a well-traveled street on his way to the athletic field. The boy crossed the street in the middle of a block where there was neither a marked crosswalk nor a sign cautioning automobile drivers about pedestrians. As in *Taylor*, the principal knew for several years that boys were in the habit of walking and running across the street at this point. Nevertheless, there was never a sign posted warning the boys against this dangerous habit, there was no teacher or other person stationed to prevent the crossing, and there was no general rule or regulation promulgated to prohibit such crossings. On occasion, however, a teacher would catch a student crossing the street (at that point rather than the appointed place) and give the student a corrective warning. A California appeals court ruled that the school authorities were liable for their failure to develop proper safety regulations.

Titus v. Lindberg[22] is another case involving a school principal's failure to adopt proper safety regulations. The case concerned a young boy who sustained serious eye damage. One morning as he entered the school grounds, he was struck in the eye by a paper clip shot from an elastic band by an older boy. The school grounds was the bus pick-up site for two other schools. Several hundred students typically gathered on the school grounds waiting for the buses to come or waiting for the school doors to open. Even though the school employed 19 full-time teachers, none of them had been assigned any responsibilities in connection with the supervision of the students before school began. The principal had taken full responsibility for the job of supervising all the children. At the time of the incident, however, the principal was inside the school building. The court found the principal negligent on the grounds that he had not established regulations concerning the congregation of students and their conduct before school, that he had not assigned any teachers to assist in supervising the pupils, and that at the time of the incident he was not actively supervising the students.

School personnel have also been held liable for injuries that were caused by a failure to follow local or state regulations (Reutter & Hamilton, 1976). The failure to follow state regulations was a primary factor in *Armlin v. Board of Educ. of Middleburgh Central School Dist.*[23] This suit concerned the injuries sustained by a fifth grade girl while in a gymnastics class. While performing stunts on gymnastic rings, the girl fell backward, injuring her back. The State Physical Education Syllabus, which was used by the school, stated that the physical education equipment and the class should be placed so as to be entirely in view of the teacher. At the time of the accident, the teacher was at the trampoline and the rings were not in sight. Although the stunt the girl was attempting was forbidden by the physical education teacher, testimony indicated that it was performed often in the class. The court found the teacher and the school district liable for the girl's injuries.

An employer or therapist may also be held responsible for injuries resulting from a failure to follow self-imposed rules and guidelines. In *Homere v.*

State,[24] the state was found guilty of negligence for its psychiatrists' failure to follow their own guidelines concerning a release decision at a state mental hospital. Because of the seriousness of a patient's previous behavior, the psychiatrists at a state hospital in New York had imposed a more stringent standard of self-review that required the evaluation of the patient by a commission composed of three psychiatrists. Following the patient's evaluation, the commission recommended that the patient be released and that he be treated as an outpatient in the community. Sixteen days after the release decision had been reached, but before the patient was actually released, the patient picked up a chair and smashed windows and a television set. As a result of this incident the patient was placed in a protective restraint for 2 days. Despite these incidents, the patient's case was not reevaluated and he was released a short time later. On the morning of his release, the patient assaulted five women without provocation. The court ruled that in light of the patient's behavior following the evaluation it was negligent to permit the patient's release without reconvening the three-member commission to reevaluate the case. The defendants were held liable for the injuries resulting from the patient's attacks.

An agency or therapist may also incur liability resulting from a failure to comply with official directives, such as court orders. In *Semler v. Psychiatric Institute of Washington, D.C.,*[25] the court held a psychiatric institute, a psychiatrist, and a probation officer negligent for their failure to comply with a court directive. A court had ordered that a man, who was on probation for having abducted a young girl, receive treatment at and remain confined in a psychiatric institute until he was released by the court. Any change in the probationer's hospital treatment status was to be approved by the court. Less than one year later, the court granted permission for the probationer to be transferred to the status of a day care patient. This meant that he would spend from 8:00 a.m. till 5:00 p.m. at the psychiatric institute and he would spend his evenings and weekends at home with his parents. Several months later the psychiatrist and the probation officer changed the patient's status to merely participating in group therapy sessions meeting twice weekly. This change allowed the man to move out of his parent's home and live alone. The court was not informed, and the new arrangement lacked the supervision and structure the court had demanded. Approximately one month later, the man killed a young girl. The girl's family sued for damages. The court found the psychiatric institute, the psychiatrist, and the probation officer guilty of negligence and liable for the girl's death.

The case of *Mounds Park Hospital v. Von Eye*[26] concerned the failure of a psychiatric hospital to follow doctor's orders. A doctor had given the hospital orders to observe a women patient closely because of her suicidal tendencies. One day the woman wandered out of her room, down corridors, and into a patient's room in another department. She jumped from that patient's second floor window. The woman sued the hospital to recover for the injuries she sustained when she jumped from the window. The occupant of the room from which the plaintiff escaped testified that she went out into the corridor to call for a nurse and that she "went down the hall yelling for a nurse," but no nurse came. The jury concluded that immediately prior to and at the time when the patient jumped from the window she was not being closely observed. The court found that the hospital was negligent for not following the doctor's instructions and that the hospital was liable for the patient's injuries.

Doctors' Hospital Inc. v. Kovats[27] involved the failure of a nurse to follow the proper policy in applying a restraint device. The lawsuit was brought by a patient against a hospital and a doctor for recovery for injuries the patient sustained when another patient struck him with a chair. The patient who wielded the chair had extricated himself on at least five occasions from the restraint device prior to the time he slipped from the restraints and struck the plaintiff. The assailant's condition clearly made him a threat to other persons. This patient's doctor had ordered the hospital nurses to keep the patient in the restraint device when he was not being observed by a nurse. Expert testimony indicated that if the restraint device had been properly applied, the patient would not have been able to escape from it. The defendants were found guilty of negligence for the failure to follow the proper and safe practices in applying the restraint device. The court awarded the injured patient $4,500.

FAILURE TO INSPECT AND
REPAIR DANGEROUS PHYSICAL CONDITIONS

An employer or therapist has a duty to inspect and to repair, if necessary, the physical facilities and the equipment used in the agency. The inspection must be as frequent and as thorough as any reasonably prudent person might make under similar circumstances and should uncover latent or concealed dangers. The employer is permitted a reasonable amount of time to remedy the situation following notice of the danger. Failure to remove dangerous conditions not discoverable with reasonable care, tests, or inspections does not ordinarily constitute negligence (Mirabel & Levy, 1962). Continued use of known dangerous or defective equipment, however, may result in the employer or therapist being held liable for injuries caused by the situation. Obviously, defects in facilities and equipment will develop sooner or later in any community center. These conditions must be found and remedied in order to adequately protect the well-being of clients, staff, public, and the center itself.

In *Dawson v. Tulare Union High School District,*[28] the court found that the defendants were negligent in maintaining a patently dangerous condition. During a physical education class a group of high school girls were playing a jumping game as instructed by the teacher. Nearby, a piano, which rested on a dolly, suddenly fell without warning and crushed the ankle of one of the girls. The student's family subsequently sued the school district for damages. During the trial, testimony demonstrated that the piano had rested on the dolly in an unstable condition for more than a year and that school officials had knowledge of the dangerous condition during that time. In fact, about a year before the accident, the piano fell backward and injured the leg of a student who was trying to move the piano. A report about the accident had been filed. Nevertheless, the school had done nothing to correct the situation. The court found the defendants guilty of negligence and liable for the injuries caused by their failure to correct the precarious positioning of the piano.

A similar incident occurred in *Kidwell v. School District No. 300, Whitman County.*[29] This case involved a 9-year-old girl whose foot was permanently maimed when an upright piano fell upon it. Testimony indicated that the piano had been stored in such a manner that it could easily be tipped over. Shortly after the accident the school installed iron supports on the piano to prevent it from falling backward again. The court found the school district negligent on the ground that the piano had been stored in such a manner as to present a foreseeable harm to children.

In *Nicholson v. Board of Education of City of New York,*[30] a New York appellate court found sufficient evidence to sustain the trial jury's conclusion that the municipality had constructive, if not actual, notice of an illegal and hazardous condition. For years, the unsupervised schoolyard was used as a meeting and play area for children in that densely populated area. On numerous occasions the school board had been informed that firecrackers were being exploded in the schoolyard after hours. Members of the community, concerned about the firecrackers, had requested that the missing gates of a high metal fence separating the schoolyard from the sidewalk be reconstructed so that the yard could be closed. The board failed to take this or any other protective measure, and as a consequence, an exploding firecracker blinded a 7½-year-old boy. The court found the Board of Education liable for the boy's injuries.

The court, in *Freund v. Oakland Board of Education,*[31] held the school board liable for injuries sustained by a 15-year-old student. While waiting for class to be dismissed, steel lockers fell on the student and injured her. A subsequent examination of the locker room revealed that some of the steel lockers in the girls' locker room were in a dangerous and defective condition in that they were not secured to prevent their falling. The principal of the school testified that the school janitor inspected the lockers twice a year. Other evidence, however, indicated that the dangerous condition existed for some time prior to the accident. After reviewing the evidence, the court found the school district guilty of negligence in maintaining dangerous conditions and therefore liable for the injuries.

Hovey v. State[32] involved a student who fell and injured herself at a state normal school. The student had attended a school-sanctioned and school-sponsored music rehearsal on the second floor of the school from 4:00 to 5:00 one afternoon in late December. From the lighted auditorium, she entered a dark hallway and started to descend an unlit stairway. The student was carrying several books when she left the auditorium. The steps and the handrail were made of black slate and black painted wood, respectively. The handrail did not come all the way to the first landing, but instead, stopped several steps short of the landing. While reaching for the short handrail the student slipped and fell down 15 steps. The court found the state negligent and liable for the girl's injuries, since the state did not provide a safe exit by failing to illuminate the hallway and stairway and by failing to provide an adequate handrail.

TRANSPORTATION ACCIDENTS

Public transportation facilities may often be inadequate, expensive, or nonexistent, particularly in smaller communities, and most clients of community centers do not have driver's licenses or automobiles. Clients must frequently rely upon the community center to provide most transportation needs. A greater legislative awareness of these transportation needs and the creation of more varied and flexible public transportation systems would help alleviate this problem. Presently, however, transportation problems exist and must be dealt with by the clients, staff, and community centers. The centers often use buses, vans, and automobiles to provide transportation to clients. Considering the hazards of road travel and the physical and mental limitations of many clients, accidents connected with transportation services are likely to occur. Traffic accidents frequently result in time-consuming, costly lawsuits. For example, in 1958, a school bus left a road, allegedly as a result of the driver's negligence, struck a culvert, exploded, and burned (*Molitor v. Kaneland Community Unit District No. 302*).[33] After more than 6 years of lawsuits, 14 of the 16 children involved in the accident were able to recover a total of $850,000 from the school district. The school district's insurance company paid only $100,000 of the damages and the school district was responsible for paying the remaining $750,000 (Nolte, 1969).

The boarding and disembarking of passengers are particularly high risk times. A survey by the National Educational Association (National Education Association Research Division, 1963) showed that in school transportation more accidents resulting in lawsuits occur during the boarding and disembarking of bus passengers than at any other time. *Wynn v. Gandy*[34] involved an action against the driver of a school bus that struck and killed a student. A 13-year-old boy sustained fatal injuries when he was shoved by other pupils and fell under a slow-moving bus. The boy and approximately 100 other students were crowding around and running after the moving bus when the boy was shoved. The school authorities and the bus driver knew that the children customarily crowded around and chased the bus; the driver had been late in arriving to pick up the children and he was preparing to stop on the opposite side of the street from the school when the accident occurred. The driver was held liable for the boy's death.

Accidents may also occur as a result of children playing in and around parked buses. In *Scott v. Thompson*,[35] a young girl died while playing in a school bus. While the bus driver was waiting to begin his second run, he went into a garage for a cup of coffee. Unfortunately, he left the bus parked on a busy highway with the door open and the motor running. Several children entered the bus and began playing. The bus driver was not able to watch the bus from his location in the garage. A 7-year-old girl, who was playing in the bus, left the bus and was struck by a truck as she attempted to cross the highway. At the trial, the bus driver admitted that he was aware of the school safety regulation prohibiting school bus drivers from leaving a bus unattended with children aboard. Evidence also showed that the defendant bus driver knew that the highway was heavily traveled and that children would be getting on the bus while it was parked. The court found that the bus driver's failure either to park a safe distance from the highway and to keep the bus doors closed or to remain on the bus constituted negligence. The court also concluded that there was sufficient evidence to substantiate a causal relationship between the driver's negligence and the child's injuries. The court awarded the plaintiff $65,000.

In *Davidson v. Horne*,[36] a bus driver was held responsible for the injuries of a student who was struck by a car immediately after the student disembarked from the bus. The 9-year-old boy was hit by a speeding car that failed to stop for the school bus as required by law. The bus driver, however, had failed to pull the bus over to the side of the road; instead, he stopped near the center of the highway. Furthermore, the bus driver failed to check the traffic conditions before he discharged the child. The court ruled that both the school bus driver and the driver of the automobile acted in a negligent manner and that they were liable for the student's injuries.

Several courts have held that school bus drivers are under a duty to exercise extraordinary or the highest degree of care for the safety of the students being transported (*Davidson v. Horne; Van Cleave v. Illini Coach Co.*[37]). Courts would very likely consider that drivers of vehicles transporting community center clients have a similar duty to exercise extraordinary care. Accidents en route, however, may happen without liability being imposed on the driver of a bus or other vehicle if the vehicle is operated in a safe and prudent manner at the time of the accident. In order to establish that the bus driver is liable for the injuries resulting from an accident, it is necessary to prove that the bus driver operated the bus in a negligent manner (National Education Association Research Division, 1963). For example, in *Van Cleave,* a bus driver and his company were found guilty of negligence and responsible for a student's injuries. The bus company had failed to provide someone other than the driver to manage and supervise the children. For a considerable length of time prior to the accident in question, many of the children on the bus were standing in the aisle and were engaged in "roughhousing." The bus driver, without warning, suddenly propellled the bus forward and one of the children, who was standing in the aisle, was thrown forward and struck and injured the 6-year-old plaintiff. The Appellate Court of Illinois affirmed a lower court decision holding that the bus driver and the bus company had operated the vehicle in a negligent manner and that they were liable for the plaintiff's injuries.

Another important issue related to traffic accidents involves the responsibility for injuries clients receive while traveling in privately owned automobiles. Depending upon the limitations of the client and the client's arrangement with the center, the center may be responsible for making certain that the private automobile is in good, safe running order and that the driver is cautious, licensed, and insured. When the community center is deriving a benefit from transporting a client, the client enjoys the status of an invitee or business visitor if he or she is being picked up for work by a staff member in a privately owned automobile. The community center owes such passengers not only the duty to exercise due care for their protection, but also the duty to warn the client of known dangers, to inspect the vehicle in order to discover and repair concealed hazards, and to take reasonable precautions to protect the client from foreseeable harm (Prosser, 1971). Failure to do so exposes the community center to liability for any accident-related injuries.

Hanson v. Reedley Joint Union High School District[38] involves a lawsuit arising from an automobile accident that killed one student and injured another while they were riding home from junior college tennis practice in another student's car. The teacher in charge of the practice arranged for one student to take other students home in his car, and the school reimbursed the driver for one gallon of gas for every 10 miles he drove. Transporting the students to another school's tennis court for practice was essential for continuing the junior college's tennis program, and similar kinds of transportation arrangements had been made with students in the past. The instructor knew that the driver of the car had a tendency toward recklessness and that the student's car was in an unsafe condition. The student's car was specially equipped for additional speed and power, it had no fenders, roof, or runningboards, it had faulty lights, speedometer, and brakes, the steering was loose, and the tires were worn smooth. Evidence indicated that the accident occurred as a result of the recklessness of the driver and the unsafe condition of the automobile. The court found that the driver, the teacher, and the junior college were all guilty of negligence and that they were liable for the death and injuries.

When a client is riding in a vehicle merely for his or her own pleasure or on his or her own business, and without making any return or conferring any benefit on the driver, he or she would probably be considered a guest (Black, 1968). For example, when a community center employee and a client go out for a drink after work in the employee's automobile, the client would probably be considered a guest. "While the driver is under a duty to exercise reasonable care for the protection of the guest in his active operation of the car, and is required to disclose to him any defects in the vehicle of which he has knowledge, he is not required to inspect the automobile to make sure that it is safe, and is not liable for defects of which he does not know" (Proser, 1971, p. 383). Thus, a community center might not be held liable for injuries to a client if she or he were a guest in a vehicle. It should be noted, however, that if the community program is a residential program, e.g., a group home, the client would most likely be considered a business visitor even if the excursion was a pleasurable one for the client. This is a result of the fact that group home supervision is continuous and can involve several different types of activities.

The Supreme Court of South Dakota considered the question of the guest status of the passengers in *Robe v. Ager*.[39] A group of high school girls were participating in a school fund raising event in another town. The superintendent allowed the dean of girls to use his car to take the girls, and he provided a credit card for expenses. After the fund raiser, they decided to take a 90-mile side trip to a swimming area. One of the girls, who was an inexperienced driver, was allowed to drive. An accident occurred in which one of the girls was injured. The evidence was sufficient to find that the driver operated the vehicle in a negligent manner and that the dean of girls was negligent in her supervision of the girls. The court, however, did not find the school district or any other school employee liable because at the time of the accident the girls were guests. The court found that the side trip had been for the mutual pleasure and enjoyment of all the occupants of the automobile and it had no rational relationship to the purpose of the intended trip. The court implied, however, that if the accident occurred on the way to or from the fund raiser, the school might have been held liable.

FAILURE TO CARE FOR AN INJURY PROPERLY

Although there may be a moral obligation to help an injured or endangered person, an individual, even a doctor, has no legally enforceable duty to aid an injured person unless a special relationship exists between them (e.g., doctor-patient relationship) (Prosser, 1971). In a limited number of cases the courts have indicated that such a duty exists as the result of a pupil-teacher relationship (*Ogando v. Carquinez Grammar School District of Contra Costa County*[40]) and a player-coach relationship (*Welch v. Dunsmuir Joint Union High School District*[41]). The courts might easily recognize the relationship between a client and the staff of community centers as constituting such a special relationship. A legal duty would, therefore, exist requiring the center's staff to take affirmative action to minimize the extent of the injuries to clients when accidents occur. Depending upon the circumstances, the staff's actions might consist of providing first aid, summoning trained medical personnel, transporting the injured person to the appropriate medical facilities, or any combination of the aforementioned (Leibee, 1965).

Ogando concerned a lawsuit against a school district for the unnecessary death of a young girl. While playing hide-and-seek during lunch recess on the school playground, the child ran her outstretched arm through a glass pane in a door and immediately jerked her arm back. The broken pane cut a deep gash across her elbow and severed an artery, causing profuse bleeding. In a confused state, the girl ran around the playground screaming until another student took her to the school nurse's office. When the nurse arrived she was able to stop the bleeding. A doctor was summoned and the girl was taken to a hospital where she died as a result of having lost so much blood before being given first aid. At the time of the accident there was no teacher on the playground. The trial court drew the inference that if a teacher had been present on the playground, the girl's life would have been saved because the teacher would have been responsible for immediately taking charge of the injured child and either arresting the flow of blood or summoning the school nurse. The court found the school district guilty of negligence and liable for the girl's death. This decision was based largely on the failure to supervise the playground properly, with the implication that teachers are required to provide necessary first aid services.

In *Welch,* a coach failed to provide first aid treatment to an injured player. After being tackled while attempting a quarterback sneak, the plaintiff was lying on his back on the field and unable to stand. The coach, suspecting that the boy injured his neck or spine, asked the boy to grasp his hand. At that time the boy was able to grasp his hand firmly. The plaintiff was carried off the field by eight unsupervised fellow players, even though a stretcher was available on the sideline. A doctor was present on the sideline, although there was contradictory testimony as to whether he examined the injured boy before he was carried off the field. During the trial, the doctor's testimony indicated that the failure to use a stretcher to remove the player resulted in the boy's permanent quadriplegia. The court ruled that the coach was guilty of negligence for failing to use the proper first aid procedure.

Mogabgab v. Orleans Parrish School Board[42] is another case that was based on a breach of school personnel's duty to provide first aid treatment to students injured in connection with school activities. During the second day of football practice in August, a 16-year-old boy collapsed while running "wind sprints." The boy was suffering from heat stroke and shock. For 2 hours after the symptoms appeared, the two football coaches kept the youth under their care and they administered inappropriate "first aid" treatment. During this time period neither the boy's mother nor a doctor was notified. When a doctor was finally summoned, he was not able to save the boy's life. Testimony indicated that if the boy had received prompt medical attention he probably would have lived. The court found the coaches and the school board liable for the boy's death.

Responsible persons with special relationships to others are expected only to provide the necessary first aid; they are not expected to have medical expertise. *Pirkle v. Oakdale Union Grammar School District*[43] involved the injuries a young man sustained following a blow to the stomach while playing touch football under the defendant's supervision. Immediately following the blow, the boy was escorted to the first aid room, covered with a blanket, and allowed to rest in the room unattended. Two hours later the instructor returned to the boy and, realizing the serious nature of the injury, sent the boy home. Five hours later the boy's spleen and a kidney were removed. The court held that the defendant instructor could not be held liable for injuries sustained. As a layman, the instructor could not have reasonably been expected to discover the seriousness of the injuries and his failure to secure prompt medical attention did not aggravate the injuries. The court did imply, however, that the instructor would have had a duty to secure prompt medical attention had the seriousness of the injury been more readily apparent.

Staff who are not medically trained should be wary of providing treatment for diseases or injuries in nonemergency situations. An example of a lawsuit arising from providing unnecessary, injury-producing treatment in a nonemergency situation can be found in *Guerrieri v. Tyson*.[44] This case involved two teachers who immersed a 10-year-old boy's hand in scalding water. The boy had an infected finger that did not require emergency treatment. The condition did not even prevent the boy from playing baseball during noon recess. Nevertheless, disregarding his protests, the teachers forcibly immersed the boy's hand in scalding water and held it there for 10 minutes. Afterward, the boy was hospitalized as a result of the severe burns he received. The court found the teachers guilty of negligence, declaring that any reasonably prudent person would have foreseen that the scalding water would aggravate the infection and produce painful permanent damage.

The potential problem areas and the examples of lawsuits presented in this chapter represent only some of the possible situations that may jeopardize the well-being of the clients, staff, and general public with regard to the administrative activities of a community center. It would be impossible to list all of the situations that could produce injury to clients or others as a result of a community center's administrative actions or inactions. In general, a particular situation should be viewed as a potential problem area if the situation would expose a client or others to an unreasonable risk of harm or injury. In the following chapter, some techniques for discovering, alleviating, and avoiding potentially hazardous situations within a treatment-oriented community center are discussed.

POINTS TO REMEMBER

1. A community center owes a duty to supervise the clients and staff properly so as to prevent the occurrence of unnecessary foreseeable harm.
2. Clients are to be supervised to an extent commensurate with the clients' abilities and commensurate with the amount of risk facing the clients.
3. A community center that accepts a client for placement in a program that presents a reasonably foreseeable harm to the client or to others may be held liable for resulting injuries.
4. A community center can be held responsible for injuries resulting from an improperly derived discharge decision. Discharge decisions must be

based on sound professional judgment following a thorough examination of adequate first-hand information.

5. The failure of a community center to adopt or follow prudent policies and regulations for the protection of clients and others may make the center liable for any resulting injuries.

6. A community center has a duty to inspect and repair if necessary the facilities and the equipment used in the agency. The failure to do so exposes the center to liability for injuries that may result.

7. A community center is responsible for making sure that their vehicles are in safe working order, that their drivers are well trained and prudent, and that when possible their clients are instructed in safe transportation practices.

8. A community center has a duty to take affirmative action to minimize the extent of the injuries to clients when accidents occur. The community center must make sure that its staff members are skilled in providing proper first aid and that they are familiar with the center's emergency procedures.

REFERENCES

Black, H.C. *Black's law dictionary* (rev. 4th ed.). St. Paul, MN: West Publishing Co., 1968.

Knaak, W. C. *School district tort liability in the 70's.* St. Paul, MN: Marric Publishing Co., 1969.

Leibee, H. *Tort liability for injuries to pupils.* Ann Arbor, MI: Campus Publishers, 1965.

Mathiason, G. (ed.). *Guardianship and protective services for older people.* Washington, DC: NCOA Press, 1963.

Mirabel, J.T., & Levy, H.A. *The law of negligence.* Amityville, NY: Acme Book Co., 1962.

National Education Association Research Division. *Who is liable for pupil negligence?* Washington, DC: National Education Association, 1963.

Nolte, M. C. *Guide to school law.* West Nyack, NJ: Parker Publishing Co., 1969.

O'Connor, G. Home is a good place: A national perspective of community residential facilities for developmentally disabled persons. *Monograph of the American Association of Mental Deficiency,* 1976, No. 2.

Prosser, W. L. *Handbook of the law of torts* (4th ed.). St. Paul, MN: West Publishing Co., 1971.

Reutter, E. E., & Hamilton, R. R. *The law of public education* (2nd ed.). Mineola, NY: The Foundation Press, 1976.

Roby, J.J. Getting caught in the "Open Door": Psychiatrists, patients and third parties. *Mental Disability Law Reporter,* 1976, *1*, 220–228.

Wolfensberger, W. *The principle of normalization in human services.* Toronto, Canada: National Institute on Mental Retardation, 1972.

ENDNOTES

[1]Excelsior Ins. Co. of New York v. State, 69 N.E. 2d 553 (App. Ct. 1946).

[2]Milton v. State (Health & Soc. & Rehab. Serv. Admin.), 293 So. 2d 645 (La. App., First Cir. 1974).

[3]Comiskey v. New York, 418 N.Y.S. 2d 233 (N.Y. Sup. Ct., App. Div. 1979).

[4]Daniels v. Conn, 378 So. 2d 451 (La. Ct. App. 1979).

[5]293 P. 2d 889 (Cal. Ct. App. 1956).

[6]See, e.g., Castello v. U.S., 552 F. 2d 1385 (10th Cir. 1977); Abille v. U.S., 482 F. Supp. 703 (N.D. Cal. 1980); Becton v. U.S., 489 F. Supp. 134 (D. Mass. 1980); Smith v. U.S., 437 F. Supp. 1004 (E.D. Pa. 1977); Frank v. Utah, 613 P. 2d 517 (Utah Sup. Ct. 1980); Bohrer v. County of San Diego, 163 Cal. Rptr. 419 (Cal. Ct. App. 1980).

[7]211 N.Y.S. 2d 560 (Supr. Ct., App. Term, 2d Dept. 1961).

[8]226 F. Supp. 129 (S.D. Iowa 1964).

[9]373 N.Y.S. 2d 696 (Sup. Ct., App. Div., 3rd Dept. 1975).

[10]314 N.Y.S. 2d 904 (Cl. Ct. 1970).

[11]227 N.Y.S. 2d 946 (1962).

[12]487 P. 2d 936 (Idaho Sup. Ct. 1971).

[13]188 N.W. 2d 868 (Minn. Sup. Ct. 1971).

[14]319 N.Y.S. 2d 783 (Sup. Ct., App. Div., 4th Dept. 1971).

[15]410 N.Y.S. 2d 99 (Sup. Ct., App. Div., 2d Dept. 1978).

[16]583 P. 2d 626 (Wash. Sup. Ct. 1978).

[17]241 N.Y.S. 2d 497 (N.Y. Sup. Ct. 1963).

[18]382 N.Y.S. 2d 128 (Sup. Ct., App. Div., 3rd Dept. 1976).

[19]127 N.Y.S. 2d 147 (Sup. Ct., App. Div., 3rd Dept. 1954).

[20]110 P. 2d 1044 (Cal. Sup. Ct. 1941).

[21]129 P. 2d 35 (Cal. App. Ct., First Dist., Div. Two 1942).

[22]228 A. 2d 65 (N.J. Sup. Ct. 1967).

[23]320 N.Y.S. 2d 402 (Sup. Ct., App. Div., 3rd Dept. 1971).

[24]361 N.Y.S. 2d 820 (Cl. Ct. 1974).

[25]538 F. 2d 121(4th Cir. 1976).

[26]245 F. 2d 756(8th Cir. 1957).

[27]494 P. 2d 389 (Ariz. App. Ct. 1972).

[28]276 P. 424 (Cal. Dist. Ct. App., 3rd Dist. 1929).

[29]335 P. 2d 805 (Wash. Sup. Ct. 1959).

[30]330 N.E. 2d 651 (N.Y. App. Ct. 1975).

[31]82 P. 2d 197 (Cal. Dist. Ct. App., First Dist., Div. Two 1938).

[32]27 N.Y.S. 2d 195 (Sup. Ct. 1941).

[33]163 N.E. 2d 89 (Ill. Sup. Ct. 1959).

[34]97 S.E. 527 (Virg. Sup. Ct. App. 1938).

[35]363 N.E. 2d 295 (Mass. App. Ct. 1977).

[36]71 S.E. 2d 464 (Ga. Ct. App. 1952).

[37]100 N.E. 2d 398 (Ill. App. Ct. 1951).

[38]111 P. 2d 415 (Cal. Dist. Ct. App., 4th Div. 1941).

[39]129 N.W. 2d 47 (S.D. Sup. Ct. 1964).

[40]75 P. 2d 641 (Cal. App. Ct. 1938).

[41]326 P. 2d 633 (Cal. App. Ct. 1958).

[42]239 So. 2d 456 (La. App. Ct. 1970).

[43] 253 P. 2d 1 (Cal. Sup. Ct. 1953).

[44]24 A. 2d 468 (Pa. 1942).

5

ADMINISTRATIVE RECOMMENDATIONS

Probably one of the most harmful effects of a community center's increased awareness of its vulnerability to accidents and lawsuits is the tendency to develop overprotective, paternalistic policies. This overprotective tendency, combined with the attitude that disabled individuals and juveniles are homogeneous groups of nonmaturing persons, results in the development of programs that do not recognize the differing abilities and needs among clients. Unfortunately, the procedures and regulations that are developed under such circumstances are usually designed to protect the most severely limited clients. For example, potentially dangerous appliances in a residence, such as a gas stove, may be ruled off limits for all clients, and the movement of all clients within the community may be prohibited unless they are accompanied by a staff member. Under these conditions, the clients may not have any greater opportunity to develop independence and autonomy than they would have had in a traditional institution.

In attempts to develop a safe community center, the staff must not lose sight of the primary goals of habilitation and the development of individual self-determination. The "safety" precautions that are imposed too often further accentuate the differences between handicapped and nonhandicapped persons, which makes the transition between dependent living arrangements and independent or semi-independent living more difficult. Individuals with handicaps have just as great a claim to a right to risk (Perske, 1972) and a right to self-determination and autonomy (Nirje, 1972) as do people without handicaps. There are, however, a variety of procedures that a community center should incorporate into the center's program that would properly protect the clients and others from undue harm and protect the center from unnecessary lawsuits, without drastically curtailing individual rights. This chapter is concerned with recommendations pertaining to the administration and organization of a legally safe community center.

PLANNING AND EVALUATION

One of the foremost and important phases of developing a safe and effective community center is the writing of a detailed delineation of the agency's program plan, including procedures for evaluating this plan. Involvement of staff members, from all levels of the organization, in the early stages of planning helps ensure the success of the resulting plan, making it more understandable and acceptable to staff members. The resulting plan should be aimed at answering the following questions: *What are the goals of the community center? How are these goals to be achieved?* and *How well are the goals being achieved?*

Surles (1977) describes a model, called an achievement planning model, that may be useful for planning a community center's overall program. This model involves outlining plans in terms of specified needs, goals to be achieved, objectives related to each goal, alternative strategies for meeting each objective, the specification of the chosen strategy, the description of the implementation methodology, evaluation procedures, and the informational feedback provided by evaluations. The agency's goals should represent the general intentions and directions of the center in view of the client's and the community's needs, whereas the objectives should be more specific with measurable indices and time tables. A community center should have two related sets of goals and objectives. One set, the *administrative set*, is concerned with the management activities of the center that must occur in order for treatment programs to be successful. Administrative goals and objectives involve, among other concerns, addressing the impact of the center on the clients and the community, safety and emergency procedures, employee concerns, and the acquisition and allocation of space and materials. These issues are the general focus of this chapter and the preceding chapter. The other set of goals and objectives, called the *treatment set*, is concerned with the treatment activities as they are related to each individual client. These client treatment-related issues are discussed in Chapters 6 and 7.

To develop appropriate plans for achieving these goals a community center must engage in costly activities, yet the failure to develop appropriate plans carefully would probably be even more costly in terms of injuries and lawsuits. Scheerenberger (1975) has detailed a planning and evaluation system that is very useful for creating a comprehensive plan for a community center. His recommendations include 10 items to be taken into consideration during planning. These are:

1. Nature of the program required to satisfy the goal
2. Characteristics (e.g., age, abilities, disabilities, health problems) of the clients and the number of clients to be served

3. Costs (e.g., manpower requirements, space requirements, maintenance, equipment, consumable supplies, transportation, and insurance) required for the program
4. Availability of funding resources for the program
5. Activities to be initiated and their sequence
6. Assignment of responsibilities
7. Time required to implement the plan
8. Duration of the program
9. Geographical location of the program
10. Monitoring and evaluation of the program

In addition, health and safety issues need to be considered.

Clients, relatives, staff members, and the general public have a right to know what programs and services are available, as well as the degree to which they are professionally delivered and their outcomes. An organizational or program plan is not comprehensive unless it incorporates an accountability system within it. An accountability system must be capable of measuring what activities are performed, evaluating the effects of those activities on the clients and others, and evaluating the progress toward specified goals, and also be able to assist in the making of qualitative and quantitative judgments as to the effectiveness, adequacy, and efficiency of the activities. In order to achieve these ends, the community center's staff must collect, record, and organize complete information regarding the conduct of the center, and must make reports that reflect the performance of the center in the achievement of its goals. Included in the evaluation should be an analysis of the effects that the community center's program has on the clients, staff, and the community in general.

The remainder of this chapter is devoted to setting forth specific recommendations concerning the development of a comprehensive plan for a community center.

DEVELOPING SAFETY REGULATIONS

One of the first steps in establishing a safe community center involves the development of written accident prevention procedures and safety regulations. These regulations should be formulated after a thorough examination of all the components of the community center's facilities, equipment, and activities. All of the different areas of the community center's organizational structure should participate in the development of these safety procedures and regulations. This cooperative effort may help ensure that the procedures and regulations will be followed once they are formulated. Life-safety experts, such as those employed by insurance companies, may also participate in the development of the safety regulations. In addition, clients, guardians, relatives, and concerned community members should participate in the formulation of these regulations. Community agencies, such as the fire department, police department, community safety council, local chapters of organizations such as the National Safety Council, American Society for Safety Engineers, and American Red Cross, the local medical society, the local health department, and educational associations should also be contacted and their assistance solicited.

After the safety rules and regulations are developed, they should be submitted to the governing body of the community center for examination and approval. The names and positions of the people who were involved in the creation of the safety policies and a brief description of the processes employed in evolving the safety policies should accompany the written policies. This information may be very useful if the adequacy of the safety policies is ever questioned. The process being suggested for the creation of the safety rules and procedures may seem arduous. A lawsuit, however, arising from injuries caused by the lack of appropriate safety regulations can destroy a community center.

In 1975, the National Safety Council presented an accident prevention technique called a *job safety analysis* (JSA) which can be very useful for analyzing and developing safety procedures for potentially hazardous jobs within a community center. The JSA procedure has five phases. Persons who are familiar with the activities of the community center should participate in the analysis. The first phase involves selecting the jobs that are suitable for a job safety analysis. Since a JSA is time consuming, only those jobs where an accident is likely to occur should be examined. Staff members involved in the various activities of the community center should be able to provide a list of such jobs.

The second phase in the analysis process involves breaking the job into a sequence of steps which describe what is being done. In order to break the job down into steps, an experienced employee should be observed performing the job under normal operating conditions. As the job is repeated, the employee's actions should be scrutinized to identify each step the employee takes toward completing the job. The steps should be recorded in sequence as they are being performed. In deriving such a task analysis, care must be taken to ensure that the steps identified are neither so large that important actions are overlooked nor so detailed that the sequence becomes unnecessarily cumbersome.

The third phase involves identifying the hazards and potential accident situations. In order to do this, the following questions should be asked about each step of the job analysis:

1. Is there danger of striking against, being struck by, or otherwise making injurious contact with an object?
2. Can a person be caught in, on, or between objects?
3. Can he [she] slip or trip? Can he [she] fall on the same level or to another?
4. Can he [she] strain himself [herself] by pushing, pulling or lifting?
5. Is the environment hazardous (toxic gas, vapor, mist, fume, dust, heat or radiation)? (National Safety Council, 1975, p. 121)

In addition, the job should be observed closely and discussed with an experienced employee.

The fourth phase of the analysis involves developing recommendations for making the job safer and preventing accidents. The principal solutions to correcting hazardous situations are:

1. Find an entirely new way to do the job.
2. Change the physical conditions that create the hazards.
3. Change the procedure of performing a task.
4. Try to reduce the necessity of doing a hazardous job, or at least, the frequency that it must be performed. (National Safety Council, 1975, p. 121)

The employees that will be performing the job should be involved in this process of developing a solution. Greater acceptance of the changes may result from this cooperative effort.

The final phase is a reevaluation of the job after the change has been implemented. This involves observing the task being performed and discussing the effects of the changes with the employees who regularly perform the job. Their insight and opinions of the changes provide valuable information. They may be able to point out problems with the solution and they may be able to suggest a more practical remedy that someone not as familiar with the job would not have realized.

A staff member, preferably someone in a supervisory position, should be made responsible for coordinating and monitoring the community center's safety program. This safety coordinator should be thoroughly familiar with the center's safety and health rules and policies, and the person should be familiar with the federal, state, and municipal safety codes, laws, and regulations that are applicable to the community center. An interest in safety, a willingness to work closely with employees and clients, and a willingness to keep abreast of safety issues are also prerequisites for this position. The safety coordinator should be directly accountable to the director of the community center. The duties of the safety coordinator include participating in the development and revision of safety policies, conducting periodic safety inspections, enforcing the safety regulations, coordinating the employees' and the clients' familiarization with the community center's safety policies, actively monitoring the safety habits component of the individual habilitation plans, and managing the accident reporting and analysis system. A detailed description of the safety coordinator's responsibilities can be found in *A Job Analysis for Safety Education Supervisors* (National Safety Council, 1959).

SAFETY INSPECTIONS

Inspections of electrical cords and machinery, smoking areas, gas-fueled items, and other potential hazards at the community center should be conducted daily at closing time. As a supplement to these regular inspections of the work areas made by the staff and clients, periodic safety inspections should be conducted by supervisors and/or the safety coordinator. A thorough safety inspection is one of the most effective methods for discovering hazardous conditions and practices. Jacobs (1964) reported a study which indicated that the number of liability claims against a school district could be reduced by 18% by providing a system-wide and periodic safety inspection of the school grounds and facilities. Possibly, inspections could serve a similar type of preventive function in a community center. Inspections should occur with little advance warning every 3 months or at intervals suitable for the community center. The more hazardous the activities in which the center is engaged, the more frequently the inspections should be conducted. During the inspection, extra attention should be paid to areas where accidents have occurred and to the little used areas of the community center. "A well-planned inspection depends upon knowing where to look and what to look for" (National Safety Council, 1975, p. 57).

The particular inspection procedures used by different community centers may vary considerably; however, inspection checklists should be developed and utilized by all community centers. A list of checklists that may be helpful to a community center in developing a safety checklist to meet its unique needs is presented at the end of this book in Appendix B. Included in all safety inspections should be inspections of fire alarm and fire emergency equipment, all emergency exits, and first aid equipment. The results of these inspections should be reported to the staff and clients. This would also be a good time to discuss and instruct the clients in safety practices and in how to identify and correct hazardous situations on their own.

After reviewing the report, staff and/or clients should initiate corrective measures where applicable. Nothing should become part of the center's regular operation until it has been checked for hazards, necessary safeguards have been installed, and safety instructions have been developed. This, too, presents an excellent opportunity for clients to practice and improve safety skills by becoming involved with the process. In addition, the community center should cooperate thoroughly with the annual inspections from state and local fire safety departments, building inspectors, and other local and state authorities involved with the protection of health, environment, and safety.

ACCIDENT REPORTING AND ANALYSIS SYSTEM

A carefully devised and supervised accident reporting and analysis system is an invaluable component in any safety program. The information that is gained from an accident reporting system can serve many useful purposes both within and outside of the community center. The information can be used to modify and evaluate the safety instruction programs for the clients and staff. The accident data can elucidate problems and solutions to the safety problems involving the community center's facilities, equipment, and procedures. Insurance companies can use the accident report information to guide decisions concerning the community center's insurance needs and to assess a policy premium fairly. State, regional, or national agencies can combine the accident information from several community centers in order to examine trends and to help formulate policies and regulations. Accurate accident records can also serve as a data base for much needed research in the area of community centers. Most importantly, the information that is gained from an accident reporting system can serve as an objective measure of the success or failure of the community center's safety program.

The National Safety Council (1975) has proposed a three-stage accident reporting and analysis system which can be an extremely useful component in a community center's safety program. This system involves accurate accident reporting, investigation of accidents, and periodic analysis of accident information.

In order to help ensure the accuracy of an accident report, the report must be made as soon as possible after the needs of the injured person(s) are met. It is often difficult or impossible to ascertain the details concerning the accident if an accurate report is not completed shortly after the accident occurred. The passage of time has a tendency to distort people's memories of what happened, and the important details can be lost forever if a report is not made promptly. If the need arises, an accurate written accident report can be very valuable for supporting statements in court. To help ensure promptness of reporting, pads of standardized accident report forms should be available in the activity areas of the community center (e.g., in the kitchen, in the workshop, and in the transportation vehicles). It is important that both injury-producing accidents, however slight, and incidents consisting of near accidents in which fortunate circumstances averted an injury be reported by the staff member responsible for managing the accident situation.

The report of an accident must be an objective description of the circumstances before, during, and after the accident. The primary purpose of an accident report is to preserve accurate information, not to assess blame (National Safety Council, 1951). Extreme care must be taken by the supervisory and administrative personnel to make sure that the prompt reporting of an accident is not the occasion for a reprimand or any other disciplinary action. Employees and clients should be praised, not punished, for prompt, accurate reporting of an accident.

The National Safety Council has developed several standard forms for reporting accidents which may be helpful in developing a community center's accident report forms.[1] A community center's accident report should include the following information:

1. Name, address, and age of the persons involved in the accident
2. Pertinent information concerning the condition of those involved in the accident (e.g., experiencing a seizure)
3. Date, time, and geographical location of the accident
4. Nature, degree, and bodily location of the injuries

5. Description of the activities the person was engaged in immediately preceding and during the accident
6. Condition of the equipment involved in the accident
7. Probable cause of the accident
8. Description of the medical attention the injured received, the name and address of the treating physician, and the name of the treating hospital
9. Name and position of the staff member in charge
10. Description of the staff member's actions prior to and following the accident
11. Recommended corrective action
12. Dated signature of the person making the report
13. Dated signature of the safety coordinator upon receiving the report (National Safety Council, 1966)

The names, addresses, and signed statements of witnesses should be obtained.

A separate accident report form should be completed for each person injured in the accident. The safety coordinator should be responsible for making sure that a copy of the accident report is placed in the accident file and in the files of all clients and staff members directly involved in the accident. The staff members must also be very careful not to release information concerning the accident to nonauthorized persons without their supervisor's permission.

The next step in an effective accident reporting system is the investigation and analysis of the accidents. Accident reports alone have limited value for evaluating and modifying a safety system; however, when combined with follow-up investigation and analysis, the accident reports serve a valuable function. The investigation and analysis of accidents is intended to reveal useful information concerning dangerous conditions that otherwise might not have been noticed. The National Safety Council (1975) stated that the purposes of an accident investigation are to: 1) learn about the causes of accidents so that environmental or procedural changes can be made to prevent the recurrence of the accident, 2) inform the employees and clients about potential hazards and direct attention toward accident prevention procedures, and 3) determine and record facts that may have a bearing on the legal liability for the accident. As with the accident report, the ensuing investigation is intended to result in unbiased, complete knowledge about the accident.

In order to achieve these purposes, care must be taken to ensure that the investigation process is carried out in a pleasant, objective, non-accusatory manner. It is important that the individuals questioned by the investigator be comfortable and relaxed during the fact-finding period. If at all possible, the safety coordinator, who is familiar with the general principles of negligence, should be responsible for conducting the investigations. If the accident resulted in a serious injury, however, then a committee of at least three people should be involved in the investigation. In order to reduce suspicions, the safety coordinator should never be involved with any punitive actions taken as the result of an accident. A separate committee should be established to handle any necessary disciplinary action. Every injury-producing accident must be investigated promptly. The near-accidents should also be promptly investigated; however, the nature of the incident and the extent of possible injuries may be considered in determining the scope of the investigation.

The National Safety Council (1975) has presented some general guidelines for conducting accident investigations. These guidelines are:

a. Go to the scene of the accident promptly.
b. Talk with the injured person, if possible. Talk with witnesses. Stress getting the fact, not placing the responsibility or blames.
c. Listen for clues in conversations. Unsolicited comments often have merit.
d. Encourage people to give their ideas for preventing the accident.
e. Study possible causes—both unsafe conditions and unsafe practices.
f. Confer with interested persons about possible solutions. The problem may have been solved by someome else.
g. Write up a report, using a printed form which allows for a narrative description.
h. Follow up to make sure conditions are corrected. If they cannot be corrected immediately, report this to all concerned.
i. Publicize any corrective action taken so that all may benefit from the experience. (p. 101)

A detailed model for conducting accident investigations and analyses also is available from the American National Standards Institute (ANSI).[2] Photographs taken immediately after the accident occurred may be very useful in an investigation. The more complete the information gathered in the investigation, the greater are the chances for developing effective countermeasures.

The final component of an accident reporting and analysis system is the periodic analysis of the accident and investigation reports. At least twice a year the reports should be analyzed by a safety committee which includes the safety coordinator. These analyses may reveal accident trends that are not otherwise observable, and the analyses may permit an objective evaluation of the progress of the center's safety program. The American National Standards Institute presents an analysis procedure that is based on selecting, cross-classifying, and summarizing the fundamental factors in accidents.

The first step in the analysis involves determining a set of general classifications into which to group the accident information. Grouping of the information is necessary in order to determine trends. Examples of the categories include: 1) the location of the accident, 2) the type of injury, 3) the activity occurring at the time of the accident, 4) the equipment involved in the accident, and 5) the occupation of the injured person (National Safety Council, 1975). After the general categories are developed, the information should be further classified into more specific categories. An attempt should be made to create as many specific categories as are necessary to prevent the loss of important information. The categories should encompass all situations pertinent to the community center. ANSI Standard Z16.2 recommends some classification categories that may be used as a guide in developing categories for grouping community center accident information.[3] Sometimes the general and specific categories can be arrived at only after the reports are reviewed by the safety committee. A unique numerical code should be assigned to each category in such a way that the codes for similar accident factors follow in a sequence. The safety committee can then sort the accident information into the different categories and tabulate the information to reveal trends. The safety committee should also examine the countermeasures that have been taken and recommend further countermeasures if necessary.

EMERGENCY PROCEDURES

In order to decrease the occurrence and the degree of injuries during an emergency, the community center and its staff should: 1) develop emergency plans, 2) maintain current medical information files, 3) educate staff and clients in emergency procedures, and 4) be prepared to provide necessary first aid.

The first step in developing emergency procedures is to determine the types of emergencies that may arise. Many types of natural disasters occur in localized areas of the country. For example, hurricanes are restricted to coastal areas. The local fire department can provide information concerning natural disasters in the area. Sokoloff (1976) has proposed a technique for protecting clients from unnecessary harm during an emergency and at the same time minimizing their "differentness." This technique involves a life-safety expert or other trained person carefully assessing the center's facilities and developing emergency plans. These emergency plans would enable persons in any part of the community center to reach a safe place without sustaining injuries. For example, in geographic areas susceptible to tornadoes, the safety expert would examine the structure of the facilities, the activities of the center, and the limitations of the clients and staff, and would then develop a plan for getting all clients, staff, and visitors to a "tornado-proof" location. This plan would be written in a detailed manner and a timed test developed. Passing the timed test would become a high priority training objective for both the staff and the clients. If after considerable training and practice an individual is not able to pass the timed test, the emergency plan should be revised. Periodically the timed test should be repeated to make sure the skills are retained.

Every community center must develop and practice a fire evacuation plan for both staff and residents. Guidelines for developing fire evacuation plans can usually be found in local and state fire prevention regulations or licensing requirements. Two important factors to remember when formulating fire evacuation plans are: 1) fires frequently happen during the night when people are asleep so that particular attention must be given to a plan that is appropriate for nighttime, and 2) because fires frequently block commonly used pathways, two emergency exits are needed for all work, living, and sleeping areas. A meeting place outside of the building must also be established so that an accurate identification of all evacuees can be made.

Appropriate fire extinguishers and fire detectors should be installed and inspected regularly. Several companies that sell fire extinguishing and detecting equipment, as well as local and state fire officials, will provide films and instruction on the use of the equipment and basic fire safety practices. Since fires occur most frequently at night, extreme caution should be used when prescribing nightly doses of anti-psychotic or mood altering drugs, muscle relaxants, or any other drugs that produce drowsiness or confusion. In the event of a fire or other emergency during the night, "medicated" clients would be at a severe disadvantage. Recently, a fire in a midwestern boarding home killed 25 residents, 17 of whom had been given medications that likely hindered their escape. Often such medication is unnecessary and used simply as a matter of custodial convenience.

Diagrams of the evacuation plan should be conspicuously posted on each floor. Fire drills should be held frequently, preferably monthly, at various times of the day, particularly nighttime. As part of these drills the usual exits should be obstructed so that the staff and clients are forced to practice alternative escape routes. Data concerning when the fire drill took place, the duration of the drill, and brief comments about the drill should be recorded. Finally, as suggested by Sokoloff (1976), mastery of the evacuation plan should become a high priority training objective.

Persons with physical or mental disabilities may need special emergency procedures in case of a fire. A booklet entitled *Wheeling to Fire Safety,* produced by the Eastern Paralyzed Veterans' Association, provides very useful information and practical suggestions concerning fire emergency procedures for disabled persons. (This booklet can be obtained by writing to the Eastern Paralyzed Veterans' Association, 432 Park Avenue South, New York, New York 10016.)

The community center should maintain a fire-resistant card file, listing pertinent medical information on each client and staff member, which can be used in an emergency. Depending upon the arrangement of the community center's physical plant, several copies of files may be needed. For example, if the residences are separated from the workshop facilities, a copy of the file should be kept at both settings. Information contained on these cards should include the individual's name, address, telephone number, age, blood type, medication being taken, allergies and medical problems, a recent photograph, the name, address, and telephone number of the nearest relative or guardian, the person's doctor's name and telephone number, the person's dentist's name and number, and the preferred hospital. These cards should be dated and signed by the individual providing the information. Twice a year these cards should be reviewed, updated, signed, and dated by the reviewer. In addition, clients and staff members must be encouraged to carry identification cards at all times. The person's name, birth date, address, telephone number, and particular medical problems or allergies should be listed on this card. If a client is so debilitated that carrying an identification card is not feasible, pertinent information should be inconspicuously placed on a medal worn around the neck, on a bracelet, or on a wristwatch.

Near all telephones should be a list of emergency phone numbers, the center's address, directions to the community center, and instructions to follow in case of an emergency. The kinds of emergencies that need to be included in this list are medical emergencies, fires, emergency rescue, poisonings, and police emergencies. Clients and staff members must be thoroughly instructed and practiced in using these emergency procedures under simulated conditions. Several special adaptations may be needed in order for some clients to learn to use these procedures, such as large print and numbers, phones adapted for physically handicapped clients, and color coding of the telephone numbers, buttons, or phone dial.

The community center must be prepared to provide prompt first aid in an emergency situation. Otherwise the injured person may suffer further harm and the center may be held legally responsible for the aggravation of the injuries. During the community center's business hours, at least one staff member in each physical structure should be certified to provide first aid (i.e., the staff member must have passed an approved first aid course). In addition, at least one staff member involved in supervising a potentially hazardous activity should be certified to provide first aid. In fact, a good policy would be to have all staff members certified as first aid providers. If a community center employs a large number of persons or if the community center is plagued with a high staff turnover rate, one of the supervisory personnel should become a certified first aid instructor so that first aid courses can be designed to meet the staff's and clients' needs. Training in cardiopulmonary resuscitation and in the Heimlich Maneuver should be included in the first aid course. When feasible, clients should also be instructed in basic first aid techniques. For further information concerning first aid training, the administrators of the community center should contact the local chapter of the American Red Cross, or the American Heart Association. In addition, appropriate first aid equipment must be readily accessible in all the activity areas of the community center.

Butler and Ballou (1974) presented examples of several release forms requesting the client's family's or guardian's permission for the community center to secure necessary services for the client. Among these release forms are: authorization to the community center and its staff to secure medical services for the client as they appear to be needed, authorization for an approved physician and hospital to provide the necessary treatment to alleviate an apparent medical emergency, authorization for the center's staff to initiate first aid procedures that are necessary for the health and safety of the client if injured while participating in the center's activities, and authorization for the center's staff to administer physician-prescribed medication. Responsibility for payment for these services must be clearly specified in these authorization forms. In the development of the release forms, the community center should consult a local attorney.

TRANSPORTATION SAFETY

Whenever clients are being transported by community center staff members or sanctioned representatives of the center (e.g., volunteer van drivers), careful attention must be given to protecting the clients' health and well-being. Seaton, Stack, and Loft (1969) have presented five basic safety considerations concerning the organization and implementation of a transportation program. The first consideration involves the use of efficient business methods in maintaining high standards in the selection of vehicles. "Efficient business methods" refers to the keeping of accurate records on drivers, equipment, routes, violations, accidents, insurance, commendations, and complaints. When purchasing vehicles for a community center, the administrators should select vehicles that serve the needs of the clients and the center, and that are also the least restrictive type of vehicles available. For example, a 20-passenger bus should never be purchased if two 10-passenger vans or several station wagons would serve the needs as well.

The second consideration involves the inspection and maintenance of vehicles. A thorough safety check of all the community center's vehicles should be made at regular intervals, at least three times a year. In addition, before using a vehicle, the driver should make a routine safety check of the vehicle. A separate checklist should be developed for both the periodic safety inspections and the driver's safety check. If a problem arises with a vehicle, it should be corrected immediately; vehicles in poor working order should never be used to transport clients or staff.

The third consideration involves the establishment and supervision of transportation areas, routes, and stops. In view of the special hazards surrounding the loading and unloading of passengers, the community center's administration must develop and monitor regulations to be followed by clients and staff. For example, a regulation should be formulated that bars the opening of a bus's doors before the bus comes to a complete stop. Checks should be made by supervisory personnel at irregular intervals to determine whether the regulations are still being followed.

The fourth consideration involves the care that should be taken in the selection, education, and placement of drivers. The National Commission on Safety Education (1964) prepared a detailed manual which presents excellent guidelines concerning the selection and education of school bus drivers. With minor modifications, these guidelines can be used by a safety-minded community center regardless of the kinds of vehicles owned by the center. The community center's drivers should participate in continuing safety education programs. Included in these driver education programs would be instructions in first aid techniques and in ways of dealing with the passengers in a crisis situation. Whenever a community center uses a bus for transporting clients, a staff member, a prudent volunteer, or a capable client should accompany the clients in order to assist if an emergency arises. Such a person would be responsible for the clients' safety if the driver becomes incapacitated.

The fifth consideration concerns the education of the clients in safe transportation practices. Clients should be taught how to enter, exit, and wait for a vehicle in a safe, orderly manner. Clients must be instructed in emergency procedures and in ways of assisting one another if the driver becomes incapacitated. In addition, an important aspect of the education program involves teaching the clients to identify safe and unsafe vehicles, driving conditions, and drivers. The clients may then be able to identify problems that have been overlooked by the staff, and be better prepared to make prudent decisions concerning independent transportation.

Considering the risks involved with private transportation, Leibee (1965) presented a list of recommendations which may be very useful for a community center. They are:

1. Select drivers with extreme care. Do not use those who are on probation or who have "bad reputations" as drivers.
2. Check the kinds and amounts of insurance on the car. Be certain the coverage is complete and adequate.
3. Determine, if you are able, the status of passengers in the car(s) on the trip. Are they "guests"?
4. If a student is a driver, have a mature adult in each car.
5. Give complete instructions for the trip—driving speed, route, meeting places, etc.
6. Be aware of the general fitness of the car(s) tires, lights, wipers, etc.
7. If the owner-driver of the car is a center employee, is the trip within the scope of the employee's employment? (Leibee, 1965, p. 67)

INSURANCE

Adequate insurance coverage has become an absolute necessity for all profit and nonprofit organizations as well as for private citizens. Insurance against loss and damage is a critical aspect of any fiscally sound community center. In fact, the state and local regulations governing the center may even require that the center purchase certain kinds of insurance. Unfortunately, during the busy process of planning and establishing a community center, sometimes administrators do not plan and obtain sufficient insurance coverage until a problem occurs. Fanning (1975) has pointed out some insurance needs of community centers, among which are the following: 1) medical insurance for clients and staff, 2) insurance coverage for the vehicles used by the community center, 3) mortgage insurance where applicable, 4) household content insurance against fire, theft, and accident, and 5) life insurance coverage for clients where appropriate. In addition, the community center and its related professionals (e.g., physicians and dentists) should carry liability insurance in the event that injuries result from the services they provide, and clients' personal possessions should be insured against fire, theft, and accident. The center should purchase liability and accident insurance for volunteers and clients.

An insurance policy is basically a contract in which the insurance company agrees to assume certain risks and be responsible for specified losses sustained by the policyholder who pays a fee to the company. An insurance policy can compensate for the loss suffered by a community center, but it does not prevent or hinder the occurrence of the loss. The policy will specify whether the insurance company will assume the risk of property loss or damage, the risk of personal injury or loss of life, and/or the risk of legal liability for services rendered in an improper manner. The policy will also specify the amount of money that the insurance company will pay to the policyholder for specific losses, and it will specify conditions under which the insurance company will compensate for a loss.

A standard liability insurance policy typically consists of five sections. These are: 1) the insurance agreement, 2) the defense and settlement, 3) the policy period, 4) the amount payable, and 5) the conditions (Pozgar, 1979). The insurance agreement involves the insurance company's promise to pay the actual monetary damages following a liability judgment against the policyholder. In the defense and settlement portion of the policy, the insurance company agrees to defend the policyholder in case of lawsuit, and the insurance company is delegated the power to reach a settlement of any claim as it deems necessary. The policy period refers to the time period when the policy is in effect. Injury-producing incidents that occurred before or after the policy period would not be covered by the insurance policy. The insurance policy specifies the maximum amount payable to an injured party covered by the policy. Finally, the policy contains several important conditions, such as the requirement that the policyholder must notify the insurance company that an injury occurred and that a claim or suit has been initiated, the requirement that the policyholder must cooperate with the insurance company in case of a claim or lawsuit, and the procedures for canceling the policy. The policyholder's failure to comply with the terms and conditions of the insurance policy can result in the insurance company's failure to pay for a claim.

The administrators of the community center should work closely with a concerned, informed insurance agent in developing insurance policies that adequately cover the individuals involved in the community center's activities, including transportation and recreation. The center should secure insurance coverage to meet the state's maximum statutory liability, remembering that the defendant is responsible for paying any difference between the court's award and the policy's amount payable. Of course, the degree of insurance coverage a center obtains must be balanced against the financial wisdom of purchasing that kind of policy. Care must be taken so that the community center is neither overinsured nor underinsured. The administrators of the community center should consult with their lawyer concerning insurance needs, and they should carefully shop around for the policies that best fit the needs of the community center. Periodically the administrators should review the center's insurance policies in order to ensure that the center's insurance needs are still being met.

RECORD-KEEPING

One of the most effective means a community center has for protecting itself from unjustified lawsuits involves the collection and storage of information. If a community center's actions are being challenged by a lawsuit, accurate records can disclose facts that are sufficient to enable the community center to demonstrate that the center used due care under the circumstances. The courts have indicated that they expect that decisions concerning the health and well-being of clients should be supported by data that would enable the court to evaluate the propriety of the decision (Roby, 1976). A community center should conduct its activities in such a manner as to document empirically the client's progress toward his or her goals and to monitor and evaluate accurately the community center's program.

A record "is a potential legal document and should be treated as such. Therefore, it should be put away for safekeeping and should be preserved under the strictest possible rule so as to preserve its legal validity on behalf of the [client]" (Hayt & Hayt, 1964, p. 44). If the client or the client's guardian disagrees with any information in the client's records and the community center decides not to amend the records, the client or the client's guardian has the right to enter a statement disputing the information. This statement must be kept side by side with the disputed information, and the statement should be considered whenever the client's records are being reviewed (*Educational Rights of Handicapped Children,* 1977). If it becomes necessary to alter records, the incorrect data should be crossed out with a single line in ink. The date of the change, the signature of the individual changing the record, and the proper information should be added to the record (Hayt & Hayt, 1964). A record that has been changed by erasure, or by use of correction fluid after it has been filed, may lead to suspicions concerning the purpose of the changes.

"The permanent preservation of all records routinely is an economic waste; some records, however, should be kept indefinitely because of their historical, research or training value" (Hayt & Hayt, 1964, p. 47). Community center administrators should consider the amount of available storage space, the future needs of the records, and the legal considerations of having the records available in the event of a lawsuit when determining how long to preserve records (Health Law Center, 1974). At the very least, records should be retained as long as the state statute of limitations for tort claims stipulates.

Throughout this book recommendations are made concerning information that should be recorded and stored. The information needs of each community center, however, are unique and the center's record-keeping system must be designed to meet those needs. Thus, the particular form and content of many of the records may vary from agency to agency. Nevertheless, it is essential that the records include information that is required for planning and evaluation. With this purpose in mind, the Child Welfare League of America (1975) has recommended that the following information always be recorded and stored for each client:

1. The nature of the client's difficulties
2. The services needed by the client and his or her family
3. The treatment plan, goals of the plan, and anticipated duration of treatment
4. The measures taken to implement the plan
5. The kinds of services that were given to the client
6. The evaluation of the services the client received
7. Vital statistics about the client such as birth records, statements of guardianship, legal custody, etc.
8. Detailed health records, psychiatric and psychological reports, educational assessments, official documentation, and financial arrangements including the client's income and expenditures related to the services provided to the client

In the following chapters, the rationale and structure of these and other important records are further discussed.

COMMUNITY CENTER RULES

In the preceding sections of this chapter, many recommendations have been made concerning the development of rules and regulations for governing specific activities and operations of a community center. Due to the diversity of activities in which community centers are engaged and due to differing client needs and goals, the task of making recommendations for each aspect of the administration of a community center becomes an overwhelming and probably unnecessary task. It is hoped that, after reading the earlier sections of this book, the reader has become sensitive to issues concerning the well-being of clients, staff, and others, and is better prepared to recognize and alleviate problem situations within his or her agency. There are some basic guidelines, however, that should be followed when establishing rules and regulations governing the conduct of staff and clients. The most basic guideline is that a rule should not restrict a fundamental right that is explicitly or implicitly guaranteed by the U.S. Constitution or statutes. If the rule does infringe upon a basic right, there must be a clear and convincing justification for doing so.

After analyzing cases from many federal and state courts, Reutter (1975) arrived at some minimum guidelines for formulating school regulations. With minor revisions, Reutter's guidelines are also applicable to developing community center regulations. These guidelines are:

1. The rule must have a legitimate habilitative or educational purpose, and it must be rationally related to achieving the goals of the community center.

2. The meaning of the rule must be reasonably clear. The rule must not be so vague as to be almost completely subject to the interpretation of the authority invoking it.
3. The rule must be sufficiently narrow in scope so as not to encompass constitutionally or statutorily protected activities.
4. If the rule infringes on fundamental constitutional or statutory rights, a compelling interest of the community center in the enforcement of the rule must be clearly shown.
5. Those persons who are governed by the regulation should be informed about the regulation, including how compliance and noncompliance are determined, the consequences for breaking the regulation, any exceptions, and if possible the rationale behind the regulation.

Persons who are familiar with the activity to be governed by the proposed regulation should participate in the development of the regulation. Serious errors can occur when administrators make regulations about matters of which they are only vaguely familiar. A carefully planned set of procedures and policies concerning the operation of the community center will help enable employees to act in a prudent, uniform manner, rather than on the spur of the moment, when an emergency situation arises. Carefully developed policies will help protect the community center and its employees from charges of negligence and misconduct, and more importantly, they will help safeguard the rights and well-being of the clients.

POINTS TO REMEMBER

1. One of the most important steps toward the development of a safe and effective community center involves the writing of a detailed delineation of the agency's program plan including procedures for evaluating this plan. This plan should answer the questions: What are the goals? How are these goals to be achieved? How well are the goals being achieved?
2. After a thorough examination of the components of the center, written accident prevention procedures and safety regulations should be developed. This examination should include a review of the center's jobs, a sequencing of the job's steps, identification of hazards, development of written safety recommendations, and reevaluation of the job after implementation of the recommendations.
3. A supervisory or administrative level employee should be appointed safety coordinator, who would be in charge of and accountable for the safety program.
4. In addition to daily inspections of critical areas, thorough safety inspections should be conducted at periodic intervals.
5. A carefully devised and competently supervised accident reporting and analysis system should be developed in order to help identify and correct dangerous situations within the center.

6. In order to decrease the occurrence and the degree of injuries during an emergency, the center should develop emergency plans, maintain current medical information files, educate staff and clients about emergency procedures, and be prepared to provide necessary first aid.
7. In regard to meeting transportation needs, the center should maintain high standards in the selection of vehicles, it should conduct thorough safety checks of all vehicles, it should develop and enforce safety regulations, it should exercise care when selecting, educating, and placing drivers, and it should educate clients in safe transportation practices.
8. The administrators of the community center should work closely with a concerned, informed insurance agent in developing insurance policies that adequately cover the individuals involved in the community center's activities.
9. The center should collect and preserve in records information that is required for planning and evaluating the center's program and evaluating each client's individual program plan. Clear-cut policies should be established for storing, amending, and altering records.
10. In regard to creating community center regulations, the most basic guideline is that the regulations should be rationally related to achieving client and center goals. The regulations should not restrict a fundamental right without being able to clearly show a compelling interest in doing so.

REFERENCES

Butler, H., & Ballou, B. Release forms. In Nisonger Center for Mental Retardation and Developmental Disabilities (ed.), *Operating manual for residential services personnel.* Columbus, OH: Author, 1974.

Child Welfare League of America. *Standards for foster family service.* New York: Author, 1975.

Eastern Paralyzed Veterans Association. *Wheeling to fire safety.* New York: Author, undated.

Educational Rights of Handicapped Children, 1977, *1*(2).

Fanning, J. W. *A common sense approach to community living arrangements for the mentally retarded.* Springfield, IL: Charles C Thomas, 1975.

Hayt, E., & Hayt, J. *Legal aspects of medical records.* Berwyn, IL: Physicians' Record Co., 1964.

Health Law Center. *Problems in hospital law* (2nd ed.). Rockville, MD: Aspen Systems Corp., 1974.

Jacobs, A.W. *The administration of California laws holding school districts liable for negligence.* Unpublished doctoral dissertation, University of California, 1964.

Leibee, H. *Tort liability for injuries to pupils.* Ann Arbor, MI: Campus Publishers, 1965.

National Commission on Safety Education. *Selection, instruction, and supervision of school bus drivers.* Washington, DC: Author, 1964.

National Safety Council. *Accident prevention manual for industrial operations* (2nd ed.). Chicago: Author, 1951.

National Safety Council. *A job analysis for safety education supervisors.* Chicago: Author, 1959.

National Safety Council. *Student accident reporting guidebook.* Chicago: Author, 1966.

National Safety Council. *Handbook of occupational safety and health.* Chicago: Author, 1975.

Nirje, B. The right to self-determination. In W. Wolfensberger (ed.), *The principle of normalization in human services.* Toronto: National Institute on Mental Retardation, 1972.

Perske, R. The dignity of risk. In W. Wolfensberger (ed.), *The principle of normalization in human services.* Toronto: National Institute on Mental Retardation, 1972.

Pozgar, G. D. *Legal aspects of health care administration.* Germantown, MD: Aspen Systems Corp., 1979.

Reutter, E. E. *The courts and student conduct.* Topeka, KS: National Organization on Legal Problems of Education, 1975.

Roby, J. J. Getting caught in the "Open Door": Psychiatrists, patients and third parties. *Mental Disability Law Reporter,* 1976, *1,* 220–228.

Seaton, D. C., Stack, H. J., & Loft, B. *Administration and supervision of safety education.* New York: The Macmillan Co., 1969.

Scheerenberger, R. C. *Managing residential facilities for the developmentally disabled.* Springfield, IL: Charles C Thomas, 1975.

Sokoloff, H. D. Architectural implications, In R. B. Kugel and A. Shearer (eds.), *Changing patterns in residential services for the mentally retarded* (rev. ed.). Washington, DC: President's Commission on Mental Retardation, 1976.

Surles, R. C. Evaluating community service programs for the handicapped. In J. L. Paul, D. J. Stedman, & G. R. Neufeld (eds.), *Deinstitutionalization—Program and policy development.* Syracuse, NY: Syracuse University Press, 1977.

ENDNOTES

[1]For information concerning standard accident report forms write to the National Safety Council, 425 N. Michigan Ave., Chicago, Illinois 60611.

[2]For information concerning the accident investigation and analysis procedure write to the American National Standards Institute, Inc., 1430 Broadway, New York, New York 10018.

[3]ANSI Standards Z16.1 and Z16.2 are available for sale from the American National Standards Institute, Inc., 1430 Broadway, New York,New York 10018.

6

CLIENT, STAFF, AND COMMUNITY RECOMMENDATIONS

Within a community there are three interrelated groups of "publics" or consumers that the center is designed to serve. First and most important are the clients. This group consists of those persons actually engaged as recipients of the community center's primary treatment programs and their guardians or representatives (e.g., parents). The second group consists of those persons who are employed by the center and upon whom the center depends for its day-to-day operation, including professional consultants. The third group consists of the members of the larger community, including those persons who donate their time and energy toward volunteer activities for the center. In this chapter, recommendations are made concerning ways in which the community center can provide effective, valuable services to these groups and at the same time protect them from unnecessary harm. Further recommendations concerning individual client treatment programs are also presented in Chapters 7 and 8.

CLIENT CONCERNS

Client Admission and Discharge

Due to the varying needs and large numbers of potential clients, and due to limited resources, a community center may not be able to serve all who request services. In order to help eliminate inappropriate referrals, to help avoid complaints filed by disgruntled applicants, and to help reduce application processing time, the community center should develop explicit written admission criteria and guidelines. The basis for developing these criteria is whether shortly after, or even before, accepting a client into a treatment program, the center's staff in cooperation with the client and the client's guardian, where applicable, is able to develop a written treatment plan. This plan should clearly describe the steps that will be taken to facilitate the client's personal development and self-actualization. If the center is not able to develop and carry out such a plan, the applicant should not be admitted. When developing application guidelines, care must be taken to ensure that the admission criteria do not discriminate against applicants on the basis of race, color, religion, sex, national origin, age (40 to 65 years old), or physical disability, without an overriding just cause (e.g., accepting a 45-year-old adult into a preschool program would obviously be inappropriate).

The admission guidelines should specify what procedures, records, tests, and family history are desired before screening the applicant. In addition, these written guidelines should clearly specify the procedures to be followed by the staff members involved in the application process. One staff member should probably be assigned the task of monitoring and supervising the application process. Whenever possible and appropriate the applicant's guardian or next of kin should also participate in the application process. Easily understandable application forms should be developed. These forms should be tailored to the specific information needs of the community center. Some of the information that may be requested would include the applicant's name, age, family background, and treatment history, name and address of the guardian or next of kin, name of the social worker, employment history, and medical history and medication. Applicants should be notified promptly concerning an admission or rejection decision, preferably shortly after all the necessary forms, interviews, and testings are completed.

Written procedures concerning an admissions waiting list should also be developed. In general, waiting lists should be based on a first come, first serve basis after an applicant has been accepted. These applicants should be notified of their placement on the waiting list, and procedures for updating this list should be formulated. In addition, procedures should be developed for identifying and safeguarding any personal belongings, including adaptive devices and medication, a successful applicant may wish to bring with him or her upon admission.

Dybwad (1969) has presented an interesting approach for attempting to ensure that a community center appropriately serves a client's needs. He suggests that before an individual is admitted into a community center's program an agreement, in the form of an actual contract, should be made between the interested parties. This agreement would concern the individual's length of stay in the program, the individual's needs, specific objectives, and proposed time lines for achieving the objectives. He suggests that if such an arrangement is not made when the individual enters the program, there is a tendency for the placement to remain a permanent one. Dybwad also suggests that if such an agreement is made, and if periodic reports concerning the client's progress toward the specified goals are made, there might be a greater commit-ment on the part of the client's relatives or guardian. In this way, some support for the client might be developed outside of the center that could help ease the client's transition from the sheltered environment of the center to a more independent arrangement. This type of admission agreement may be particu-larly beneficial for guarding against "institutionalizing" clients by community centers. Care must be taken when forming such an agreement, however, because the center's failure to fulfill its part of the agreement may constitute a legally actionable breach of contract. Before making such agreements, the community center should consult a qualified lawyer, in that geographic area, concerning the development of guidelines for making admission agreements.

More recently, the Institute of Judicial Administration (1977), sponsored by the American Bar Association, has made recommendations concerning the admissions of juvenile offenders to training centers, which are similar to Dybwad's (1969) recommendations. As they would apply to a residential community center, these recommendations are:

1. Whenever feasible, the community center and the client and/or the client's guardian should make arrangements for frequent visitations of relatives and friends.
2. The admission documents should include a description of the specific ser-vices that will be provided by the community center to aid the client and to ease the transition to the larger community.
3. A description should be formulated of the behavioral and/or the physical changes that are needed in the larger community in order for the client to return to the larger community.
4. Whenever feasible, admission documents should include provisions for helping the family or friends to participate in the care of the client while he or she is residing at the center.

Community centers need clear-cut authority to allow clients to test their abilities outside of the center and to provide opportunities for greater freedom of movement and self-direction. This may include trial visits to their natural homes and to independent environments. In order to achieve these goals the center must be willing and able to provide assistance to the client during the crucial transition period. This assistance may involve helping the client to secure employment, financial aid, support services, and living arrangements.

Community centers must also have the freedom to discharge from their care clients 1) who have recovered from the disability that led to their place-ment, 2) who have improved to such an extent that they no longer need care or supervision beyond what they can arrange or consent to for themselves, 3) who have not improved but cannot benefit from further care and treatment at the center, either because they are able to manage without the center's assistance or because the center does not have the ability to meet the client's current physical, nutritional, emotional, or behavioral needs, or 4) who present such a foreseeable hazard to themselves, others, or the operation of the center that they cannot remain in the program. Such termination or discharge decisions should be made only after careful examination and evaluation of the client's condition and the client's probability of success outside of the center. The client, the client's guardian or next of kin, and the agency that originally referred or placed the client in the center should be given sufficient notice, at least 30 days, before the discharge is to occur. Whenever possible, the client, the client's guardian, and the referring agency should also participate in the examination and evaluation process prior to the making of the actual discharge decision. In cases of emergency where the client's physical or mental well-being is endangered (e.g., the client is the target of abuse by other clients or staff members), or when the client's excessive behavior problems present a hazard to himself or herself or others, the discharge process may be greatly accelerated. Termination decisions should be clearly supported by an objective assessment of the client's current condition, careful professional judgments, and written records. The client's written valid consent and/or the consent of the client's guardian, and the consent of the referring agency should be sought for the client's discharge. Those persons should also be allowed to contest the decision and have their written statements included in the client's records. When the client, the client's guardian, or the referring agency chooses to terminate the treatment relationship with or without the approval of the community center, this decision and the circumstances surrounding it should be carefully documented.

Search and Seizure

The Fourth Amendment of the United States Constitution ensures citizens that their person, property, and home will not be invaded by government officials without reasonable cause. The U.S. Supreme Court in *Katz v. U.S.*[1] declared that, for the most part, only those searches that are conducted pursuant to a valid, judge-approved search warrant are presumed to be reasonable. Since the 1960s there has been an increased recognition that even students are entitled to protection by the Fourth Amendment. Likewise, community center clients are protected against unreasonable searches and seizure of their property. Those persons involved with an unconstitutional search and seizure can be held liable for any resulting injury.

Circumstances may arise in a community center involving a potentially dangerous condition, but administrators may not wish to involve the police or judiciary by obtaining a warrant because of the stigma attached to such procedures, or because that process takes considerable time and the dangerous situation may demand prompt action. The courts have reasoned that because of the special relationship between school personnel and students, and because guardians have a right to expect that the school will maintain certain safeguards to protect their children from "harmful and dangerous influences," schools have not only the right but also an obligation to investigate a presumably hazardous condition on the premises even without a warrant (National Association of Secondary School Principals, 1979). A similar relationship and obligation exists between a community center and its clients.

If the center's employees suspect that a client has possessión of a forbidden or dangerous item, such as a gun or illicit drugs, the employee may wish to search for and seize the dangerous item. Care must be taken, however, not to abuse the obligation to protect clients and others. When making the determination of whether to make warrantless search, the center's administrators must consider the duties of the center, the purpose and necessity of the search, the client's age and record, and the seriousness of the potential problem. When the danger of the situation warrants it and when the urgency of the situation allows it, the center's administrators may decide to involve the police and obtain a search warrant.

The staff of each community center should formulate a policy concerning search and seizure of dangerous or forbidden items. This policy should specify what items are forbidden, how a search is to be conducted, who makes the final decision concerning whether or not to conduct a search, when a warrant should be sought, when police should be involved, and what disciplinary actions can be taken. Periodic searches should not be conducted. The National Association of Secondary School Principals (1979) has presented five recommendations for developing a search and seizure policy. First, warrantless searches should be conducted only upon the basis of a reasonable suspicion that a specific client is concealing something, possession of which is either in violation of a law or a center regulation. Second, the center's employees should seek the voluntary disclosure of the suspected item or the client's consent to make the search before beginning an involuntary search. Third, the greater the abridgment of the client's right to privacy that will result from the search, the greater the justification that must exist in order to conduct the search. Fourth, the danger presented by the item being sought, the client's age, condition, and record, and the urgency of making the search without delay are factors that must be considered when making the decision to search a client. Finally, the primary purpose and justification for the search should be the protection of the health, safety, and welfare of the clients, employees, and others. Extreme caution must be used when coercing a client to cooperate with a search. If excessive force must be used in order to conduct a search, a warrant and the assistance of the police should be sought before conducting the search.

EMPLOYEE CONCERNS

Employee Selection and Hiring

The caring staff members who work closest with the clients are probably the most valuable component of any community center. These staff members must act as mediators between the community center and the general public.

Occasionally they may be called upon to act as advocates for the clients, particularly if the clients' rights are being abused by the community center itself. In addition, it is those staff members who work closest with the clients who will be able to give feedback and invaluable suggestions concerning the client's individual habilitation plans. The selection and training of caring staff members are critical factors in the success of any community center.

One important quality of potential staff members, which is difficult to specify and which is frequently overlooked, is the applicant's attitude toward the clients.[2] The staff members of a community center must "believe" that the clients are citizens and that they are entitled to the same rights and privileges due all citizens. In addition, the staff members must "believe" that the clients are dynamic human beings who are capable of growth and development. The task of determining an applicant's beliefs and attitudes toward disabled persons or juveniles is quite difficult. There is often a discrepancy between what people believe and what they say, particularly in an interview situation.

There are some techniques, however, that may reveal some clues about an applicant's attitudes. One such technique involves carefully examining the applicant's reports of previous experiences with disabled persons or juveniles and asking the applicant questions concerning the experiences. Another technique for examining beliefs and attitudes is to present the applicant with some hypothetical situations involving disabled persons or juveniles and ask the applicant questions as to how he or she would deal with the situation. It is important to remember that, although an applicant may have an impressive educational and work background, if the person does not consider the clients to be human beings and citizens, he or she may do the clients more harm than good.

Viewing clients as objects of pity also is a destructive attitude in a community center. Recently, an otherwise competent administrator at an institution for retarded individuals told one of the authors that she would not want to eat with the residents and that she certainly would not want to have to come in contact with them in the community. This "second class citizen" attitude was clearly expressed in the policies developed by that administrator. Such individuals can hinder the client's growth in subtle ways that are difficult for supervisors to control. For example, such a staff member may not bother to make suggestions concerning ways to further normalize the client's environment. Probably a good administrative policy would be to hire a cooperative applicant with minimal educational experience but with a caring healthy attitude toward the clients, than to hire a well-educated, highly skilled person who viewed disabled persons or juveniles as second class citizens. It is probably more difficult to change an adult's attitudes than to teach a cooperative adult new skills.

Discriminating in regard to employment is forbidden in the United States. There are both constitutional and statutory prohibitions against discrimination on the basis of race, color, religion, sex, national origin, age (40 to 65 years old), or physical disability concerning the hiring, compensation, promotion, discipline, and discharge of employees. An employee or potential employee can seek compensation for damages if an employer illegally discriminates in these matters.

Peres (1978) has pointed out that the first step in lessening an employer's chances of a discrimination complaint with regard to a hiring decision is to develop a written set of hiring guidelines. He provides excellent recommendations for developing these guidelines. These guidelines must contain policies concerning hiring standards, qualifications, recruitment, screening, application forms, interviews, and rejection of unsuccessful applicants. An administrator who is knowledgeable in the area of unlawful discrimination should be responsible for the process of employee selection. The duties of this administrator and others involved in the selection process, such as secretaries who handle incoming job inquiries, should be specified in the guidelines.

In addition to the previously mentioned clearly impermissible categories for judging applicants, employers should also avoid making inquiries into height and weight measurements, citizenship, credit background, marital status, or spouse's background except where it is necessary to do so for clearly bona fide job-related requirements. Inquiries into these areas may be viewed as discriminatory in nature. In order to determine appropriate skill requirements for the job, the community center should carefully examine the job in question and evaluate those indicators that correctly predict a prospective employee's ability to perform the job. The relative importance of these predictors or job requirements should be determined and then assigned priorities. For example, educational requirements must be examined to determine if they are necessary and whether related experiences or on-the-job training could be substituted. It is critical that these hiring standards be applied uniformly.

The way in which the job is advertised may present a problem if this process is discriminatory in nature. For example, advertising a position opening only in a university newspaper or through an employment agency may be discriminatory. An excellent publication entitled *Affirmative Action and Equal Employment—A Guidebook for Employers* (obtained by writing to the Office of Voluntary Programs, Equal Employment Opportunity Commission, 1800 G. Street, N.W., Washington, D.C. 20506) presents recommendations for eliminating discriminatory recruitment practices. The position announcements should include a brief description of the job responsibilities and expectations.

In order to help ensure that the hiring standards are uniformly applied for all prospective employees an application form must be developed. Peres (1978) has suggested that the following topics be included on application forms:

1. Name, address, telephone number, and Social Security number
2. Work experience, including dates of employment, job title, nature of duties, salary, immediate supervisor, and reasons for leaving
3. Education and training

4. Driver's license number, if applicable
5. Reason(s) for interest in position
6. Other qualifications and experiences related to the position
7. Any factors that would prevent adequate performance of the job in question
8. Personal and employment references

In addition, special information pertinent to the job should be included in the application form. A reasonable period of time must be allowed in which to obtain and complete a job application. No one should be denied an opportunity to complete an application for the job.

After a reasonable time period has elapsed, the applications may need to be screened to facilitate the hiring process in order to filter out those applicants who are obviously not qualified for the job. Those persons involved in the screening should be thoroughly familiar with the priorities assigned to the job requirements. Standards must be uniformly applied and an application must not be rejected until it has been thoroughly evaluated. Once a manageable number of applications has been reached, the applicants should be personally interviewed if possible. The purpose of these interviews is to gather more meaningful information about an applicant's qualifications so that a more informed hiring decision can be made. These interviews should be concerned with only relevant factors regarding an applicant's ability to perform the job. The interview should be somewhat structured and brief notes should be recorded. Often the application form itself can be used as the basis for developing a structured interview.

Finally, care must also be used when establishing a tactful, uniform procedure for rejecting unsuccessful applicants. Applicants should be informed of their status in the hiring process only after a definite decision is reached. Applicants, however, should be told when they will be informed of the decision. A rejection should be thoroughly explained in a tactful and understandable manner.

Employee Training

Staff training must be an integral part of the community center's general program. Training programs should be developed for the preparation of new employees and for providing existing employees with continuing education. The new employee training should include: 1) familiarization with the community center's philosophy, organization, policies, activities, programs, practices, and goals, 2) training in first aid and accident prevention techniques, 3) training in the implementation of the normalization principle, 4) training in tactfully dealing with clients, relatives or guardians, visitors, and the media, 5) training in meeting the needs of the clients with whom the employee will be working, and 6) training in any skill areas in which the individual has not yet reached the level of competence required for the job (AC/MR-DD, 1978).

This training should meet the same high standards required for client training. The training that a new employee receives should be described and properly documented in the employee's personnel file. The successful completion of this training program must be viewed as absolutely necessary for all new employees. Those responsible for conducting the orientation program should develop a system for evaluating the effect of the orientation program. Such a system may involve written examinations, pre- and posttests, answers to objective questions, and completion of practicum exercises. As in other areas of employment, employees have a right to confidentiality regarding their performance in the training, and their performance should not be discussed or gossiped about to others (National Institute on Mental Retardation, 1978).

In order to assist in the training of new employees and to serve as a reference source for existing employees an employee handbook should be developed. All employees should be given a copy of the handbook. This handbook should contain the center's policies and procedures. A formal but brief description setting forth the duties, responsibilities, and limitations in authority, as well as the principal measures of accountability and performance, should also be included (Katz, 1977). The handbook should be written in an easily understandable form in a looseleaf format to facilitate updating. The employees who will be governed by the handbook should participate in the formulation of the handbook. This affords the employees an opportunity to examine and learn more about the rationale behind the policies. This cooperative effort may also result in the development of greater support for the policies among employees. The handbook should be periodically reviewed and changes discussed at staff meetings. In their 1973 book, *Community Placement of the Mentally Retarded,* Mamula and Newman presented an example of such a care providers' handbook.

Continuing education programs are essential to the success of a community center. Through continuing education programs the staff can keep abreast of new techniques related to habilitation, and they can sharpen the skills they already possess. Local colleges and universities, the state social services administration, and local agencies such as the American Red Cross may be able to provide a variety of continuing education programs for the staff of a community center. In these programs, attention should be given to local experiences and policies related to the community center and to specific problems that the center's employees have faced. Other than those courses that are critical to maintaining certification or to maintaining an adequate quality of care, employees should have the opportunity to choose among various options, taking advantage of the various local and regional educational opportunities. In addition, the community center's employees should be given the opportunity to attend seminars, conferences, workshops, and institutes, to visit other agencies, to participate in professional organizations, to conduct and publish research, and to have access to a professional library (AC/MR-DD, 1977).

Evaluation and Recognition

It is extremely important that the community center develop uniform procedures for evaluating the performance of its employees. Haphazard or spur of the moment evaluation procedures can lead to discrimination and claims filed by disgruntled employees. The information that is gathered by evaluation procedures is critical for making promotion, recognition, training, and disciplinary decisions. The primary purpose of the evaluation, however, is to assist the employee in improving his or her performance. Peres (1978) has provided several excellent suggestions for developing a staff evaluation policy. These include:

1. Those conducting the evaluation should be thoroughly familiar with the functions and responsibilities of the particular job, and familiar with the employee in question.
2. Evaluations should be conducted in an honest, uniform manner, and performance standards should be well explained to all employees.
3. Evaluations should be conducted several times a year.
4. Evaluations should be concerned with all aspects of the employee's job performance, paying particular attention to results rather than methods. There are often several methods of producing an equally acceptable result. Of course, in order for the alternative procedure to be suitable it must also be ethically, professionally, and legally appropriate.
5. The evaluator should be able to support conclusions with direct factual data rather than impressions.
6. Keep a record of the performance evaluation, and give a copy of the evaluation to the employee. Both the evaluator and the employee should sign and date the evaluation, the employee should be allowed the opportunity to comment upon the evaluation, and those comments should be appended to the original evaluation record.

By developing an evaluation form or a standard evaluation format, the community center's administration can be better assured that evaluations are conducted in a uniform manner. In addition, during the evaluation process the employee and the evaluator should arrive at some realistic job performance goals for the employee. The employee's progress toward these goals should be assessed during the next evaluation.

All too frequently the primary results of an evaluation are either simply oral feedback concerning the employee's job performance or the initiation of some corrective action. Favorable evaluation results can also serve as the basis for honoring or recognizing an employee's achievement. Community center administrators must remember that their employees often give more to their work in terms of time, effort, and dedication than do workers in other trades and professions. In order to encourage and maintain these needed high levels of dedication the center's administrators may need to provide good employees with recognition of their work and incentives, in addition to their wages, for exceptional job performances and achievements. This recognition may consist of formal acknowledgments, such as a Recognition Luncheon, plaques, and certificates, or less formal acknowledgments, such as a privileged parking space. A community center can also periodically publish a newsletter both to recognize the accomplishments of employees and clients and to inform relatives and community members about the operation of the community center.

Employee Discipline and Discharge

The discharge of an employee represents a loss to the community center and it represents a failure somewhere in the employee management process (e.g., an error in employee selection, training, or evaluation). The community center not only loses the services of that employee, but an investment of both time and money in the selection, training, and evaluation is also wasted. A community center's first step in regard to discharging problem employees is to develop a uniform discharge policy. Among the issues that should be addressed by a discharge policy are the reasons for discharge, how the discharge policy is to be initiated, and by whose authority will discharges become final (Peres, 1978). These procedures must be uniformly applied to all discharge actions. Delon (1977) has presented a list of reasons for initiating disciplinary actions and discharges. Included in this list are issues such as excessive unauthorized absences, failure to submit reports or falsification of records, neglect of duty, unprofessional conduct, and abuse of clients. Of course, disciplinary actions or discharges based on one of the forbidden discriminations must never be permitted.

The community center administrators should develop a set of gradual, constructive procedures that are to be implemented when employees do not fulfill their responsibilities properly. These procedures should be written down, disseminated, and applied uniformly for all employees. Peres (1978) has described a gradual step process that may serve as a model for developing guidelines to follow when an employee is not performing properly. The first step in the process involves an informal oral conference between the supervisor and the employee. This conference is to occur following ordinary unacceptable behavior in relation to a commonly understood or formerly adopted standard or regulation. The supervisor should make a factual record of the conference by recording the date, time, place, persons involved, and the substance of what is said. At this point in the process, however, the record should not be placed in the employee's personnel file. Instead, the record should be kept in a separate temporary file which is destroyed if the employee's behavior improves or is referred to if the improper behavior continues. Second, if the employee persists in breaking the clearly specified regulation, a formal conference between the supervisor and the employee should be held in order to discuss the problem behavior. At this meeting the supervisor should clearly specify what behaviors do not meet the standards and what behaviors must be changed, offer specific counseling and assistance, and set a time frame for correcting and evaluating the problem (French, 1978). This conference should be recorded, detailing the date and nature of the first informal meeting (from the temporary file), and the date, time, location, and persons involved in the formal conference, indicating specific guidelines that the employee must follow, describing the employee's improper behavior, and specifying the time frame for correction and evaluation. This memo should be placed in the employee's personnel file and a copy should be sent to the employee. The employee should also have the opportunity to respond in writing to the memo and his or her responses must be appended to the memo. A written reprimand may also be issued. This reprimand must be clearly directed to the specific behavior to be corrected, and it must not deal with extraneous issues that can be misunderstood. In order to ensure that the employee has indeed viewed the written report, memo, or reprimand the employee should sign the copy that is kept in the personnel files. If the employee persists in the improper performance, the third step in the corrective process would involve suspending the employee without pay for a few days. The suspension notice should clearly explain the nature of the suspension and why it is being imposed with reference to the past warnings. A copy of the suspension notice should be given to the employee and a copy must be placed in the employee's folder. The supervisor may also wish to orally explain to the employee the suspension and the reasons behind the suspension. Of course, before the employment relationship deteriorates to a point necessitating suspension, the employer or supervisor should carefully examine the situation from the employee's viewpoint in hopes of reaching an acceptable solution to the presenting problem.

If, following the previously described corrective and disciplinary actions, the employee persists in the improper behavior which presents a hazard or seriously disrupts the functioning of the center, the employee may have to be discharged. As with the other steps in the disciplinary process, the reasons for the discharge must be documented. This documentation should accurately reflect the employee's past performance. Among the items that may be used as documentation are previously issued written warnings, memos, evaluations, incident reports, complaints from clients and others, and absenteeism records. Documentation that is created after the discharge occurs or after legal action ensues may appear less credible in court. The employer should also explain the reasons for the discharge to the employee in as tactful and straightforward a manner as possible. Under those circumstances when clients or others are exposed to harm or injury as a result of an employee's deliberate improper behavior, the progressive disciplinary steps may be bypassed and the employee summarily discharged. For example, an employee who is found guilty of maliciously striking clients must be discharged promptly for the protection of clients from unnecessary foreseeable harm and for the protection of the center from devastating publicity and legal action. Credible documentation, however, must also accompany this type of summary discharge.

COMMUNITY CONCERNS

Community Education and Board Involvement

One result of the movement toward providing services for disabled persons and troubled juveniles in their own communities, rather than in remote institutions, has been to place great importance upon the reactions, apprehensions, and attitudes of community members toward these persons. Training and assisting clients to function as fully as possible in the major life areas is only part of the habilitation or rehabilitation process. The other part of the process involves educating and assisting the larger community to accept the clients and to encourage them to live in the mainstream of life (Nelson, 1978). The success of the community center's program may be more dependent on establishing positive community relations, public understanding of the clients' abilities and limitations, and acceptance of the center's service philosophy than on the clients' actual progress. In addition, having the support of the community can be a priceless asset should the center become involved in an incident resulting in injuries to clients or others.

Unfortunately, the importance of creating change within the community has been given little attention by the training universities and colleges. The result has been that many professionals involved in the service delivery field are not adequately trained in community change strategies. Therefore, while a community center administrator may give careful thought and skill to developing effective training programs for altering the clients' behaviors, that same adminsitrator may not develop effective programs for changing community member behavior toward the clients. One reference source that administrators may find particularly useful in this regard is a book by Roberta Nelson, *Creating Community Acceptance for Handicapped People.* In this book the author details strategies for teaching community members to be more tolerant and supportive of people with differences. She presents several steps that are necessary for effecting societal change. They are:

> (1) broadening the targets for community education and involvement to all members of the community, (2) developing a plan for organizing and educating the community, (3) developing mechanisms to involve the community in achieving the social changes necessary to integrate disabled people into the community, and of extreme importance, (4) specifically enlisting the support of influential people and decision makers in the community to achieve the established goals (Nelson, 1978, p. 32).

Like other activities of the center, the community education program should be a carefully planned and constructively organized endeavor that is diligently supervised and monitored under the direction of a responsible staff member. When creating such a program, one must remember that it is facetious to think that the larger community will "naturally" understand the needs and abilities of the center's clients when, frankly, many "trained" professionals and parents do not. Most likely the public will harbor some misconceptions and scientifically unfounded beliefs about the clients, resulting in the perpetuation of certain negative attitudes. The center's community education program must be aimed at shattering these myths. In order to do this, there must be a clear understanding of the political, religious, economic, and social nature of the community (Fanning, 1975). Without such an understanding, it is extremely difficult to create a successful educational plan. Some informal surveying of the community's attitudes toward the clients can be made by talking with grocers, clergy, doctors, neighbors and friends of staff members and board members, and others in the community. This information gathering should be the first phase in a community education plan.

There have been a number of approaches to the next phase. At the present time, however, there does not seem to be any single logical sequence to follow. What will be done will greatly depend upon the community's unique culture, needs, attitudes, and resources. Fanning (1975) has suggested several alternatives. These include a speakers' bureau, radio and television broadcasts, newspaper and magazine articles, letters, phone calls and door-to-door meetings, open houses, and public hearings. A speakers' bureau consists of a group of informed persons who are prepared to speak about and represent the center to other organizations in the community. A prepared slide program about the center can be a very useful tool for a speakers' bureau. Radio and television stations are required by law to provide opportunity, even during prime listening and viewing time, for both spot announcements and feature programs for charitable and public service activities. Newspapers and magazines can print news items about a coming event in the center and feature articles about the community center.

Good working relationships should be developed with program managers and the editors of the local media. Through letters, phone calls, and door-to-door meetings an important personal contact can be made with people who might otherwise not have been reached. These types of contacts are very expensive, however, in terms of the amount of time required. By inviting community members to an open house at the center, the community members can view the center's activities and the clients on a first-hand basis. In order to protect the clients' privacy and to avoid excessive disruption of the program, a set of policies governing public visitation must be established. A public hearing involves providing the opportunity for community members to come and question the center's administrators and to express their own ideas, support, and concerns. This is not always a beneficial educational tactic, since persons who bitterly oppose the center will probably come to the meeting and be vocal whereas those who are not opposed may be less likely to come and express their views. Such an unbalanced meeting can be particularly harmful to the public's view of the center if the meeting receives media coverage. Fanning (1975) has reported that three experienced group home administrators did not recommend this approach. More recently, an article in *Mental Retardation News* ("Group Homes," 1979) discussed the disheartening and at times cruel responses of community residents at a public hearing to talk over a proposed group home in De Kalb County, Georgia.

In addition, properly organized and conducted fund raising can and should be used both as a revenue source and as a means for educating community members. Since fund raising usually involves considerable advertising campaigns and personal contacts, these avenues can be utilized for educational purposes as well. Too frequently, however, fund-raising approaches further help to perpetuate misconceptions by attempting to evoke pity or sympathy rather than encouragement and empathy.

One the the most potentially effective community education resources a center can have is the board of directors or the policymaking board of the center. This board should be composed of approximately equal numbers of clients and/or client representatives, service providers and professionals, and influential citizens. By involving the influential or powerful leaders of the community early in the planning process, the leaders can help to accelerate the attitudinal change process within the community. "The image of your agency held by power groups will depend upon who among them is actively involved in the workshops as well as by the results which can be pointed to with pride" (Loomis, 1977, p. 77). The involved leaders, as well as the clients, their families, and professionals in the field, can provide voices to put the voices of dissidents into perspective. When prominent and influential community members contribute their time and ideas to a center, they begin to create an image of the center to the public. The board members will speak about the center and its achievements to their influential friends and colleagues, and they can help to focus the general public's attention on the advantages of having the center within their community. Prominent board members can also be valuable economic consultants, providing information that enables the center to adjust to meet current and future demands. In addition to participating on the board of directors, prominent citizens can also be enlisted to serve as trustees of the center. The trustees would be concerned with developing long range planning and with mobilizing resources.

After the board members are selected, the next step involves educating the board members about the needs and resources of the clients, the center, and the community. New board members should be given a thorough orientation to the operation of the center. They should be informed about the center's goals and activities, and they can even be given a copy of the center's policy manual. New board members will also need to be given background information concerning the board's and the center's activities before becoming involved. Robertson (1971) recommends that all new board members should be given a "board manual" which should include the following information:

1. Names and addresses of all board members
2. Statements of the center's goals and objectives
3. Historical information about the center
4. Description of the basic responsibilities of board members
5. Names and responsibilities of the center's key staff members
6. Names and responsibilities of key volunteers

7. Important organizations and individuals who provide support
8. Current financial information and important data
9. Rules and by-laws governing the board
10. Some "official" replies to questions that are frequently asked

New board members should become involved with the board's activities as soon as possible so they do not lose their initial zeal. Finally, minutes or key notes should be recorded at all board meetings and an information system, such as a newsletter, should be developed in order to keep board members informed about pertinent topics.

Volunteer Programs

Volunteer workers from the general community can be valuable assets for a community center. Through their dedication, interest, time, expertise, and connections with other community members, volunteers can contribute worthwhile services to a community center and its clients. A volunteer program should be an organized and carefully supervised activity in which the varied skills of unpaid personnel are used to support and supplement the efforts of paid community center staff (Nelson, 1978). An improperly organized, poorly supervised, or inadequately evaluated volunteer program can be more injurious than helpful to the clients, the center, or others. "A dedicated volunteer who is made to feel needed and useful will be an invaluable public relations asset: those whose time is wasted take home a negative view of your agency and become a liability" (Loomis, 1977, p. 75).

In his discussion of involving volunteers in rehabilitation facilities, Levin (1977) presented numerous benefits that can be realized by a planned volunteer program. One benefit from a volunteer program is the ability to provide increased services to the clients. Carefully trained and constructively supervised volunteers can relieve paid staff members from various tasks, such as transporting a client to a doctor's office, thereby allowing the staff to spend more time with clients and more time preparing and evaluating individual programs. Since volunteers frequently have special talents and expertise, the center can utilize these skills in order to expand the variety of services. Volunteers can provide paid staff with technical assistance and professional consultation. Volunteers can help ease the transition from the security of the community to the demands of the mainstream of society by helping the clients to increase their exposure and contact with the larger community. Through frequent contact, volunteers may be able to form much needed bonds of friendship with clients. The type of kindness, encouragement, understanding, and support resulting from an honest friendship can be a valuable element in a client's movement toward self-actualization. Well-informed volunteers can be valuable public relations agents for the community center. Volunteers can help increase public awareness of the center and its clients by making informal and formal presentations to friends, neighbors, and other organizations in the community. Volunteers can also act as spokespersons for the center by correcting misconceptions about the center or its clients as they arise. Volunteers can serve as powerful advocates for the clients by helping to bring about needed societal changes. As advocates, volunteers can speak out on matters that significantly affect the clients' abilities to function in society, and volunteers can influence the formulation and revision of policies at all levels of government. Finally, volunteers can greatly benefit the center and its clients by assisting in various fund-raising activities, such as helping to organize and run a raffle.

Creating such beneficial volunteer programs requires careful planning, diligent supervision, and systematic evaluation by the center's administrators. The same organizational principles governing other aspects of the center's program should also be applied to the development of the volunteer program. Levin (1977) has listed eight components that should be incorporated into a volunteer program in order to attain operational efficiency and high quality results. These components are:

1. Volunteer job descriptions
2. Recruitment
3. Interviewing
4. Placement
5. Preparation (orientation and training programs)
6. Supervision
7. Evaluation
8. Recognition (Levin, 1977, p. 185)

The very first step in developing a volunteer program involves appointing a knowledgeable, concerned staff member to the position of director of volunteer services. This individual must be given enough administrative authority and autonomy to be able to develop, carry out, and enforce policies effectively. The director must meet with other staff members and with clients (when possible) to specify the center's and the clients' needs and to determine how volunteers can assist in meeting these needs. From these meetings, a list of goals and objectives for the volunteer program should be developed and recorded. Next, the descriptions of the roles that volunteers can play in meeting those goals should be formulated and job descriptions created.

The same general guidelines regarding job descriptions, advertising, recruitment and training that were mentioned previously in regard to staff employment should also be applied to volunteer programs. Procedures for carefully recruiting volunteers must be developed and applied fairly. In general, the same high standards required of potential employees should also be required of potential volunteers, particularly if the volunteers will have frequent direct contact with the clients. The director and other administrators must remember that the community center and its staff can be held legally responsible for the negligent acts of volunteers as well as for those of employees. Of course, the competencies demanded of a volunteer worker should be tailored to match the particular job the volunteer will be performing for the center. For example, the requirements to be a volunteer groundskeeper should be considerably different from the requirements to be a volunteer bus driver.

Volunteers must be provided with an appropriate orientation to the community center and a carefully evaluated training program. A soundly organized and capably conducted orientation and training program can help to prevent or minimize the likely harm that could be caused by an untrained volunteer. A volunteer manual and other written materials can be distributed to help each volunteer understand the center's policies. The activities of volunteers must be carefully supervised and the outcomes of the volunteers' actions must be evaluated. In order to help maintain high standards and interest by volunteers, the achievements of the volunteers should be recognized by the center's staff by giving awards or certificates, including articles in the newsletter and bestowing other indicators of appreciation. The director of volunteer services should keep confidential records of each volunteer's application form, orientation and training, evaluations, achievements, and other pertinent information. Finally, in order to create a valuable, rather than a detrimental, volunteer program the center's administration must recognize that an effective volunteer program requires a certain amount of investment of time, effort, money, and other resources. In particular, the administrators must not overlook the necessity to purchase liability insurance coverage for the volunteers.

In order to assist agencies in developing volunteer programs, the Goodwill Industries of America, in cooperation with the U.S. Department of Health, Education, and Welfare, has prepared a series of handbooks covering the administration, interviewing, placement, training, supervision, and evaluation of a volunteer program. (These useful handbooks are available through the Goodwill Industries of America Inc., National Auxiliary to Goodwill Industries, 9200 Wisconsin Avenue, Washington, D.C. 20014.)

Protecting Endangered Third Parties

"Under general principles of civil liability, one who creates a situation involving a foreseeable peril not readily discoverable by endangered persons has a duty to warn those persons of the potential peril" (Rose, 1978, p. 59). In 1960, a California court affirmed this principle in *Johnson v. State*.[3] This lawsuit concerned the actions of a foster placement agency. The agency placed a child in a foster home without adequately informing the foster mother about the child's violent characteristics and past record of violence. The court held that the agency could be held liable for the injuries sustained by the foster mother when she was attacked by the child. More recently, in the controversial *Tarasoff v. Regents* case,[4] the California Supreme Court held that a therapist who knew, or had reason to know, that a patient presented a serious danger to a third party had a duty to exercise reasonable care to protect the foreseeable victims and warn them of the danger. This duty may also include alerting the police or taking other necessary steps to protect the endangered person (Pozgar, 1979). Likewise, a community center has a duty to take reasonable steps to protect third parties from foreseeable harm caused by the center's clients. This can include warning a client's employer or potential employer about the client's likelihood to cause harm and warning a potential victim of a client's threats.

The center's staff must use careful, prudent judgment regarding decisions to warn a third person about a client's likelihood to cause him or her harm. Before such a decision is reached, thoughtful consideration must be given to the need to prevent direct or indirect harm to the client from the disclosure of such upsetting information and the client's right to protection of his or her privacy. Confidential information must never be disclosed to persons who have no legitimate use for that information. Staff members must distinguish between and act appropriately upon a client's idle and real threats. In making such decisions, the client's past records, in particular the client's behavior under circumstances similar to the present circumstances, and the client's present behaviors must be carefully reviewed. The client's most recent behaviors should be given the greatest weight in this decision making. A client should not be continually haunted by an isolated incident that occurred several years earlier.

Indiscriminate disclosure of personal information about clients and/or unnecessary warnings of nonexistent dangers will quickly destroy the confidence that clients and the general public have in the center. When disclosing information to a third party, the center must be careful not to disclose more than what is necessary for the third party to protect himself or herself, since overbroad disclosure can violate the client's right to privacy. Also, the disclosure will most likely alter the relationship between the client and the third person(s). The center should establish clear policies concerning the disclosure of information to endangered third persons. These policies should specify who makes decisions concerning warning third persons, when police should be contacted, and how the information is to be transmitted. In addition, a system must be devised for keeping a record of the decisions, disclosures, and the contacts with third parties. Finally, whenever possible, the client should be tactfully informed about the disclosure before it is made.

POINTS TO REMEMBER

1. In order to help avoid client admission problems, the center should develop equitable, explicit, written admission criteria and guidelines that include client prerequisites, admission procedures, and waiting list procedures.
2. Clearly specified procedures should also be developed for discharging clients from the center's care. Included in these procedures must be a careful examination and evaluation of the client's condition and the client's probability of success outside of the center.

3. The center must establish procedures both to protect the clients against unreasonable searches of their persons or property and to protect persons associated with the center against harm as a result of dangerous contraband.

4. Discriminating against employees in regard to hiring, compensation, promotion, discipline, and discharge decisions should be avoided. The first step in avoiding employee discrimination is to develop a written set of hiring guidelines.

5. Training programs should be developed for the preparation of new employees and for providing existing employees with continuing education. In addition, a staff handbook containing the center's policies and procedures should be developed.

6. Uniform procedures should be developed to evaluate employees' performance of their duties. Based upon these evaluations, the center's administration should develop mechanisms for recognizing employee achievements.

7. The community center should develop uniformly applied, gradual, constructive procedures that are to be implemented when employees do not fulfill their responsibilities. All disciplinary actions should be carefully documented.

8. A critical aspect of the center's program should involve educating and assisting community members to understand the client's abilities, limitations, and needs, and to develop an acceptance of the center's service philosophy. This community education program should be a carefully planned, supervised, and evaluated endeavor. Efforts should also be made to enlist the support of influential community members and to create an active, informed policymaking board.

9. The same high standard organizational principles governing other aspects of the center's program should also be applied to the development of a volunteer program. The volunteer program plan should contain the following components: volunteer job descriptions, recruitment, interviewing, placement, preparation, supervision, evaluation, and recognition.

10. The center and its staff have a legally enforceable duty to exercise reasonable care to protect others when they are in foreseeable danger as a result of client or staff actions. There is also a duty, however, to use prudent judgment regarding decisions to warn third parties so as not to cause unnecessary harm to the client. The center should establish carefully planned policies governing the disclosure of information to or the warning of third parties.

REFERENCES

Accreditation Council for Services for Mentally Retarded and Other Developmentally Disabled Persons (AC/MR-DD). *Standards for services for developmentally disabled individuals.* Chicago: Joint Commission on Accreditation of Hospitals, 1978.

Delon, F. G. Legal controls on teacher conduct: Teacher discipline. *NOLPE Second Monograph Series, No. 2.* Topeka, KS: National Organization on Legal Problems of Education, 1977.

Dybwad, G. Action implications, U.S.A. today. In R.B. Kugel & W. Wolfensberger (eds.), *Changing patterns in residential services for the mentally retarded.* Washington, D.C.: President's Commission on Mental Retardation, 1969.

Fanning, J. W. *A common sense approach to community living arrangements for the mentally retarded.* Springfield, IL: Charles C Thomas, 1975.

French, L. L. Teacher employment, evaluation, and dismissal. In R. D. Stern (ed.), *The school principal and the law.* Topeka, KS: National Organization on Legal Problems of Education, 1978.

Group homes stir controversy. *Mental Retardation News,* September/October, 1979, *28,* 7.

Institute of Judicial Administration. *Standards relating to youth service agencies.* Cambridge, MA: Ballinger Publishing Co., 1977.

Katz, I. Concerns in labor relations. In J. G. Cull & R. E. Hardy (eds.), *Considerations in rehabilitation facility development.* Springfield, IL: Charles C Thomas, 1977.

Levin, S. Involvement of volunteers in rehabilitation facilities. In J. G. Cull & R. E. Hardy (eds.), *Considerations in rehabilitation facility development.* Springfield, IL: Charles C Thomas, 1977.

Loomis, G. P. Considerations in the development of a public relations program. In J. G. Cull & R. E. Hardy (eds.), *Considerations in rehabilitation facility development.* Springfield, IL: Charles C Thomas, 1977.

Mamula, R. A., & Newman, N. *Community placement of the mentally retarded.* Springfield, IL: Charles C Thomas, 1973.

National Association of Secondary School Principals. *A legal memorandum: Search and seizure in the schools.* Reston, VA: Author, February, 1979.

National Institute on Mental Retardation. *Residential services: Community housing options for handicapped people* (2nd ed.). Downsview, Ontario: Author, 1978.

Nelson, R. *Creating community acceptance for handicapped people.* Springfield, IL: Charles C Thomas, 1978.

Peres, R. *Dealing with employment discrimination.* New York: McGraw-Hill Book Co., 1978.

Pozgar, G. D. *Legal aspects of health care administration.* Germantown, MD: Aspen Systems Corp., 1979.

Robertson, R. L. Public relations for the non-profit organization. In P. Lesley (ed.), *Lesley's public relations handbook.* Englewood Cliffs, NJ: Prentice-Hall, 1971.

Rose, C. M. *Some emerging issues in legal liability of children's agencies.* New York: Child Welfare League of America, Inc., 1978.

Yuker, H. E. Attitudes of the general public toward handicapped individuals. In *The White House Conference on Handicapped Individuals, Volume one: Awareness papers.* Washington, DC: U.S. Government Printing Office, 1977.

ENDNOTES

[1]389 U.S. 347 (1967).

[2]"Attitudes represent a tendency to act. If the beliefs and feelings are positive, there will be a tendency to move toward the object of the attitude, and to say and do nice things. If the beliefs and feelings are negative, there will be a tendency to avoid the object, or to say or do negative things. If the beliefs and feelings are ambivalent, the

person's actions will vacilate [sic], sometimes they will be positive, other times they will be negative.

Behavior does not always correspond to beliefs and feelings. Often there is a discrepancy between what people think, what they say, and what they do. What people do, the action component of an attitude, including its verbal expression, is influenced by social environmental factors that are present when the attitude is expressed or the action taken" (Yuker, 1977, p. 89).

³447 P. 2d 352 (1960).

⁴551 P. 2d 334 (Cal. Sup. Ct. 1976).

7

POTENTIAL PROBLEM AREAS IN PROVIDING TREATMENT AND DIRECT CARE

The previous chapters have addressed the issues of developing and operating a program that is physically safe and legally sound. One must, obviously, give much attention to the considerations discussed in Chapters 1 through 6 before attempting to initiate any type of community-based program. It is not an easy task to ensure that the program's physical facility meets all federal, state, and local requirements, that it remains in good repair, that safety regulations have been developed and are continuously maintained, that transportation safety procedures are followed, that records are kept in good order, and that client, employee, and community concerns are constantly addressed and evaluated. An administrator or director of a community program can feel overwhelmed attempting to attend to and monitor all the day-to-day operational tasks of the program. In executing all these tasks, however, one must never lose sight of the objectives of the program or the reasons for its existence. Normally, the primary goal of the agency will be to provide care, treatment, rehabilitation, or a learning or creative work environment for the clients. Often, one will find that it is an even more difficult task to provide the appropriate care and treatment than it is to maintain a safe and legally protected environment. For the continued survival of a program, in this age of accountability, however, an administrator must address all the issues, including providing appropriate treatment and learning experiences. To protect the program's existence, one cannot have one without the other. A safe environment without treatment is no better than a program providing treatment in an unsafe facility using negligent procedures. It is a burden, no doubt, but with lawsuits increasing daily, it is an obligation that every administrator must meet. The purpose of this chapter, therefore, is to outline the primary problem areas that may arise when attempting to provide treatment and direct care in a community-based program.

TREATMENT VERSUS CUSTODIAL CARE

In establishing a community-based program, an administrator attempts to develop an environment that is both pleasant and safe for the clients and staff. The question arises, however, as to whether there is a duty to provide anything more than good custodial care. To answer this question adequately, one must briefly review the legal history, including both cases and statutes, of the "right to treatment" for the mentally ill, developmentally disabled persons, and juvenile offenders.

Under the doctrine of *parens patriae,*[1] the government is allowed (and in some instances required) to establish facilities to care for those individuals who are unable to care for themselves. For decades, hundreds of institutions were built to house mentally ill and developmentally disabled persons. Often, the living conditions in these institutions were so deplorable (Blatt, 1969) that the issue of providing treatment was not even relevant. This situation began to change in the 1960s when courts began examining institutions and first recognized a right to treatment for involuntarily confined or incarcerated mentally ill and mentally retarded persons.[2]

One of the earliest and most famous cases was *Wyatt v. Stickney,*[3] a federal district court suit in Alabama seeking a right to treatment for individuals confined in a state mental hospital and a public institution for the mentally retarded. The court, in a landmark decision, held that a constitutional right to treatment did exist for these individuals. It should be noted that there is no right to treatment that actually exists in the U.S. Constitution per se. When the court speaks of a constitutional right to treatment, the court is referring to the "package of rights which the involuntarily confined mental patient is guaranteed by the due process and equal protection clauses, and the cruel and unusual punishment prohibition" (Friedman & Halpern, 1974). This right to treatment was first described by Dr. Morton Birnbaum (1960).

Equally as important as recognizing this right to treatment were the standards that the *Wyatt* court promulgated as minimum conditions for prerequisites for treatment programs for mentally retarded or mentally ill persons. In addition to specifying that a humane psychological and physical environment exist with qualified and sufficient staff, the court ordered that each resident must receive an individualized *treatment* program. The *Wyatt* case, in addition to several others,[4] appeared to acknowledge that treatment must be provided, and that this treatment constituted the *quid pro quo,* or justification, for confining these individuals who had committed no crime. Recently, the *Wyatt* court was asked to modify its original order and to allow the state to merely provide an "enriched environment" instead of habilitation programming for some of the more severely debilitated residents. The court clearly rejected this proposal holding that each individual has a right to programming that is designed to maximize the resident's human ability to cope with the environment.[5] This is probably one of the most emphatic statements issued by a court that clearly indicates that treatment, as opposed to custodial care, must be provided.

The Supreme Court has never directly addressed the issue of whether a confined mentally ill or developmentally disabled individual has a constitutional right to treatment. In the famous *O'Connor v. Donaldson* case,[6] however, the Supreme Court did issue an important decision in the area of mental illness tangentially relating to the issue of the right to treatment. The original case involved the question of whether involuntarily confined mental patients have a right to treatment. It appeared that Donaldson had been institutionalized several years earlier, and although he was not dangerous and had friends who were willing to take care of him and accept responsibility for his actions in the community, the institution refused to release him. Additionally the only treatment that Donaldson was receiving was described as "milieu therapy," which, in this case, primarily consisted of allowing Donaldson to exist in the "milieu" of the mental hospital. The court, in its opinion, focused on the constitutional right to liberty rather than on the right to treatment. It held that "a State cannot constitutionally confine without more [than custodial care] a nondangerous individual who is capable of surviving safely in freedom by himself or with the help of willing and responsible family members or friends."[7] Thus, although not directly considering whether an individual has an absolute right to treatment, the Court obviously felt that something *more* than custodial care would be required if a nondangerous individual was being involuntarily confined when that individual could safely survive in the community.

The *Donaldson* decision left many questions unanswered. For example, would an individual who could not safely survive in the community be guaranteed a right to treatment in order to be able to move successfully into the community? This issue has far-reaching implications for developmentally disabled persons, many of whom could not survive in the community if they had not first received the necessary and appropriate treatment and education. The issue of whether developmentally disabled individuals who are residing in programs supported, or partially supported, by federal funds have a right to treatment (as opposed to custodial care) was answered when Congress enacted the Developmentally Disabled Assistance and Bill of Rights Act.[8] One section of this act specifically states that developmentally disabled persons "have a right to appropriate treatment, services, and habilitation. . . ."[9] The law further requires the federal government to ensure that "public funds are not provided to any institutional or residential program for persons with developmental disabilities that does not provide treatment, services, and habilitation which is appropriate to the needs of such persons."[10]

States receiving monies under the act must ensure that individual habilitation plans are written for every person receiving services. Clearly, Congress intended that programs serving developmentally disabled persons provide more than a pleasant living environment with custodial care; treatment and habilitation programs must be developed and implemented. Obviously, the law applies only to those agencies and programs receiving public funds since the penalty for noncompliance would be withholding those funds. It is unlikely, however, that many community programs exist today that do not, in one way or another, receive public funds.

Recent cases in the *development disabilities area* reflect this mandate to provide treatment to those individuals who are placed in residential settings. Several cases in New York, for example, have held that when the state assumes responsibility for a person under the doctrine of *parens patriae,* the state must provide the necessary and proper care and treatment for that individual.[11] In a recent case in Maine, *Wuori v. Zitnay,*[12] the court established standards for the care and treatment of mentally retarded individuals who reside in *community placements.* One of the standards enumerated involved developing an individualized plan of care, education, and training for each client who resided in the community. The court went into great detail in describing how a client's "prescriptive program plan" was to be developed and implemented. Thus, it appears that treatment has been judicially, as well as professionally, recognized as necessary when providing services, especially residential services, for developmentally disabled persons.

Although, until recently,[12a] no specific federal legislation, similar to the Developmentally Disabled Assistance and Bill of Rights Act, addressed the right to treatment for *mentally ill adults* (whose mental illness first occurred in adulthood rather than childhood), most cases addressing the issue have found that residents in mental institutions have a right to an individualized habilitation plan designed to improve their conditions. In fact, the earliest decisions in the area of the right to treatment were cases involving persons committed to mental institutions.[13] Recent cases, including updates of previous decisions, reiterate the right that mental patients have to appropriate treatment as opposed to mere custodial care.[14] Some courts have even found that dangerous mental patients, committed through the criminal justice system as opposed to a commitment proceeding, have a constitutional right to be provided with treatment designed to allow them the opportunity to improve their conditions.[15] Often, individualized habilitation plans are required. Some courts distinguish between the voluntarily committed patient and the involuntarily committed one, finding that only the involuntarily committed patients have a right to treatment.[16] Most courts, however, do not make this distinction. Additionally, in a recent Massachusetts consent decree, *Brewster v. Dukakis,*[17] a right to individualized treatment was found to exist for all residents of the Northampton State Hospital. Since the decree also required the discharge of institutionalized persons concurrent with placement in community-based facilities, this right to treatment has been extended to mentally ill individuals residing in community-based programs. The Massachusetts legislature essentially codified this consent decree in regulations promulgated by the Department of Mental Health.[18] Thus, in Massachusetts, for example, it is clear, either by case or statutory law, that mentally ill individuals in community programs must be provided with treatment.

When working with *juvenile offenders* in community programs, there appears to be little doubt that some form of treatment or rehabilitation should be provided since the juvenile justice system is based on a rehabilitative model as well as on the *parens patriae* doctrine, which requires the state to care for and protect children. All states have separate juvenile codes that classify juveniles who are encapsulated into the juvenile justice system in a very different manner from adults who come within the jurisdiction of the criminal court. Obviously, children who have been abused, mistreated, or who have not received the proper care, custody, or support from their parents or guardians need to be placed in an environment where they will receive the needed nurturance and proper training. These children should be provided with learning opportunities that are similar to what "normal" children receive in their homes.

Providing treatment has not been as obviously indicated for those children who commit what would be crimes if they were adults. Over the years, service providers (especially those persons who operated institutions for juvenile offenders) have had a tendency to forget the ideals on which the juvenile court was established and have often substituted punishment for treatment. When presented with the issue, however, courts readily acknowledge that juveniles who come through the juvenile court system, even those who commit delinquent acts, have a right to treatment.[19]

Finally, the argument has been made that *elderly persons residing in nursing homes* have a right to more than mere custodial care. Some professionals have argued that elderly individuals have a right to be provided with treatment designed to restore necessary skills that have been lost due to illness, non-use, or dependency on others (Edwards & Sheldon-Wildgen, in press). If the elderly person is physically capable of relearning or reengaging in these daily living skills, the environment could be arranged in a manner that would be conducive to aiding the person in attaining this goal. Although the living environment should always be pleasant and all residents provided with their basic rights, it would not be inappropriate to provide the type of care that would encourage and perhaps retrain independent, rather than dependent, skills.

Over the last decade, it has become increasingly clearer that a right to treatment exists in programs serving dependent populations. Congress has judicially recognized this right for the developmentally disabled, and lower courts and legislatures have recognized the right for mentally ill patients. The right to rehabilitation is one of the main doctrines upon which the juvenile justice system is based and is being argued as a needed right for elderly residents. Community facilities, therefore, should design their programs in such a manner as to provide treatment, whether it be therapy, programming, or education, that will meet the individual needs of the clients being served. The remainder of this chapter is devoted to specifying and discussing the major considerations in developing an appropriate treatment program.

THE USE OF APPROPRIATE ASSESSMENT
INSTRUMENTS FOR PLACEMENT AND EVALUATION

One of the first steps that a community program should complete in an attempt to provide treatment is developing and utilizing an appropriate assessment instrument. While Chapter 6 addressed the issue of assessing which people would be appropriate for a particular community program, this chapter is concerned with the issue of assessing a person's behavioral, intellectual, or social skills after that person has become a client in the community program. Assessing a person's entry skills and subsequent performance level is critical in evaluating how successful a program is in providing services that meet each individual's needs. Although it is necessary that all clients be assessed, the evaluations should always be carried out in an appropriate manner. The following issues are considerations that should be addressed when developing or using assessment instruments. Recommendations concerning assessment procedures are given in Chapter 8.

Nondiscriminatory Assessment Instruments

Community program directors should take care in choosing, developing, or using an assessment or testing instrument to ensure that it does not unfairly discriminate against a particular class of people. IQ tests are an example of an instrument that has been recently attacked as discriminatory against black children. In *Larry P. v. Riles,*[20] a United States District Court in California ruled that standardized intelligence tests could not be used for the identification or placement of educable mentally retarded (EMR) children. The suit was originally filed in 1971 when it was found that a disproportionately large percentage of black children existed in EMR classrooms in San Francisco. The case was subsequently expanded to include all black children in California who, in the future, could be classified as mentally retarded on the basis of IQ tests.[21] As of 1977, data indicated that although black children comprised only 10% of the school population in California, they accounted for 25% of the EMR enrollment. The court accepted a "cultural bias" theory to explain why black children performed worse than white children on the standardized intelligence tests which in turn led to the placement of more black than white children in EMR classrooms. This theory presumes that the IQ tests, as they now exist, are designed to measure intelligence as demonstrated by white, middle class children. The language used on the tests is standard English which is predominantly used in white, middle class families; black children may speak a language other than this standard English. Additionally, the court found that black children's intelligence may be demonstrated in areas and ways other than what the tests indicate. Thus, black people have a heritage and culture that may never be tapped by an intelligence test designed primarily for white, middle class people.

The court found the California schools to be in violation of three federal statutes, Title VI of the Civil Rights Act of 1964,[22] Section 504 of the Rehabilitation Act of 1973,[23] and the Education for All Handicapped Children Act of 1975,[24] since they had used IQ tests that were culturally and racially biased to place black children, in a disproportionate number, in EMR classrooms. An injunction was issued prohibiting the use of standardized intelligence tests for use in placing children in EMR classes. In addition, each school district was ordered to reevaluate all black children currently in EMR classrooms. Standardized IQ tests could not be used in this evaluation.

Service providers should also be aware that some assessment instruments or tests, which may not be inherently discriminatory, can be administered in such a way as to have a discriminatory impact on certain people. Congress, for example, recognized this when writing the Education for All Handicapped Children Act of 1975. This law specifically provides that "testing and evaluation materials and procedures utilized for the purposes of evaluation and placement of handicapped children will be selected and administered so as not to be racially or culturally discriminatory."[25] This law also requires that any evaluation be administered in the child's native language or mode of communication and that no single procedure be the sole criterion for determining an appropriate educational placement. Evidence presented in court has also demonstrated that a child's performance on a test, for example, an IQ test, can be greatly improved when administered in the language spoken in the home.[26]

Therefore, in selecting assessment instruments and in administering any type of evaluation, program personnel should be able to demonstrate that their instruments are nondiscriminatory in nature or in effect. Conscious effort should be made to ensure that when tests are given, they are given in a manner that does not unfairly bias the results. Keep in mind that a test or assessment measure can, and often should, discriminate *between* individuals; it should not, however, discriminate *against* them (Schwitzgebel & Schwitzgebel, 1980).

Valid and Reliable Instruments

Any evaluation or assessment instrument should be both valid and reliable. The *validity* of an instrument or test generally refers to whether or not the instrument accurately measures what it intends to measure. Thus, for example, an assessment checklist used to evaluate community living skills would be considered valid if mastery of the items on the checklist was positively correlated with successful community living and nonmastery of the items was negatively correlated with success in the community. The *reliability* of an instrument or test normally refers to the consistency of the results obtained when using the instrument. For example, a test is said to be reliable if it produces similar results when administered at different times to the same individual (given that the administration of the tests occurs within a period of time during which no changes of behavior would presumably have occurred). Reliability can also refer to the agreement between two or more independent observers who are recording a behavior simultaneously. Thus, when assessing a person, scores obtained on the assessment instrument are said to be reliable if there is a high percentage of agreement between the observers who were rating or scoring the person's behavior. Many professional groups, whose members are involved in the testing and evaluation of people, require that members administering tests be able to demonstrate the evidence in support of the validity and reliability of the test and, thus, show the appropriateness of the test or evaluation for its intended use.[27]

A recent New York case illustrates the problems that can arise when a testing instrument is not reliable or when the instrument does not produce reliable results. In *Hoffman v. Board of Education of the City of New York,*[28] an intermediary appeals court upheld a jury verdict against the New York City Board of Education for misfeasance in failing to retest a child who was placed in a class for the mentally retarded. It appears that the plaintiff, who was 26 when he brought the suit, had been given an intelligence test when he was in kindergarten by a clinical psychologist. The child had been previously evaluated but the results were not clear-cut since one entry in the child's file indicated he was retarded while another noted that he was of normal intelligence (IQ 90). When tested in 1956, the plaintiff was in kindergarten and the results indicated that his IQ was 74, but the psychologist recommended that the boy should be retested within 2 years, due to the uncertainity of his findings. As a result of this IQ test, the child was placed in special class for the mentally retarded. He was never reevaluated as requested. Years later, he was reevaluated and it was discovered that the plaintiff was not retarded.

In bringing the suit, the plaintiff argued that his incorrect placement had retarded his educational and emotional growth which consequently affected his future ability to earn a living. A jury awarded the plaintiff $750,000 which was reduced to $500,000 by the intermediary appellate court. The court held that since the school placement was so critically important, the school district had a duty to reevaluate the plaintiff's intelligence as recommended by the psychologist.

In 1979, this decision was overturned by New York's highest court.[29] The basic premise in this court's ruling was predicated on the idea that the court should not interfere with the professional judgment of those who are directly responsible for the administration and operation of the school system. Nonetheless, the lower court decision, read in light of the recent California case, *Larry P. v. Riles,* seriously questions the validity and usefulness of certain test instruments, e.g., standard intelligence tests. Community center personnel should use extreme care in selecting (and evaluating) any assessment tool employed by the program. The fact that it has widespread use does not mean that it is free of problems, as evidenced by the cases involving intelligence tests. Likewise, new testing instruments should be evaluated to demonstrate that they are both valid and reliable.

Community centers should additionally select or develop instruments that "accurately assess the characteristics required for success in the program" (Schwitzgebel & Schwitzgebel, 1980, p. 124). Thus, one would not want to use an instrument that rated someone as inappropriate for a program who really was appropriate for the program. Nor would one want to employ an assessment instrument that found that someone was not ready to leave the community center's program when the person actually was ready. Conversely, the instrument should not show that a person has the skills necessary to leave when the person actually does not. Once again, it is easy to see that a situation can arise where either the test instrument itself is invalid or unreliable or the assessment or test is administered or interpreted in such a way as to make the results invalid or unreliable. Obviously, either case is undesirable. Assessment instruments should accurately assess an individual's behavior, and the results of the test should provide a valid and reliable indication of the performance level of the person in relation to a particular skill or set of skills.

Assessment Procedures That
Do Not Invade a Person's Right to Privacy

Often, only a thin line separates an intervention into a person's life to assess that person's skill level accurately from an intervention that invades that person's right to privacy. When assessment or evaluation instruments ask the client to reveal personal information, the client should be informed of the use of the information, assured of the confidentiality of the information obtained, and be explicitly informed of his or her right not to reveal any information. This is especially true when the information given could have detrimental or negative consequences for the client. For example, community programs should be particularly careful about the type of personally identifiable information they obtain from clients who are part of a drug rehabilitation program or a program for abusive parents. If confidentiality cannot be ensured, clients or potential clients should be specifically informed of this so they can decide if they want to reveal any information or even participate in the program.

In *Merriken v. Cressman*,[30] questionnaires were sent out to students which asked intimate questions about family relationships as well as asking the students to identify other students who behaved unusually. Information obtained from the questionnaire was to be used in a drug abuse program, and although the information was not to be made available to the general public, school personnel did have access to it. A consent letter was sent out to parents, but they were not told specifically how the information would be obtained or used nor were they told who would have access to this information. The court did not feel this consent was adequate because of these oversights as well as the fact that the parents were not required to make an affirmative response indicating they wanted their child to participate. Rather, the parents were only to indicate that they did not want their child to participate by contacting the principal. Finally, the court felt that the program lacked sufficient credibility in doing what it said it would to justify the invasion of privacy.

Any assessment instrument used should assess *only* those behaviors that are relevant to a client's problem and related to the reason the person is in the community center. Additionally, the assessment instrument should not measure personal and private behaviors unless this aspect is an integral part of the treatment program and the clients have been informed and have consented. The use of an assessment instrument was recently challenged in *Phoenix Place, Inc. v. Department of Mental Health.*[31] In 1977, the Department of Mental Health in Michigan mandated that all programs serving developmentally disabled persons and receiving state funding use Progress Assessment Charts (PAC) to evaluate their clients. The use of PAC required the direct observation of the behavior of the mentally retarded clients, including their toilet habits, private hygiene skills, and other personal functions. When a community treatment agency objected to using the assessment system, the agency was threatened with a cutoff of funds. It was then that the agency brought suit challenging the use of PAC as violative of developmentally disabled persons' right to privacy and statutory protections of "human dignity" (Michigan, similar to several other states, has a statutory requirement that the provisions of the Mental Health Code be construed to "protect and promote basic human dignity").[32] A temporary restraining order was issued and the court found that the right to privacy had been invaded by the uninvited observations required by the use of PAC. In addition to finding that several of the behaviors measured were those fundamental to marriage, procreation, and family relationships,[33] the court found that the assessment data regarding the intimate details of the clients' lives were often unrelated to any type of treatment received. Thus, a community center should be cautious about the type of assessment done and the need for the particular information in addition to obtaining informed consent and maintaining the confidentiality of any information obtained.

FAILURE TO PROVIDE ADEQUATE AND APPROPRIATE TREATMENT

At the beginning of the chapter, the issue of whether to provide custodial care or treatment was discussed, with most evidence indicating that treatment (as opposed to only custodial care) should be provided in community center programs. With that in mind, it may be useful to determine what constitutes treatment and what is necessary in order to state that the program is, in fact, providing treatment to its clients.

Soon after recognizing that a right to treatment did exist for mentally ill or developmentally disabled individuals and for juveniles, courts and legislatures began to mandate that appropriate,[34] adequate,[35] effective,[36] proper,[37] or suitable[38] treatment be provided (Schwitzgebel, 1973). Some argued that the courts did not possess the expertise to determine what constituted appropriate treatment, but this argument received little support. Judge Bazelon, a prominent judge in the mental health field, noted that courts make decisions daily in areas where they are not inherently competent; they therefore rely on expert testimony to aid in decision making (Bazelon, 1969). The area of mental health is essentially no different from any other area where expert testimony may be required.

Often, when defining appropriate treatment, the courts have included several elements. For example, in *Wyatt v. Stickney,*[39] the court specified three major areas of concern that a facility should address when providing treatment. These three conditions that the court established as prerequisites for a treatment program included: 1) a humane psychological and physical environment, 2) a sufficient number of qualified staff, and 3) individualized treatment programs for each resident. The court in *Rone v. Fireman*[40] held that determining what constituted minimally adequate treatment was not beyond judicial competence. This court noted four standards by which treatment could be measured: 1) a humane and therapeutic environment, 2) qualified staff in sufficient number, 3) individualized treatment plans, and 4) planned therapeutic programs and activities. The court also stated that high staff ratios alone would not ensure that quality care was being provided. The staff must be qualified, and one way to ensure qualified staff would be by providing inservice training and continuing education.

In recent years, courts have mandated the placement of developmentally disabled individuals in community settings.[41] The first case to issue standards for the care and treatment of developmentally disabled persons in community facilities was *Wuori v. Zitnay.*[42] Among other things, the standards in the consent order specified that clients residing in community placements had a right to certain environmental, food and nutritional, and staffing standards, a right to professional services, and a right to individualized prescriptive program plans. Daily living and clients' rights were also outlined as were prohibitions on the use of medication, labor, and restraints and abuse. The standards were quite comprehensive. Community standards addressing the needs of mentally ill persons were outlined in a consent decree in *Brewster v. Dukakis.*[43] Included in the consent decree was the requirement that all clients have a written Individual Service Plan which should detail the clients' capabilities and needs for services and the method in which services are to be provided. The areas of personnel and training were addressed, and the Department of Mental Health was instructed to promulgate regulations for environmental standards in order to protect the legal and civil rights of each client.

The considerations in staffing a community center have been addressed in previous chapters. It is important to reiterate that there should always be a sufficient number of staff in order to provide adequate services. Staff should be well trained and qualified, with the center providing continual inservice training and evaluation to ensure that the staff are aware of any new treatment procedures or relevant information and are performing their jobs in the best suitable way. The issue of providing a humane psychological and physical environment is considered in the following section. The remainder of this section addresses the development and implementation of appropriate treatment plans.

Several terms and phrases have been used when courts, legislatures, and professionals have described treatment plans. These include: "individualized treatment plan," "individualized prescriptive program plan," "individualized service plan," "individualized program plan," and "individualized habilitation plan." Independent of the label assigned, it appears that there is general agreement that certain procedures are to be followed in drawing up the plan and certain items should be included in it. Many of the following requirements are from *Wuori v. Zitnay*,[44] but similar ones can be found in other cases as well as in the federal law, the Developmentally Disabled Assistance and Bill of Rights Act.[45] The requirements are generally laid out below; recommendations on how to follow and implement them are provided in Chapter 8.

It is clear that treatment plans should be individualized, tailored to a particular person's needs and abilities. It would be inappropriate, therefore, for a community center to mimeograph treatment plans to be used for a number of clients. The treatment plans should be developed after an interdisciplinary team of professionals, along with the client and/or the client's guardian, meets to discuss the client's capabilities and needs. After evaluating the client's strengths and weaknesses, the team should develop overall program goals for the client, with short- and long-range objectives. An explanation should be given outlining which staff members will be responsible for carrying out the different treatment programs as well as describing how the program is to be implemented.

One of the most important considerations is determining how the program can be implemented in the least restrictive manner possible. *The least restrictive means of treatment* refers to the principle stating that although the government may have a legitimate goal to accomplish when treating a person, that goal should be accomplished by means that curtail individual freedom to the least extent possible (Chambers, 1974). The principle of using the least restrictive means has been employed in a number of cases concerning residents in mental institutions. In *Lake v. Cameron*,[46] the court ruled that before committing someone to an institution, the court should seek less restrictive alternatives. Many courts have ruled that the state, in deciding on a treatment placement, should seek the least restrictive type of environment that is also consistent with the client's needs.[47] This principle applies not only when considering the placement of an individual but also when determining what type of treatment modality to use. As the court in *Covington v. Harris*[48] said, "It makes little sense to guard zealously against the possibility of unwarranted deprivations prior to hospitalization, only to abandon the watch once the patient disappears behind hospital doors."[49] Whenever describing how to develop individualized treatment plans, most courts now commonly require that the plan be made with the least restrictive form of treatment in mind. For example, in *Wuori v. Zitnay*,[50] the court required that "the recommendations included in each client's prescriptive program plan, both as to residential and programming placements, shall in all cases be the least restrictive placements suited to the client's needs."[51] When describing the Individual Service Plan required in *Brewster v. Dukakis*,[52] the court stated that the plan should "address the individual's residential and nonresidential program needs, with particular emphasis on the determination of the least restrictive residential environment and suitable nonresidential treatment, training, and support services appropriate to meet those needs."[53]

In developing the individualized treatment plan, all relevant skill areas should be considered, including grooming and personal hygiene, health, household maintenance, meal planning and preparation, money management, social communication, and community-living skills. If the client has several skill areas that need to receive training, it might be wise to assign priorities to the goals or objectives and to work first on those that may jeopardize the person's health and on those that result in the most restrictions being placed on the client. A staff member should be identified as being responsible for teaching each skill, and programming should be specifically scheduled for certain times each day. Reevaluations and assessments should be done periodically throughout the year with a team meeting once a year to determine the client's progress and to develop a new treatment plan for the forthcoming year. The *Wuori v. Zitnay* standards also specify a detailed procedure to follow if the client or client's guardian wishes to object to or appeal any portion of the treatment plan.

Although it is critical that these individualized treatment plans be developed, they alone do not ensure that appropriate, adequate, or suitable treatment has, indeed, taken place. It may be that community center personnel may become quite adept at writing treatment plans, yet treatment may not actually be provided or the treatment provided may not result in an increased probability that the client will improve his or her condition (Sheldon-Wildgen, 1976). Likewise, periodic reports can be written without actually observing the client if one is only concerned about written records. As one expert once commented, "A sterling record says nothing about a patient's likelihood of recovery" (Schwitzgebel, 1973, p. 527).

Treatment plans may be necessary, but not sufficient, requirements in an attempt to ensure that appropriate treatment occurs. One of the best ways to ensure that treatment has occurred is to evaluate the outcome: determine whether objectives and goals have been accomplished. In order for effective treatment to have occurred, "goals must have been accomplished and changes in behavior must have occurred . . . " (Sheldon-Wildgen, 1976, p. 70). As more and more courts and legislatures are mandating that treatment programs be designed to assist and maximize a client's abilities in acquiring, maintaining, and improving the skills necessary to enable that client to cope adequately with his or her environment,[54] more emphasis will be placed on evaluating the outcome of treatment programs, e.g., to determine if clients do acquire more of the needed skills. With these mandates in mind, if appropriate changes in the client's behavior do not occur, one can argue that the client's right to treatment has been denied. In Chapter 8, recommendations are given to aid a community center in determining whether appropriate treatment is being provided to the clients.

FAILURE TO PROVIDE A HUMANE
PHYSICAL AND PSYCHOLOGICAL ENVIRONMENT

As mentioned earlier in this chapter, when the judicial system first became involved in lawsuits concerned with residential programs for developmentally disabled persons, mentally ill patients, juvenile offenders, or the elderly, one of the first areas the courts addressed was the physical environment in which persons resided. The conditions in many of the facilities were often dehumanizing.[55] Courts reacted to the deplorable situations by ordering that minimum standards be imposed and certain rights guaranteed.

To understand why the courts felt it important to mandate these standards, it is necessary to describe what they found in their examination of the facilities serving these dependent populations. Burton Blatt (1969) described some of the atrocities that he found when he and Fred Kaplan visited some public institutions for the mentally retarded.[56] They found children locked in tiny cells (often in solitary confinement) who were naked and lying in their own urine and feces. They found dayrooms where the odor was so overpowering that their clothes had to be sent to the cleaners to have the stench removed. The dayrooms often had a series of bleacher-like benches where residents sat, nude, jammed together, without any communication or interaction and with no activities. Often, the only form of activity or entertainment in the dayrooms was watching a television set that was mounted to a wall and fixed to one channel. It was not unusual for the television set to be in disrepair, but the residents still sat watching a blank tube. The staff in the dayroom appeared to do very little with the exception of periodically hosing down the floor in order to wash excretions into a sewer located in the center of the room. Residents were normally unwashed and unkept; many of the older ones were toothless. Food was often fed to residents in a mush-like form, taking only a few minutes per feeding per resident. Privacy was nonexistent and abuse a common occurrence. In short, the care of the retarded was bordering on barbaric. Perhaps, Blatt reasoned, the attendants and supervisors were not intentionally evil but just did not regard the residents as really human. Whatever the reason for this type of treatment, whether intentionally or benignly imposed, it was intolerable.

Courts were appalled when presented with similar descriptions of institutions in question. Ironically, there was rarely a question of fact as to whether these conditions actually existed. It was not uncommon for the defendant institution to stipulate to the fact that many of these things did occur. And these dehumanizing psychological and physical abuses occurred in facilities that housed people who had been deprived of their freedom, not because they had broken any law, but because of their condition. Most were placed in residential facilities without the constitutional safeguards afforded those individuals charged with committing a crime. If the government was going to intervene into their lives and confine them, it had to do so in a humane way that would be appropriate for any human being. So strong was the belief that dependent populations should be provided with a humane environment that most courts, legislatures, and even Congress, when faced with the issue, mandated that certain basic rights must be provided.

Specific standards for institutions were first delineated in *Wyatt v. Stickney*.[57] Later, Congress gave more force to the impetus to provide basic rights by requiring that public funds could not be used in programs that did not provide specified minimum standards.[58] Some of the most comprehensive and detailed descriptions of client rights can be found in the recent standards for community-based facilities that have been promulgated both by case law and state law regulations. Chapter 8 gives a more in-depth examination of what client rights should be provided; these rights are only briefly outlined here. The following are taken in large part from the consent decree in *Wuori v. Zitnay*[59] and from the Massachusetts Department of Mental Health Regulations for community residential alternatives.[60] The major impetus for the Massachusetts regulations was the consent decree in *Brewster v. Dukakis*.[61] Both *Wuori* and *Brewster* were concerned with standards in community-based facilities.

1. Clients have a right to live and receive services in the least restrictive environment possible.
2. Facilities should emulate normalized living conditions and conform to practices prevalent in the community.
3. Clients have the right, at all times, to be treated with dignity and respect.
4. Clients have the right to be free from discomfort, distress, or deprivation.
5. Clients have the right to be provided with appropriate psychological, medical, dental, and other therapeutic services as are necessary.
6. Clients have the right to vote, unless under guardianship.
7. Clients have the right to religious worship of their own choosing.
8. Clients have the right to engage in private communication with others, including the right to send and receive mail, the right to visit others and to

have visitation from others, the right to use the telephone, and the right to associate with others of one's choice.

9. Clients should have the right to interact socially with persons of the client's choosing.
10. Clients have the right to engage in physical exercise.
11. Clients have the right to have their own clothing, which is seasonally appropriate, clean, and neat.
12. Clients have the right to manage their own funds.
13. Clients have a right to have their own bed, dresser, and storage areas.
14. Clients have a right to attractive and private sleeping areas.
15. Clients have a right to privacy in the bathroom.
16. Clients have a right to live in facilities that have normal temperatures and adequate ventilation.
17. Clients have a right to live in a facility that has physical characteristics and behavior patterns similar to what would be found in a typical family residence.
18. Clients have a right to access to public media.
19. Clients have a right to adequate and proper food and nutrition with meals and foods being served at appropriate times and in as normal a fashion as possible.
20. Clients have a right to be free from unnecessry medication. Medication given shall not be used as punishment, as a substitute for treatent, for the convenience of the staff, or in quantities that interfere with the client's program or work. The use of any medication should be described in the client's individualized treatment plan.
21. Clients have a right to be free from mechanical, chemical, or physical restraints. Physical restraints will only be used in situations where it is necessary to protect the client from self-destructive behavior or to protect others. The physical restraints will only be used after less restrictive forms of treatment have been considered or attempted.
22. Clients have a right to protection from mistreatment. Mistreatment includes "any intentional action or omission which exposes an individual to a serious risk of physical or emotional harm." 104 Code of Massachusetts Reg. § 14.03(4).
23. Clients have a right to be free from involuntary servitude. They shall not be required to perform labor that involves the operation or maintenance of the residence or program. Nor will they be required to supervise other clients. They may, however, be required to perform labor that involves normal housekeeping and home maintenance. They also may be required to participate in a planned and supervised program of vocational and rehabilitation training, provided it is compensated at wages commensurate with its economic value and that it is in compliance with the Fair Labor Standards Act.[62]

IMPROPER USE OF AVERSIVE TECHNIQUES

When courts examined the conditions of facilities serving developmentally disabled individuals, juveniles, or mentally ill persons, they found that many residents had not only been denied basic privileges and appropriate treatment but had also been exposed to harmful or potentially dangerous conditions and procedures. It was not unusual, for example, to see residents being subjected to corporal punishment, long periods of isolation, sterilization, electric shock, mind-controlling drugs, or electroconvulsive shock. Aversive procedures were often justified as disciplinary procedures or as treatment techniques. The conditions, however, were frequently so unacceptable to either professional or societal scrutiny that issues of cruel and unusual punishment (prohibited by the Eighth Amendment) were raised.

Various procedures have now been judicially examined and prohibitions placed on the use of several techniques. The restrictions and prohibitions must be considered in light of what a particular facility is attempting to accomplish. Thus, one might find that certain procedures are strictly prohibited (unless expressed, uncoerced, and informed consent had been given) in some settings, while other procedures have guidelines that must be followed in order for their use to be allowed. One of the critical issues that courts and legislatures address is the intrusiveness or aversiveness of a procedure. Some procedures, e.g., lobotomies, are irreversible and the effects of that operation can be powerful as well as long term; thus, courts have banned the use of such procedures unless the patient has given expressed, uncoerced, and informed consent.[63] Another concern is the manner in which aversive techniques are applied. When they are applied in an arbitrary and indiscriminate manner, courts have been reluctant to find them acceptable. Thus, the court in *Wheeler v. Glass*,[64] found that spreading and tying mentally retarded children to a bed for 77½ hours and requiring them to scrub floors for 10 consecutive hours as a punishment for engaging in a homosexual act constituted cruel and unusual punishment. Another court prohibited requiring institutionalized delinquents from doing repetitive nonfunctional tasks, e.g., pulling grass without bending their knees, for no other purpose than punishment.[65] Courts have not been pleased when presented with such exotic punishment. Following is a discussion of some of the more common techniques and court reactions to those techniques.

Electric Shock

Electric shock usually involves the contingent application of a brief presentation of electric shock following some undesirable behavior, e.g., self-injurious behavior. As Budd and Baer (1976) point out, electric shock, when presented appropriately, does not produce lingering pain or tissue damage. Although electric shock has been extremely useful,[66] courts have not viewed its use favorably, perhaps because it is susceptible to misuse and because it is a procedure that appears somewhat inhumane. When the court in *Wyatt v. Stickney* considered the use of shock with mentally retarded residents, the court stated that electric shock could only be used in "extraordinary circumstances to prevent self-mutilation leading to repeated and possibly physical damage to the resident and only after alternative techniques have failed."[67] Because the *Wyatt* court felt that electric shock was both an aversive stimulus and a research technique, the court imposed additional restrictions on its use including obtaining approval from the human rights committee, obtaining the express and informed consent of the resident and the resident's guardian after providing opportunities for consultation with legal counsel, and obtaining a direct and specific order for its use by the superintendent of the institution.[68] By imposing all of these restrictions, the court obviously was not encouraging the use of electric shock; rather, it was suggesting that other, less intrusive and more positive techniques be used, and that only in special cases should the use of shock even be considered.

In standards for community facilities for the developmentally disabled, promulgated by the court in *Wuori v. Zitnay*, the use of aversive conditioning (which was not defined by the court) is not permitted unless positive and less drastic procedures have been tried and their failure documented. Similar to the *Wyatt* standards regarding shock, approval for the use of any aversive conditioning procedure must be obtained from the client's interdisciplinary team, the client (if able to give informed consent) or the client's correspondent, and a three-person special committee on aversive conditioning.[69]

Corporal Punishment

Corporal punishment involves any infliction of physical punishment on the body. Included in corporal punishment would be spanking, hitting, kicking, beating, or whipping a person. Using instruments to inflict physical punishment could also be considered corporal punishment.[70] Although the Supreme Court has allowed spanking as a disciplinary procedure to be used in the public schools, the Court did say that only reasonable, and not excessive, force was to be used and that teachers using spanking could be prosecuted under local criminal laws or sued under civil laws.[71] The court in *Morales v. Turman*,[72] however, prohibited the use of beating, slapping, kicking, or other physical abuses in a correctional institution for juvenile offenders. The court held that those procedures degraded human dignity and were usually inflicted in such an arbitrary fashion that they served no necessary purpose. One may be able to distinguish between spanking in the public schools, where the facility is much more open to public scrutiny, and beatings in institutions where few, if any, outsiders normally view what is going on.

Developmentally disabled and mentally ill persons have received much greater protection from corporal punishment. In standards for conditions in institutions for developmentally disabled individuals, several different courts have absolutely prohibited the use of corporal punishment.[73] In *Wuori v.*

Zitnay, the court specified that a client in a community program for developmentally disabled persons shall never be subject to corporal punishment.[74] In the Massachusetts regulations for community programs for mentally ill individuals, community programs are specifically prohibited from intentionally or negligently exposing a client to mistreatment. Included in the definition of mistreatment is the use of corporal punishment or "any other unreasonable use or degree of force or threat of force not necessary to protect the client or another person from bodily harm."[75]

Physical or Mechanical Restraints

Restraining a client's movement has not been an uncommon means of controlling individuals. People have been tied to beds or wheelchairs, have been straitjacketed, have had their arms and hands bound to their body, or have been forcibly held either contingent on dangerous or destructive behavior or as a daily measure to prevent such behavior from occurring. Courts have not viewed the use of restraints in a positive light, probably because of their restrictive nature. When presented with the issue, the court in *Welsch v. Likins* labeled the use of physical restraints (which included the use of cribs, straitjackets, or tying residents to physical objects) as cruel and unusual punishment if less restrictive techniques had not been previously tried.[76] The *Wyatt*[77] court prohibited the use of mechanical or physical restraints as punishment procedures, for the convenience of the staff, or as a substitute for treatment, and required that less restrictive forms of treatment be attempted before utilizing restraints. The *Wyatt* standards allowed restraints to be used for up to 12 hours with 30-minute checks by trained staff. Because of the long period of time during which restraints could be used, those standards also required that the resident have the opportunity for exercise for at least 10 minutes every 2 hours. *Wyatt* also specified that any mechanical restraint used had to be designed and employed in a manner that would not cause physical injury and that would cause the least possible discomfort. Finally, daily reports to the superintendent were required summarizing the use of the restraints that day, the type of restraints used, the reason for their use, and the duration.

In a more recent case, *New York State Association for Retarded Children v. Carey,*[78] a consent decree was issued that strictly prohibited the use of straitjackets or tying residents spread-eagled to a bed. The recent guidelines for community programs outlined in the *Wuori* standards[79] and in the Massachusetts regulations[80] are much stricter in their restrictions on the use of restraints than are those of the *Wyatt* court. *Wuori* (following the *Carey* consent decree) absolutely forbids the use of straitjackets, camisoles, and tying clients to their beds. The only permissible forms of restraint under those guidelines are: physically holding the client, placing the client in a room with an attendant, or placing a client in a room alone with an attendant outside. Restraints can only be in use for a maximum of one hour. Under the Massachusetts regulations, mechanical restraints can never be used. Physical restraint, which includes bodily holding the client, can only be used in emergency situations and must be used for the shortest period necessary with the least force needed. Emergency situations are limited to substantial risk or the occurrence of self-destructive behavior or serious physical assault. When possible, prior written authorization to use physical restraints must be obtained from the head of the community residence or program or a designated physician. In any event, authorization must always be obtained within 4 hours after the initial use. Extensive documentation must always occur. *Wuori* and the Massachusetts regulations specify that physical restraint cannot be used as a punishment technique, for the convenience of staff, or until less restrictive forms of treatment have been attempted or failed. Finally, and perhaps most importantly, federal law prohibits the use of restraints with developmentally disabled persons unless it is absolutely necessary, and physical or chemical restraints can never be used as punishment, as a substitute for treatment, or in a way that interferes with treatment or habilitation.[81]

Thus, it appears that the most recent guidelines for community programs prohibit the use of mechanical restraints and strictly limit the use of physical restraints. Additionally, any program receiving federal monies must comply with the federal mandate. Restraints should only be used as part of a treatment plan (but not as a substitute) or to protect the client or others from harm, and when restraint is used, it should be only for a brief period of time.

Seclusion

One of the most prevalent aversive techniques employed in facilities for developmentally disabled individuals, mentally ill persons, or juvenile offenders has been seclusion. Seclusion normally involves placing a person in a room or enclosed space and not allowing the person the freedom to exit. Several courts have addressed the issue of seclusion.

The court in *Inmates of Boys' Training School v. Affleck*[82] addressed the use of solitary confinement. Although strongly urging against its use, the court did not prohibit it. The court, however, did establish detailed standards of the minimum conditions that must be in existence during solitary confinement. These included sufficient lighting to read, access to school reading material and correspondence materials, adequate bedding and personal hygiene supplies, and daily showers.[83] In another case regarding juvenile offenders, *Morales v. Turman,*[84] the court distinguished between three types of seclusion: dormitory confinement, solitary confinement, and security. Limitations were placed on the use of these and strict time limits were established.

Wyatt v. Stickney issued extensive guidelines for the use of isolation with mentally ill clients. The court found that clients had a right to be free from isolation, and isolation (or restraints) should only be used in emergency situations where the clients could cause harm to themselves or others. Under the *Wyatt* guidelines, a person should be placed in isolation only after a Qualified Mental Health Professional has seen the person and has written an order explaining the rationale for the use of isolation. In emergency situations, a person can be placed in isolation without the order of the Qualified Mental Health Professional but permission must be obtained within 1 hour. While in isolation, the person's physical and psychiatric condition must be charted every hour by ward personnel. The resident, while in isolation, must have bathroom privileges at least every hour and be bathed once every 12 hours.[85] When addressing the rights of the mentally retarded residents, the *Wyatt* court prohibited the use of "seclusion," which it defined as "the placement of a resident alone in a locked room. . . ."[86] The court, however, did distinguish "legitimate time-out" procedures from seclusion. Legitimate timeout procedures were allowed if used under "close and direct professional supervision as a technique in behavior-shaping programs."[87] Unfortunately, the court did not define what constituted legitimate timeout procedures.

Both the *Wuori* standards and the Massachusetts regulations define seclusion and prohibit its use. In *Wuori,* seclusion is defined as "placing a client alone in a locked room, which he [or she] cannot leave at will."[88] In the Massachusetts regulations, seclusion means "the retention of an individual alone in a room or a [sic] enclosed space with closed doors from which the individual cannot fully exit."[89]

The use of seclusion is being scrutinized more every year. There are a variety of reasons why courts disapprove of seclusion, one of which may be that treatment cannot be provided while the person is in isolation. Thus, all the time a client is in seclusion, the client is being denied any form of appropriate treatment. Additionally, the psychological and physical conditions to which people are exposed in seclusion are often not conducive to the general welfare of clients. The following two cases describe some of the problems that can occur when clients are placed in seclusion and point to the potential liability community centers may face.

In *Mary and Crystal v. Ramsden et al.,*[90] a jury awarded monetary damages to two juvenile girls who had been placed in solitary confinement for allegedly attempting to escape from a juvenile correctional facility. On the day of the alleged attempt to escape, Mary and Crystal appeared before a three-person disciplinary panel. The girls were not allowed to have an advocate present at this hearing nor were they allowed to present witnesses on their behalf or confront witnesses against them. Mary and Crystal were confined to solitary rooms for 29 days and 19 days, respectively. During this time, they were required to stay in separate solitary rooms for 24 hours a day except for opportunities to go to the bathroom or to take a shower. The two girls were not allowed to interact or communicate with others and could not participate in recreational or treatment activities. The only clothing they were allowed were pajamas, and the girls asserted that the rooms were extremely hot, inadequately ventilated, and insect infested. The girls were not routinely given reading materials nor were their rooms routinely cleaned; on occasion when they requested these things, the items were denied. Mary further asserted that she had become ill and requested to see her psychologist but that he refused to see her. Crystal made a suicidal gesture during the first few days of her isolation and, by the fifth day, tests given to her by a corrections psychologist clearly indicated that continued isolation could have serious and detrimental effects on her. Crystal remained in isolation for an additional 2 weeks.

The court ruled that the girls had been denied due process in the hearings they had. More important, perhaps, was the jury's decision on the issue of whether the isolation constituted cruel and unusual punishment. Experts had testified that the isolation had no treatment value, was severely harmful to each girl, was unnecessary, and should not have been used in a juvenile correctional facility. The jury found that the length and conditions of the solitary confinement did, in fact, constitute cruel and unusual punishment and that this punishment caused injury to the girls. Mary and Crystal were awarded $2,400 and $1,600, respectively.

In another case involving seclusion, a psychologist had criminal charges brought against him for restricting a client to her room and denying her family contact.[91] The client, Susan Findley, was in a behavior modification program for adolescents in a state mental health institute. The treatment program for Susan involved making family contact, such as visitation or telephone calls, and room restriction contingent on Susan's behavior. Denial of family contact was chosen because Susan valued little else. Room restriction was used even though Susan had hanged and injured herself while she was in seclusion at another institution. She had also tied a scarf around her neck and the other end to a wall lamp when she was placed in room restriction at the present institution. On March 11, 1977, following an incident at the work center where Susan was allegedly observed shortchanging a woman who wanted change for a quarter, Susan's treatment staff decided to place Susan on a 2-day room restriction. Susan was found the next day hanging from a wall lamp. She was in a coma until she died the following August.

Criminal charges were brought against the psychologist, who was in charge of Susan's treatment program, for violating a Wisconsin statute that prohibits an employee of a mental institution from abusing, neglecting, or ill-treating a patient. The Wisconsin Court of Appeals, in refusing to define "ill-treat" as improper treatment because of the criminal sanctions involved, affirmed the lower court's dismissal of the criminal charge.[92] Although the criminal charges were dismissed, professional action and/or a civil suit could be brought against the psychologist.

Mental or Emotional Abuse

Most often, the easiest type of abuse to observe is physical abuse because it usually produces an observable permanent product, e.g., a person locked in a room or bruises and lacerations on a person's body. Mental and emotional abuse can occur just as frequently, perhaps more easily, and with repercussions just as serious as those associated with physical abuse. Although several courts, when issuing standards, have either alluded to or briefly mentioned the issue of mental or psychological abuse, it has not received as widespread attention as physical abuse. Few lawsuits have been brought alleging intentional infliction of mental distress or mental or emotional abuse, probably because of the difficulty in proving such charges. Nonetheless, this is an important issue to consider, and as courts become more sophisticated in addressing psychological questions and as more clients become aware of their rights, more lawsuits in this area may be brought.

The courts that have considered the issue of mental or emotional abuse have usually prohibited it. For example, in a consent decree issued in *Horacek v. Exon*,[93] verbal threats or abuse were strictly prohibited. One of the major sections in the *Wyatt* standards is called the "Humane *Psychological* and *Physical* Environment" (emphasis added).[94] In the standards for mentally retarded residents, *Wyatt* specifically prohibits mistreatment, neglect, or abuse in any form of any resident.[95] This could easily be interpreted to include emotional or mental abuse. In the *Wuori* standards, similar language can be found that forbids the mistreatment, neglect, or abuse of clients in any form.[96] Finally, the Massachusetts regulations specifically address the issue of mental abuse since mistreatment is defined as including the "[i]nfliction of mental or verbal abuse, such as screaming, name calling, or any other activity which is damaging to the individual's self-respect."[97]

Physical and Psychological
Danger Caused by Institutional Conditions

Walker and Peabody (1979) point out that courts have held that the Eighth Amendment prohibition on cruel and unusual punishment extends to ensuring basic conditions of safety, sanitation, and security.[98] They have provided a list of examples of evidence to look for in a facility to determine if the conditions are such that they might constitute cruel and unusual punishment. Some of the evidence to look for includes: 1) physical abuse of residents, either by employees of the facility or by other residents, 2) a higher incidence of suicide, suicide attempts, or self-mutilation among residents as compared with the national rates or rates in other institutions which meet the "minimum standards," 3) unsanitary living conditions including poor heating, lighting, ventilation, or plumbing, insect or rodent infestation, or inadequate facilities for personal hygiene, 4) overcrowding of residents that results in an increase of violence or abnormal behaviors or an increased likelihood of disease transmission, 5) inadequate medical or health-related services, or 6) poor nutrition (Walker & Peabody, 1979, p. 573).

Considering the above types of evidence, it was not surprising that the court, in *New York State Ass'n for Retarded Children, Inc. v. Rockefeller*,[99] specifically held that persons residing in mental institutions have a right to protection from harm. In this case, more than 1,300 incidents of abuse, injury, patient assaults, or patient fights were reported in an 8-month period. Injuries included, to name but a few, the loss of eyes, breaking of teeth, loss of an ear (bitten off by another resident), and numerous bruises and scalp wounds.[100] It is to be hoped that most conditions in facilities would not be this blatantly abusive. Nonetheless, lawsuits may be filed based on conditions that exist in a facility, including the condition of clients. The courts will most likely begin to look for less obvious abuses and their symptoms such as clients who are very unhappy in a program and wish to leave, clients who are overly meek and withdrawn, or clients who are so heavily medicated that they cannot function in their daily living skills.

FAILURE TO OBTAIN INFORMED CONSENT

In providing any type of treatment, the issue of informed consent is raised. *Informed consent* refers to the right of a person to be informed about what a particular treatment involves including the potential risks and benefits and, with this knowledge, to make a voluntary and uncoerced decision about whether or not to participate in the treatment program. The consent decision would normally be made by the person who is to receive the treatment, provided the person is competent to do so, i.e., is of the age of majority and is mentally competent. Otherwise, the consent of someone acting in the best interests of the client is required. The issue of informed consent originally began in the area of medicine when doctors were required to obtain the written consent of their patients before operating. Cutting into a person, without that person's permission, could be considered to constitute the tort of battery (Schwitzgebel & Schwitzgebel, 1980). The idea of requiring informed consent was gradually extended to nonmedical forms of treatment, especially those treatments that have a large effect on one's thinking processes or behavior. Obviously, the more intrusive the treatment procedure is, the more need there is for informed consent. Thus, the earliest court cases addressed the use of psychosurgery, electroconvulsive shock therapy, and psychotropic drugs.

When Consent Is Needed

The more intrusive the treatment procedure, the greater the need for informed consent. In fact, some procedures have been considered so intrusive, especially in light of where the patient resides, that the procedure has been strictly prohibited. For example, the court, in *Kaimowitz v. Department of Mental Health*,[101] prohibited the use of experimental psychosurgery with involuntary patients, even if consent was given by a legally appointed guardian. In addition to finding that psychosurgery seriously interfered with a person's mental processes including the generation and communication of ideas (which is protected by the First Amendment), the court also found that the institutional environment was inherently coercive. Because of the subtle psychological coercion that exists and because patients cannot reason equally with doctors and administrators, voluntary informed consent cannot be given.

Wyatt v. Hardin also addressed intrusive surgical procedures designed to affect a person's mental condition and specifically prohibited the use of any such procedure including psychosurgery or lobotomies.[102]

Wyatt v. Hardin furthermore issued guidelines on the use of electroconvulsive shock therapy. In addition to requiring that informed, voluntary, and intelligently made written consent be obtained (with the option of immediately withdrawing that consent), approval had to be obtained from the medical director of the institution, another mental health professional, and a five-member review committee. Complete neurological and physical examinations had to be given prior to the treatment, the patient had to be represented by legal counsel at all hearings, and a limit was placed on the number of treatments that could take place in any 12-month period.[103] With as stringent requirements as these, it appears that the court did not want electroconvulsive shock therapy to be used frequently.

Other courts have addressed less intrusive procedures and have required that informed consent be obtained before implementing the therapy. For example, in *Wyatt v. Stickney,* the court required that informed consent be obtained before allowing the use of any treatment that involved aversive stimuli, experimental techniques, or hazardous procedures.[104] The *Carey* consent decree required both the informed consent of the resident and the approval of a special committee established to review aversive conditioning techniques before any aversive conditioning procedure could be used or any behavioral research or experimentation could be conducted.[105] The number of procedures that require informed consent, according to *Wyatt* and *Carey,* is, therefore, large.

What Must Be Included in the Informed Consent

The *Wyatt* court defined expressed and informed consent as "the uncoerced decision of a resident who has comprehension and can signify assent or dissent."[106] The court in *Knecht v. Gillman* (a case that involved administering a nausea-inducing drug to an inmate of a medical-penal facility) required written consent that consisted of the following: 1) a description of the nature of the treatment, 2) a description of the reason for the treatment along with the presumed effects and possible risks, and 3) a notification of the inmate's right to withdraw consent at any time. A further requirement was that the person must be mentally competent to give consent.[107]

Schwitzgebel and Schwitzgebel (1980) list some provisions that should be included in a consent form for electroconvulsive shock therapy. The conditions listed would be appropriate for any type of aversive, intrusive, or experimental therapy. They include: 1) a detailed description of the procedure —what specifically it involves, how it will be done, and how long it will last, 2) an explanation of all the potential risks and anticipated benefits, 3) a statement as to why this treatment is proposed as compared to other less intrusive treatments or no treatment at all, 4) a statement that the client or client's guardian has read and discussed the consent form with the physician, 5) the patient's or guardian's dated and witnessed signature, and 6) the client's right to refuse further treatment at any time. This consent should be obtained immediately before the treatment is performed.

Finally, the Massachusetts regulations for community-based programs require that informed and voluntary consent be obtained in the following circumstances: 1) prior to medical or other treatment ("other" is not defined), 2) prior to involving the client in any approved research, 3) prior to admitting a client to any community program, either residential or nonresidential, and 4) prior to releasing personal information about a client to persons other than those who are involved with the treatment program or the evaluation of the quality of the program. Whenever informed consent is required, the following conditions must be met: 1) the consent must be in writing and noted in the client's record, 2) when consent for medical treatment or research is desired, the person securing the consent must be different from the person who is to perform the treatment or conduct the research, and 3) no coercion or "overbearing inducement" can be used in order to obtain the consent. The person who is attempting to secure the consent should explain the following to the client: 1) the nature of the procedures to be used and the intended outcome, 2) the risks, including side effects, of the treatment or research, 3) the risks of not proceeding with the treatment, 4) any alternatives to the treatment especially those that are less intrusive or that have fewer adverse effects, and 5) the fact that consent may be withheld or withdrawn at any time without any punitive repercussions taken against the client.[108] This last element is not to be construed as meaning that a client cannot be asked to leave the program if the client refuses to take advantage of or participate in any of the individualized treatment programs made available by the community center to the client (this is described in more detail below under the section entitled "The Program's Duty to Third Parties").

Right to Refuse Treatment

Along with considering the right to informed consent is the issue of whether people in treatment programs have a right to refuse treatment. One of the most common forms of "treatment" in facilities for mentally ill individuals and also for developmentally disabled persons is the use of medication, especially psychotropic drugs. Often this medication is routinely given as a method to control patients or as a substitute for treatment.[109] In the past, clients have had little, if any, option to refuse this medication. Two recent court cases, however, have dramatically changed the law on the right of institutionalized patients to refuse medication. The first decision, *Rennie v. Klein,*[110] found that mentally ill patients have a *qualified* right to refuse treatment in a nonemergency situation, based on the constitutional protection of the right to privacy. The four factors that the court found that should be considered in determining the patient's qualified right to refuse treatment included: 1) the patient's physical threat to himself or herself or to others, 2) the patient's capacity or ability to understand the consequences of treatment and, therefore, to decide on a particular treatment, 3) the existence of less restrictive forms of treatment, and 4) the risk of permanent side effects from the proposed treatment. In a more recent decision, *Rogers v. Okin,*[111] a Massachusetts court found an *absolute* right to refuse treatment in nonemergency situations for both voluntary and involuntary patients. Based on the constitutional protection of the right to privacy, the court held that the use of psychotropic medication has the potential to affect and alter a person's capacity to think, a person's mood, and a person's attitude. Because of the powerful consequences that these drugs can have on one's thought processes and the potential it gives the government or institution for thought control, the institution has the right to use these drugs only in emergency situations. Emergency was defined as "a substantial likelihood of physical harm to that patient, other patients, or to staff members of the institutions."[112] Additionally, the court rejected the idea that placement in a mental institution meant the patient was incompetent and, therefore, unable to make treatment decisions. Absent a court finding of incompetence, a person was presumed competent. For those who had been adjudicated incompetent, a guardian should be appointed to act in place of the patient and exercise the right to refuse treatment.

These two recent decisions, especially the *Rogers* holding, may have important implications for treatment programs that in the past did not feel it necessary to get the informed consent of clients before administering psychotropic drugs. It would appear that this type of medication now falls under the same requirements as have been imposed on other intrusive types of treatment and on experimental or research procedures.

FAILURE TO GATHER, RECORD, AND UTILIZE ADEQUATE INFORMATION AND TO MAINTAIN PROPER RECORDS

Record-keeping is an extremely important function of any community center. It includes the written documentation of what treatment has been implemented, how this particular treatment was selected, and what progress the client has made. Keeping good records can offer a great protection to community centers, but record-keeping also raises many issues, such as what types of records should be kept and who should have access to these records.

What Records Should Be Maintained

Few cases have dealt specifically with what records should be maintained, although this issue has been addressed in guidelines promulgated by various courts. For example, *Wyatt* had a specific section covering the type of records that should be maintained. Prior to that section, however, was a statement that one should not be admitted to an institution without a previous determination that the institution is the least restrictive setting feasible for that person.[113] That statement implies that evaluations of the person's skill levels should have taken place in addition to considering other types of placement. For the protection of the program, all these facts should be documented and placed in the client's individual records.

The *Wyatt* guidelines specify certain records that should be maintained for both mentally ill and mentally retarded residents. They include the following type of information: 1) identification data including legal status of the resident, 2) the resident's history including family data, educational background, and employment records along with physical and mental medical histories and a record of any prior institutionalization, 3) complaints or grievances listed by the resident in addition to complaints made by others about the residents, 4) a listing of the daily living skills in which the resident can engage, 5) for the mentally ill, an evaluation noting when the onset of the illness occurred, the circumstances that led to the admission, and a description of the person's intellectual, emotional, and behavioral functioning, 6) a summary of the results of all physical examinations given, 7) a copy of the resident's individualized treatment plan with any modifications made, 8) a summary of every review of the treatment plan which outlines the successes and failures of the habilitation program, 9) a copy of the post-institutionalization plan designed for the resident and a description of the steps taken to implement the plan, 10) a medication history, 11) a summary of each contact a resident has with a qualified Mental Health or Retardation Professional, 12) a detailed summary of the resident's progress and/or response to the treatment plan, done on a weekly basis for mentally ill residents and on a monthly basis for mentally retarded residents, 13) a summary of the resident's work activities, done on the same time basis as specified in #12, and the effect of these work activities on the resident's progress on the treatment plan, 14) any signed orders for physical restraints, isolation, or restrictions on visitations or communication, 15) a description of any extraordinary incidents or accidents involving the residents, 16) for the mentally retarded, a summary of family visits, a summary of the resident's leaves from the institution, and a record of any seizures, illnesses, treatments for illnesses or seizures, and immunizations, and 17) for the mentally ill, a summary of the findings, made by the superintendent, of the 15-day review undertaken after the person is committed to the hospital to determine if the person requires further hospitalization or institutionalization.[114] It is apparent that extensive records are required by the *Wyatt* court. The guidelines listed by the court in *Wuori v. Zitnay* are similar to those required by the *Wyatt* court but also include a physical description of the client and a more detailed record of activities spent outside the residential facility including the amount of time spent outdoors.[115]

Client's Right of Access to Records

Whenever records are kept, the question arises as to whether the client has a right to inspect those records that pertain specifically to the client. The question is not an easy one to answer since the right may vary from jurisdiction to jurisdiction depending on statutes and case law.

There are two federal laws that may have some effect on certain community center records. The Freedom of Information Act[116] allows the right of access to anyone who wants to inspect or receive copies of any document or record in the possession of the federal government. There are certain types of information that are exempted from this right to access including information of a personal or medical nature. It is not clear whether this last exemption would apply to a person who is attempting to have access to only that person's own personal information. Nonetheless, this law applies only to those records that the federal government has in its possession. It is extremely unlikely that the federal government would have any personal file on an individual as a result of his or her placement in a community center. Thus, this law probably will have little impact on community centers and will only affect those centers that receive federal grants or federal monies which require the center to submit reports, and then only those reports would be open to public inspection.

A second federal law, the Family Educational Rights and Privacy Act of 1974[117] (referred to as the "Buckley Amendment"), provides that students 18 or older, or parents of younger students, have the right to inspect school records that have been kept on that particular student. Some records are not available for inspection by either the student or the student's parents. Included among such records are those records "created or maintained by a physician, psychiatrist, psychologist, or other recognized professional or paraprofessional acting in his or her professional or paraprofessional capacity"[118] and which are created and used in connection with the provision of treatment to the student and which cannot be disclosed to anyone other than those persons involved in providing the treatment.[119] Some commentators (Schwitzgebel & Schwitzgebel, 1980) interpret this to mean that if the information is released to people other than treatment personnel, then the student or student's parent would have access to the information. In any event, this law is applicable only to educational institutions and may, therefore, have very little impact on community centers.

Case law varies as to a client's right to access to treatment information. In *Gaertner v. State,*[120] a Michigan court held that a state hospital could not deny the guardian of a mentally incompetent minor access to the minor's records on the basis of the physician-patient privilege since the privilege was held by the patient. The court did recognize that in some instances certain portions of a mentally ill patient's record may be necessarily suppressed in order to protect the patient from becoming severely upset. Absent a showing of this type of information in the records, the patient, or the patient's legal representative, should have access to the patient's hospital records. In *Gotkin v. Miller,*[121] however, the Second Circuit Court of Appeals denied a former mentally ill patient and her husband access to her records at one state and two private mental hospitals in New York. Janet Gotkin had been hospitalized from 1962 to 1970 and had not received treatment since 1970. In 1973, the Gotkins contracted to write a book about Janet's experiences and wanted her records in order to verify her recollections about her experiences. The court found that mentally ill patients did not have a constitutionally protected property interest in the direct and unrestricted access to their records.

Schwitzgebel and Schwitzgebel (1980) make a distinction between information in which the client may have a proprietary interest, such as transcripts or test results, and the more informal professional products, such as a professional's notes or comments. These latter products are often considered the property of the professional.

Each community center should examine the laws and regulations governing client access to records in the center's own state since jurisdictions vary on this issue. It should be noted, however, that many of the recent guidelines and regulations specifically provide that the client shall have access to his or her records. For example, the Massachusetts regulations provide the following:

1. The client or legal guardian shall be permitted to inspect and copy the client's records on request.
2. An attorney, advocate or other designated representative shall be permitted to inspect the entire record of a client, provided that the requesting party furnishes written authorization by the client or legal guardian.
3. When necessary for the understanding of the client, legal guardian, or representative, the staff shall read or interpret the record.[122]

Client's Right to Confidentiality

The issue of confidentiality is a broad one, including a variety of topics ranging from the nondisclosure of information given by a client to a therapist to the protection of information contained in the treatment records in a community center. Although some of these topics are covered by state law (e.g., the privileged communication between a certified psychologist or psychiatrist and a client), a large part of the issue of confidentiality remains under the auspices of professional ethics. It is not the purpose of this section to detail the different concerns about information given by a client to a therapist;[123] rather, the issue of concern is the confidentiality of any client records maintained by a community center.

Records kept on clients in community centers obviously contain much personal information about the clients. To release this information non-discriminately, one might argue, would constitute an invasion of privacy. Additionally, ethical and professional standards normally require that records remain confidential and should be released only to those people who have a legitimate interest or need for the information. The court in *Wuori v. Zitnay* recognized this by holding that "[t]he confidentiality of any records identifying individual clients shall be respected."[124]

The Massachusetts regulations for community programs devote an entire section to access to records and the privacy of them.[125] According to these regulations, the records of a client are private and should not be open to public inspection, with the following exceptions: 1) the client, or legal guardian, can give informed consent to allow another person to inspect the records, provided the client, or legal guardian, has had the opportunity to examine the information that is to be disclosed and has been given the name of the recipient and the possible uses of the information, 2) in the case of a medical emergency, the records can be made available to the physician who treats the client, but the client must subsequently be given notice of this inspection of records, 3) records of the client can be inspected upon proper judicial order, 4) client records can be available to people authorized by the department of mental health to monitor the quality of services being provided in the community program, 5) client records can be made available to persons approved by the program or residence director, authorized by a human rights committee, and under departmental regulations to engage in research, and 6) records of clients, who are legally competent but who have been determined, in fact, to be incapable according to their treatment plan, can be made available to certain people (e.g., staff or professional personnel intending to provide rehabilitation services to the client; an attorney or advocate of the client; agencies, insurers, trustees, or other persons through whom legal or financial assistance may be made available to the client) who demonstrate a clear and substantial need to have access to the records in order to serve the client's best interests.[126]

Several other protections are given to clients who have records maintained by a community facility. A client or legal guardian can challenge the decision of a program or residence director as to the inspection of the client's records. If a court order has been issued asking for the records to be produced, the client or legal guardian must be informed and also told of the right to request the court to quash or modify the order. All records maintained by a community program must contain "accurate, complete, timely, pertinent and relevant information."[127] The regulations have established a procedure that can be followed if a client or legal guardian believes the information is inaccurate or misleading or if the client or legal guardian objects to the collection or dissemination of any information. Whenever a client is the subject of a record system maintained by a community program, the client or legal guardian must be informed. Finally, a list must be kept of any person or organization who inspects a client's records. This list should contain the person's name who inspected the records, the reason for inspecting the records and what was to be done with the information obtained, and the person who authorized the inspection. The list must be placed in the client's record and made available to the client, legal guardian, or human rights committee. At all times, the confidentiality of the client should be protected.[128]

THE PROGRAM'S DUTY TO THIRD PARTIES

Treatment programs do not exist in isolation; they exist in society. Often the programs are supported through the help of public monies; therefore, one can argue that society can expect the money to be put to reasonable use. Furthermore, since the clients in these programs participate in community activities and are, it is hoped, integrated into society, society has a right to be protected whenever treatment personnel feel that a client may cause harm to someone. This section briefly addresses these two issues.

Client Responsibility to Participate in Treatment

Most of this chapter has addressed clients' rights, including the right to treatment in the least restrictive and least intrusive manner and the right to refuse treatment. In light of programs that for decades, even centuries, ignored the fact that clients had any rights, it is extremely critical to recognize these rights and to ensure that they are, in fact, provided. What if, however, a client in a community center refuses all types of treatment, including treatment that has been specifically designed for the client and is the least intrusive, yet appropriate, form of treatment that the program has to offer the client? Does the client have the absolute right to refuse all types of treatment and remain in the custodial care of the program? Does society have an interest in ensuring that the client takes advantage of all reasonable forms of appropriate treatment since it is the taxpayers who pay for a large part of the treatment program through their tax dollars?

Few, if any cases, have directly addressed these questions. At one point in time, the answer would have been that the client does not have a right to refuse any treatment, especially treatment that has been specifically designed for client and is part of the client's individualized treatment plan. With all the emphasis on the right to participate in developing one's own treatment plan and the right to refuse treatment, however, it can no longer be assumed that a client must accept just any type of treatment. Yet there must be a balance between what society expects and what the client feels is appropriate. A good compromise is offered by the Massachusetts regulations. As outlined above, those regulations require that several people, including the client, meet together to decide on the treatment goals for the client and the short- and long-term objectives. After deciding how the goals or objectives will be obtained, who will be responsible for them, and that these goals meet the client's needs and are provided in the least restrictive way possible, treatment is to begin. The regulations provide that "[e]very client shall be responsible, to the extent of his/her ability, for making responsible use of the treatment offered by the community residence or program."[129] If the client fails to fulfill this responsibility and the program has tried less drastic means of resolving the situation and has failed, the client can be asked to leave the program. If a client feels that he or she has been treated unfairly, the client may ask the human rights committee to review the decision.[130]

What the above essentially means is that an individualized treatment plan must be developed for each client, and once developed (with the input from the client), the client must make attempts, within the client's ability, to work toward the objectives and goals of the treatment program. A client who is being partially or totally supported by public monies has a duty to make a reasonable effort to learn the skills that would allow the client to become more independent and possibly to leave the program.

Program's Duty to Protect the Community

Chapter 4 addressed many of the administrative considerations in attempting to protect a program against having liability imposed because of a failure to supervise clients properly or a failure to follow prudent policies and regulations. This section does not reiterate what was stated in that chapter but, instead, offers a discussion of the specific issue of a program's duty to protect individuals in the community. Within this issue is the consideration of whether a client has revealed an intention to harm some person or commit some type of crime as opposed to a situation in which the client makes no statement of intention to do harm but the treatment staff have knowledge that the client is dangerous.

The most famous case addressing the duty of a professional (working with people) to warn third parties of the foreseeable harm that could be caused by a potentially dangerous client is *Tarasoff v. Regents of the University of California*.[131] In this particular case, a student from India, Poddar, became enamored with Tanya Tarasoff while both were attending the University of California. Although they dated for awhile, she indicated that she did not want to become intimately involved with Poddar. Upon hearing this, Poddar became very depressed and obsessed with the break-up. Poddar went to the student health facility where a psychiatrist referred him to a psychologist for help. While meeting with the psychologist, Poddar described his depression over Tanya and also stated his intention to purchase a gun. Although Poddar discontinued the therapy sessions, the psychologist, who was concerned about some of Poddar's statements, notified the campus police that he felt Poddar was dangerous and in need of commitment. The campus police interviewed Poddar and found him to be rational; he also agreed to stay away from Tanya. A few weeks later, Poddar went to Tanya's home and first shot her, then fatally stabbed her as she fled from her home. Tanya's parents brought suit against the psychologist and psychiatrist arguing that they should have warned Tanya of Poddar's threats to harm Tanya. The California State Supreme Court held that once a therapist determines, or should have reasonably determined, that a client poses a serious danger to others, the therapist has an affirmative duty to exercise reasonable care in protecting the foreseeable victim.[132] This has been translated into "a duty to warn or protect third parties."[133] The court held that a therapist could not discharge or delegate this duty of informing the police. Ironically, however, informing the police was used as evidence to indicate that the therapist had reasonably determined that Poddar posed a danger to others.

A New Jersey court followed the *Tarasoff* holding in *McIntosh v. Milano*.[134] In this case, a psychotherapist, Dr. Milano, was treating a teenage youth who was involved with drugs. Over the 2-year treatment period, the youth related fantasies of threatening people with a knife. He also indicated his sexual involvement with a woman 5 years older than he was, his jealousy when she dated other men, and the fact that he had fired a BB gun at her while she was in the car. During the youth's last therapy session, he stole a prescription form and tried to obtain some drugs. When the pharmacist became suspicious and called Dr. Milano, Milano told the pharmacist to send the boy home. Milano then tried to reach the boy, but by that time he had already shot and killed the older woman whom he had previously dated.

The court, in this case, was not convinced by the arguments that dangerousness was too unreliable to predict; that a "duty to warn" would jeopardize the client's confidentiality and, thereby, interfere with treatment; that such a duty would deter therapists from treating potentially violent patients; and that this duty would result in more persons being committed to institutions. Rather, the court held that while a therapist cannot be 100% accurate in predicting dangerousness, he or she should be held to a standard of accepted professional diagnosis. Additionally, although the issue of confidentiality is important, it is not the only consideration. The safety and welfare of the community and individuals must come first when there is a possibility of imminent danger. Thus, the duty to protect confidential communications is outweighed by the duty to protect society from harm.

Courts, on the other hand, have not held institutions or the state liable for releasing patients if it was not foreseeable that the patient would harm someone. Therefore, in *Harris v. State*,[135] the state was not held liable for a released patient's assault when the assault occurred more than 2 years after the patient's release. In *Januszko v. New York*,[136] a man named Baldi was arrested for attempted murder and sent to a state mental hospital. Due to an unfortunate mix-up in release procedures, Baldi was negligently released from the hospital. Six months after his discharge he stabbed and killed a 15-year-old girl. Interestingly, the court held that although Baldi had been negligently released, it was not foreseeable that he would murder anyone (even though he had been arrested for attempted murder) and, thus, the state was not liable for damages.

This chapter has presented the major issues that a community center should address in attempting to establish good treatment programs. Many of the areas have been extensively addressed by different courts and legislatures. Some of the requirements may, at first blush, appear overwhelming and difficult to meet. If, however, a program develops systematic and standard procedures that can be used with all clients, the task will be made much simpler. The following chapter describes some methods by which these court and legislative mandates can be fulfilled.

POINTS TO REMEMBER

1. Community centers should provide treatment, rehabilitation, or training to their clients rather than mere custodial care.

2. Nondiscriminatory, valid, and reliable assessment instruments should be used for the placement and evaluation of clients in community centers.
3. Assessment instruments should not invade a client's right to privacy.
4. Each client served in community programs should have an individualized treatment plan that meets the requirements of the federal law.
5. Appropriate and adequate treatment must be provided for each client, and this can be determined by evaluating the outcome of the treatment programs.
6. Each community center must provide a humane physical and psychological environment for the clients.
7. The use of aversive techniques, including electric shock, corporal punishment, restraints, and seclusion, has been strictly scrutinized by the courts and, if used improperly, can constitute cruel and unusual punishment.
8. Community centers should use aversive procedures only when less intrusive procedures have failed and only after safeguards have been provided.
9. Mental and emotional abuse as well as the physical or psychological danger that is caused by the facility's conditions can constitute cruel and unusual punishment.
10. Informed consent must be obtained before any aversive, intrusive, or experimental procedure is used with a client.
11. Clients should have the right to refuse psychotropic medication in nondangerous situations.
12. Community centers should keep adequate records on all clients.
13. Community centers should regard all client information as confidential and treat it as such.
14. A client in a community program has a responsibility to participate in treatment.
15. Community center personnel have a duty to society to protect people in the community from any foreseeable harm that may be caused by a client in the program.

REFERENCES

Bazelon, D.L. Implementing the right to treatment. *University of Chicago Law Review*, 1969, *36*, 742.

Birnbaum, M. The right to treatment. *American Bar Association Journal*, 1960, *46*, 499.

Blatt, B. Purgatory. In R. Kugel & W. Wolfensberger (eds.), *Changing patterns in residential services for the mentally retarded*. Washington, DC: President's Committee on Mental Retardation, 1969.

Budd, K.S., & Baer, D.M. Behavior modification and the law: Implications of recent judicial decisions. *The Journal of Psychiatry and Law*, 1976, Summer, 171–244.

Chambers, D. Right to the least restrictive alternative setting for treatment. In B. Ennis & P. Friedman (eds.), *Legal rights of the mentally handicapped*, Vol. 2. New York: Practicing Law Institute, 1974.

136 / Liability Issues in Community-Based Programs

Edwards, K.A., & Sheldon-Wildgen, J. Providing nursing home residents' rights. In J.T. Hannah, H.B. Clark, & W.P. Christian (eds.), *Clients' rights: A handbook for the mental health practitioner.* New York: Free Press, in press.

Friedman, P., & Halpern, C. The right to treatment. In B. Ennis & P. Friedman (eds.), *Legal rights of the mentally handicapped,* Vol. 1. New York: Practicing Law Institute, 1974.

Schwitzgebel, R.K. Right to treatment for the mentally disabled: The need for realistic standards and objective criteria. *Harvard Civil Rights–Civil Liberties Law Review,* 1973, *8,* 513–535.

Schwitzgebel, R.L., & Schwitzgebel, R.K. *Law and psychological practice.* New York: John Wiley & Sons, 1980.

Sheldon-Wildgen, J. Rights of institutionalized mental patients: Issues, implications, and proposed guidelines. *Kansas Law Review,* 1976, *25,* 63–85.

Walker, L., & Peabody, A. The right of the mentally disabled to protection from harm and to services in institutions and in the community. In P. Friedman (chairman), *Legal rights of mentally disabled persons,* Vol. 1. New York: Practicing Law Institute, 1979.

ENDNOTES

[1] *Parens patriae* is a Latin phrase meaning "parent of the country." It refers to the sovereign power of guardianship over persons under a disability, e.g., developmentally disabled, mentally ill, or minors (*Black's Law Dictionary,* St. Paul, MN: West Publishing Co., 1968). Its use in cases involving mentally ill individuals, developmentally disabled persons, and juveniles can be traced to early English times. The doctrine allows the state to intervene to protect or care for those individuals who are unable to care for themselves. The doctrine is very much in existence today, and most states, as well as the federal government, have legislation allowing the state to treat and care for those individuals who require such protection, care, or treatment.

[2] *See, e.g.,* Covington v. Harris, 419 F. 2d 617 (D.C. Cir. 1969); Tribby v. Cameron, 379 F. 2d 104 (D.C. Cir. 1967); Millard v. Cameron, 373 F. 2d 468 (D.C. Cir. 1966); Rouse v. Cameron, 373 F. 2d 451 (D.C. Cir. 1966); Nason v. Commissioners of Mental Health, 351 Mass. 94, 217 N.E. 2d 733 (1966). *Rouse v. Cameron* was the first judicial decision to recognize a right to treatment. Although the holding itself was based on statutory rather than constitutional grounds, the court suggested that the constitutional protections of due process, equal protection, and the prohibition against cruel and unusual punishment might be violated if a person were confined in an institution without treatment. 373 F. 2d at 453.

[3] 325 F. Supp. 781, *aff'd on rehearing,* 334 F. Supp. 1341 (M.D. Ala. 1971), *aff'd on rehearing,* 344 F. Supp. 373, *aff'd in separate decision,* 344 F. Supp. 387 (M.D. Ala. 1972), *aff'd sub nom, Wyatt v. Aderholt,* 503 F. 2d 1305 (5th Cir. 1974), *aff'd sub nom, Wyatt v. Ireland,* Civ. No. 3195-N (M.D. Ala. Oct. 25, 1979).

[4] *See, e.g.,* Sinhogar v. Parry, No. 14138/77 (N.Y. Sup. Ct. Jan. 16, 1979) as reported in 3 *Mental Disability Law Reporter* 236 (1979); Wuori v. Zitnay, No. 75-80-SD (D. Maine July 14, 1978); Davis v. Watkins, 384 F. Supp. 1196 (N.D. Ohio 1974); Welsch v. Likins, 373 F. Supp. 487 (M.D. Minn. 1974).

[5] Wyatt v. Ireland, Civ. No. 3195-N (M.D. Ala. Oct. 25, 1979).

[6] 422 U.S. 563 (1975).

[7] *Id.* at 576.

[8] 42 U.S.C. § § 6001 *et seq.*

[9] 42 U.S.C. § 6010(1).

[10] 42 U.S.C. § 6010(3)(A).

[11]*See, e.g.,* Sinhogar v. Parry, No. 14138/77 (N.Y. Sup. Ct. Jan. 16, 1979) as reported in 3 *Mental Disability Law Reporter,* 1979, *3,* 236–237; Matter of Lavette M., 35 N.Y. 2d 136 (1974); Martarella v. Kelly, 349 F. Supp. 575 (S.D.N.Y. 1972).

[12]No. 75-80-SD (D. Maine July 14, 1978).

[12a]*Note added in proofs:* In October, 1980, the Mental Health Systems Act (P.L. 96–398) was signed into law in an attempt to improve services to all chronically mentally ill individuals. Although the act does not include a mandatory bill of rights, many rights (including the right to appropriate treatment) are identified as ones that states should seriously address. This law, however, should be distinguished from the Developmentally Disabled Assistance and Bill of Rights Act, which provides a set of mandatory and enforceable rights for developmentally disabled persons.

[13]*See, e.g.,* Covington v. Harris, 419 F. 2d 617 (D.C. Cir. 1969); Tribby v. Cameron, 379 F. 2d 104 (D.C. Cir. 1967); Millard v. Cameron, 373 F. 2d 468 (D.C. Cir. 1966); Rouse v. Cameron, 373 F. 2d 451 (D.C. Cir. 1966); Davis v. Watkins, 384 F. Supp. 1196 (N.D. Ohio 1974); Welsch v. Likins, 373 F. Supp. 487 (M.D. Minn. 1974); Nason v. Commissioners of Mental Health, 351 Mass. 94, 217 N.E. 2d 733 (1966).

[14]*See, e.g.,* Welsch v. Likins, 550 F. 2d 1122 (8th Cir. 1977). See also Bowring v. Godwin, 551 F. 2d 44 (4th Cir. 1977); Wyatt v. Aderholt, 503 F. 2d 1305 (5th Cir. 1974).

[15]*See, e.g.,* Eckerhart v. Hensley, 475 F. Supp. 908 (W.D. Mo. 1979).

[16]*See, e.g.,* Rone v. Fireman, No. C75-355A (N.D. Ohio June 18, 1979).

[17]No. 76-4423-F (E.D. Mass. Dec. 6, 1978).

[18]104 Code of Massachusetts Regulations § § 14.00 *et seq.*

[19]Pena v. New York State Division for Youth, 419 F. Supp. 203 (S.D. N.Y. 1976); Morales v. Turman, 364 F. Supp. 166 (E.D. Tex. 1973); 383 F. Supp. 53 (E.D. Tex. 1974); *vacated* 535 F. 2d 864 (5th Cir. 1976), *rev'd and remanded* 430 U.S. 322 (1977), *reh. den.* 430 U.S. 988 (1977); Martarella v. Kelly, 349 F. Supp. 575 (S.D. N.Y. 1972), 359 F. Supp. 478 (S.D. N.Y. 1973).

[20]No. C-71-2270 RFP (N.D. Cal. Oct. 16, 1979) as reported in 3 *Mental Disability Law Reporter* 397 (1979).

[21]*See* Larry P. v. Riles, 343 F. Supp. 1306 (N.D. Cal. 1972), *aff'd* 502 F. 2d 963 (9th Cir. 1974).

[22]42 U.S.C. § 2000d.

[23]29 U.S.C. § 794.

[24]20 U.S.C. § § 1401 *et seq.*

[25]20 U.S.C. § 1412.

[26]*See, e.g.,* Diana v. State Board of Education, C.A.N. C-70 37 RFP (N.D. Cal. Feb. 3, 1970).

[27]*See, e.g.,* APA *Ethical standards of psychologists.* Washington, DC: American Psychological Association, 1977; APA *Standards for educational and psychological tests.* Washington, DC: American Psychological Association, 1974.

[28]410 N.Y.S. 2d 99 (N.Y. App. Div. 2d Dept. 1978).

[29]Hoffman v. Board of Education of the City of New York, No. 562 (N.Y. Ct. App. Dec. 17, 1979).

[30]364 F. Supp. 913 (E.D. Pa. 1973).

[31]No. 77-737-260CZ (Cir. Ct. Wayne County, Mich. June 20, 1978), *appeal denied* No. 78-3877 (Mich. Ct. App. Jan. 20, 1979), as reported in 3 *Mental Disability Law Reporter* 96 (1979).

[32]Mich. Comp. Laws Ann. § 330.1704.

[33]The Supreme Court has found that many of these personal and private behaviors fall under the penumbra of rights that should be constitutionally protected.

See, e.g., Griswold v. Connecticut, 381 U.S. 479 (1965) (case involving the use of contraceptives) and Roe v. Wade, 410 U.S. 113 (1973) (case involving the right to have an abortion).

[34]*See, e.g.,* Clatterbuck v. Harris, 295 F. Supp. 84, 86 (D.D.C. 1968); Nason v. Superintendent, 353 Mass. 604, ____, 233 N.E. 2d 908, 914 (1968). *See also* Developmentally Disabled Assistance and Bill of Rights Act, 42 U.S.C. § 6010.

[35]*See, e.g.,* Millard v. Cameron, 373 F. 2d 468, 472 (D.C. Cir. 1966); Rouse v. Cameron, 373 F. 2d 451, 456, 459 (D.C. Cir. 1966); Welsch v. Likins, 373 F. Supp. 487, 499 (D. Minn. 1974); Wyatt v. Stickney, 325 F. Supp. 781, 785 (M.D. Ala. 1971); Cook v. Ciccone, 312 F. Supp. 822, 824 (W.D. Mo. 1970); Nason v. Superintendent, 353 Mass. 604, ____, 233 N.E. 2d 908, 914 (1968).

[36]*See, e.g.,* Wyatt v. Stickney, 344 F. Supp. 373, 375 (M.D. Ala. 1972); Wyatt v. Stickney, 344 F. Supp. 1341, 1343 (M.D. Ala. 1972); Clatterbuck v. Harris, 295 F. Supp. 84, 86 (D.D.C. 1968).

[37]*See, e.g., In re* Jones, 338 F. Supp. 428 (D.D.C. 1972).

[38]*See, e.g.,* Millard v. Cameron, 373 F. 2d 468, 472 (D.C. Cir. 1966); Rouse v. Cameron, 373 F. 2d 451, 456, 459 (D.C. Cir. 1966).

[39]344 F. Supp. 373, 379-86, *aff'd in separate decision* 344 F. Supp. 387, 395–407 (M.D. Ala. 1972). The court additionally specified that "residents shall have a right to habilitation . . . suited to their needs, regardless of age, degree of retardation or handicapping condition." 344 F. Supp. at 396.

[40]No. C75-355A (N.D. Ohio June 18, 1979) as reported in 3 *Mental Disability Law Reporter* 306 (1979).

[41]*See, e.g.,* Halderman v. Pennhurst, 446 F. Supp. 1295 (E.D. Pa. 1977) (ordering the deinstitutionalization of the residents of the Pennhurst School in Pennsylvania). The Third Circuit Court of Appeals in *Halderman v. Pennhurst*, Nos. 78-1490, 1564, 1602 (3rd Cir. Dec. 13, 1979) as reported in 4 *Mental Disability Law Reporter* 14 (1980), affirmed the major components of the original decision but reversed the part of the lower court decision that banned all future admissions and required the eventual closing of Pennhurst. The Third Circuit Court of Appeals essentially restricted the original holding, which had been interpreted by some to mean that large institutions were inherently unconstitutional, in finding that deinstitutionalization would not be required in all cases. Rather, each person should be assessed individually and a determination made as to whether that person would be better served in an institution or in a community facility. This case is presently on appeal to the Supreme Court of the United States. It should be decided in the spring of 1981.

[42]No. 75-80-SD (D. Maine July 14, 1978) as reported in 2 *Mental Disability Law Reporter* 729 (1978).

[43]No. 76-4423-F (E.D. Mass. Dec. 6, 1978) as reported in 3 *Mental Disability Law Reporter* 45 (1979).

[44]No. 75-80-SD (D. Maine July 14, 1978) as reported in 2 *Mental Disability Law Reporter* 729, 732-734 (1978).

[45]42 U.S.C. § 6011.

[46]364 F. 2d 657 (D.C. Cir. 1966).

[47]*See, e.g.,* Lynch v. Baxley, 386 F. Supp. 378, 392 (M.D. Ala. 1974); Welsch v. Likins, 373 F. Supp. 487, 502 (D. Minn. 1974); Lessard v. Schmidt, 349 F. Supp. 1078, 1096 (E.D. Wis. 1972); Wyatt v. Stickney, 344 F. Supp. 373, 379 (M.D. Ala. 1972).

[48]419 F. 2d 617 (D.D.C. 1969).

[49]*Id.* at 624–625.

[50]No. 75-80-SD (D. Maine July 14, 1978) as reported in 2 *Mental Disability Law Reporter* 729 (1978).

[51]*Id.* at 732.

[52]No. 76-4423-F (E.D. Mass. Dec. 6, 1978) as reported in 3 *Mental Disability Law Reporter* 45 (1979).

[53]*Id.* at 47.

[54]*See, e.g.,* Wyatt v. Ireland, Civ. No. 3195-N (M.D. Ala. Oct. 25, 1979); Department of Mental Health, Mental Health Community Residential Alternatives, 104 Code of Massachusetts Regulations § 14.03 as reported in 4 *Mental Disability Law Reporter* 126 (1980).

[55]*See, e.g.,* the conditions described in Morales v. Turman, 383 F. Supp. 53, 72–105 (E.D. Tex. 1974); New York State Ass'n for Retarded Children, Inc. v. Rockefeller, 357 F. Supp. 752, 756 (E.D. N.Y. 1973); and Wyatt v. Stickney, 334 F. Supp. 1341, 1343–1344 (M.D. Ala. 1971).

[56]*See,* Blatt, B., & Kaplan, F. *Christmas in purgatory: A photographic essay on mental retardation.* Boston: Allyn & Bacon, 1967.

[57]*See,* 344 F. Supp. 373, 379–386; 344 F. Supp. 387, 395–407 (M.D. Ala. 1972).

[58]Developmentally Disabled Assistance and Bill of Rights Act, 42 U.S.C. § 6010 (3).

[59]No. 75-80-SD (D. Maine July 14, 1978) as reported in 2 *Mental Disability Law Reporter* 729 (1978).

[60]Department of Mental Health, Mental Health Community Residential Alternatives, 104 Code of Massachusetts Regulations § 14.03 as reported in 4 *Mental Disability Law Reporter* 126 (1980).

[61]No. 76-4423-F (E.D. Mass. Dec. 6, 1978) as reported in 3 *Mental Disability Law Reporter* 45 (1979).

[62]29 U.S.C § § 201 *et seq.*

[63]*See, e.g.,* Wyatt V. Stickney, 344 F. Supp. 373, 380 (M.D. Ala. 1972).

[64]473 F. 2d 983, 984 (7th Cir. 1973).

[65]Morales v. Turman, 364 F. Supp. 166 (E.D. Tex. 1973), *vac.* 535 F. 2d 864 (5th Cir. 1976), *rev'd* 430 U.S. 322 (1977); *remanded for evidentiary hearing* 562 F. 2d 933 (5th Cir. 1977).

[66]*See, e.g.,* a study by Lovaas, O.I., & Simmons, J.Q. Manipulation of self-destruction in three retarded children, *Journal of Applied Behavior Analysis,* 1969, *2,* 143–157.

[67]344 F. Supp. 387, 401 (M.D. Ala. 1972).

[68]*Id.* at 400–401.

[69]No. 75-80-SD (D. Maine July 14, 1978) as reported in 2 *Mental Disability Law Reporter* 729, 739 (1978).

[70]The use of electric shock could be considered corporal punishment. It was discussed separately because it, more than other techniques that impose physical punishment, has been used as a treatment procedure. Additionally, some therapists have advocated the use of electric shock over other procedures that inflict physical pain because it can be more easily controlled and does not risk physical damage (Budd & Baer, 1976).

[71]Ingraham v. Wright, 525 F. 2d 909 (5th Cir. 1976), *aff'd* 97 S.Ct. 1401 (1977).

[72]364 F. Supp. 166 (E.D. Tex. 1973). *See,* also, Nelson v. Heyne, 355 F. Supp. 451 (N.D. Ind. 1972) where the court prohibited the use of beatings with a thick board in a correctional facility for juvenile offenders.

[73]*See, e.g.,* New York State Ass'n for Retarded Children v. Carey, Nos. 72-356 and 72-357 (May 5, 1975); Davis v. Watkins, 384 F. Supp. 1196 (N.D. Ohio 1974); Wyatt v. Stickney, 344 F. Supp. 387 (M.D. Ala. 1972).

[74]No. 75-80-SD (D. Maine July 14, 1978) as reported in 2 *Mental Disability Law Reporter* 729, 739 (1978).

[75]Massachusetts Department of Mental Health, Mental Health Community

Residential Alternatives, 104 C.M.R. § 14.03(4)(a)(1) as reported in 4 *Mental Disability Law Reporter* 126, 128 (1980).

[76]373 F. Supp. 487 (D. Minn. 1974).

[77]*See* Wyatt v. Stickney, 344 F. Supp. 387, 401 (M.D. Ala. 1972).

[78]Nos. 72-356 and 72-357 (May 5, 1975).

[79]*See* Wuori v. Zitnay, No. 75-80-SD (D. Maine July 14, 1978) as reported in 2 *Mental Disability Law Reporter* 729, 738 (1978).

[80]Massachusetts Department of Mental Health, Mental Health Community Residential Alternatives, 104 C.M.R. § 14.03(4)(a)(6) and § 14.03(5) as reported in 4 *Mental Disability Law Reporter* 126, 128–129 (1980).

[81]Developmentally Disabled Assistance and Bill of Rights Act, 42 U.S.C. §6010(3)(B)(iii) and (iv).

[82]346 F. Supp. 1354 (D.R.I. 1972).

[83]*Id.* at 1373.

[84]364 F. Supp. 166, 177–178 (E.D. Tex. 1973).

[85]344 F. Supp. 373, 380 (M.D. Ala. 1972).

[86]344 F. Supp. 387, 400 (M.D. Ala. 1972).

[87]*Id.*

[88]Wuori v. Zitnay, No. 75-80-SD (D. Maine July 14, 1978) as reported in 2 *Mental Disability Law Reporter* 729, 738 (1978).

[89]Massachusetts Department of Mental Health, Mental Health Community Residential Alternatives, 104 C.M.R. § 14.02 (19) as reported in 4 *Mental Disability Law Reporter* 126, 127 (1980).

[90]No. 77-C-208 (W.D. Wis. March 24, 1978) as reported in 2 *Mental Disability Law Reporter* 556 (1978).

[91]State of Wisconsin v. Leff, Vol. 256, p. 347 (Dane County Ct., Wis., filed Oct. 25, 1977) as reported in 2 *Mental Disability Law Reporter* 184 (1978).

[92]Wisconsin v. Leff, No. 78-145-CR (Wis. Ct. App. Aug. 24, 1979) as reported in 3 *Mental Disability Law Reporter* 416 (1979).

[93]No. 72-L-299 (D. Neb. Aug. 6, 1975).

[94]Wyatt v. Stickney, 344 F. Supp. 373, 379; 344 F. Supp. 387, 399 (M.D. Ala. 1972).

[95]*Id.* at 401.

[96]Wuori v. Zitnay, No. 75-80-SD (D. Maine July 14, 1978) as reported in 2 *Mental Disability Law Reporter* 729, 738 (1978).

[97]Massachusetts Department of Mental Health, Mental Health Community Residential Alternatives, 104 C.M.R. § 14.03(4)(a)2, as reported in 4 *Mental Disability Law Reporter* 126, 128 (1980).

[98]*See, e.g.,* Halderman and the United States v. Pennhurst, 446 F. Supp. 1295 (E.D. Pa. 1977); Wyatt v. Stickney, 325 F. Supp. 781, *aff'd on rehearing,* 334 F. Supp. 1341 (M.D. Ala. 1971), *aff'd on rehearing,* 344 F. Supp. 373, *aff'd in separate decision,* 344 F. Supp. 387 (M.D. Ala. 1972), *aff'd sub nom, Wyatt v. Aderholt,* 503 F. 2d 1305 (5th Cir. 1974); NYSARC and Parisi v. Carey, 393 F. Supp. 715 (E.D. N.Y. 1975) (consent decree approved).

[99]357 F. Supp. 752 (E.D. N.Y. 1973).

[100]*Id.* at 756.

[101]Civ. Action No. 73-19434-Aw (Cir. Ct. Wayne County, Mich., July 10, 1973).

[102]Wyatt v. Hardin, No. 3195-N (M.D. Ala. Feb. 28, 1975, modified July 1, 1975) as reported in 1 *Mental Disability Law Reporter* 55 (1976). This case is formerly known as Wyatt v. Stickney, 344 F. Supp. 387 (M.D. Ala. 1972).

[103]*Id.*

[104]Wyatt v. Stickney, 344 F. Supp. 373, 380; 344 F. Supp. 387, 400, 402 (M.D. Ala. 1972).

[105]New York State Ass'n for Retarded Children v. Carey Nos. 72-356 and 72-357 (May 5, 1975) (consent decree).

[106]Wyatt v. Stickney, 344 F. Supp. 387, 396 (M.D. Ala. 1972).

[107]Knecht v. Gillman, 488 F. 2d 1136, 1140 (8th Cir. 1973).

[108]Massachusetts Department of Mental Health, Mental Health Community Residential Alternatives, 104 C.M.R. § 14.03 (10) as reported in 4 *Mental Disability Law Reporter* 126, 131–132 (1980).

[109]*See, e.g.,* the evidence produced in *Rennie v. Klein,* No. 77-2624 (D.N.J. Sept. 14, 1979) as reported in 3 *Mental Disability Law Reporter* 390 (1979).

[110]462 F. Supp. 1131 (D. N.J. 1978).

[111]No. CA 75-1610-T (D. Mass. Oct. 29, 1979) as reported in 4 *Mental Disability Law Reporter* 11 (1980).

[112]*Id.* at 12.

[113]Wyatt v. Stickney, 344 F. Supp. 387, 396 (M.D. Ala. 1972).

[114]Wyatt v. Stickney, 344 F. Supp. 373, 385; 344 F. Supp. 387, 398–399 (M.D. Ala. 1972).

[115]Wuori v. Zitnay, No. 75-80-SD (D. Maine July 14, 1978) as reported in 2 *Mental Disability Law Reporter* 729, 736 (1978).

[116]5 U.S.C. § 552.

[117]20 U.S.C. § 1232g.

[118]20 U.S.C. § 1232g(a)(4)(B)(iii).

[119]*Id.*

[120]385 Mich. 49, 187 N.W. 2d 429 (1971).

[121]514 F. 2d 125 (2d Cir. 1975).

[122]Massachusetts Department of Mental Health, Mental Health Community Residential Alternatives, 104 C.M.R. § 14.03(8)(b) as reported in 4 *Mental Disability Law Reporter* 126, 130 (1980).

[123]For an excellent summary of this topic *see,* Confidential communications. In R.L. Schwitzgebel & R.K. Schwitzgebel, *Law and psychological practice.* New York: John Wiley & Sons, 1980.

[124]Wuori v. Zitnay, No. 75-80-SD (D. Maine July 14, 1978) as reported in 2 *Mental Disability Law Reporter* 729, 736 (1978).

[125]Massachusetts Department of Mental Health, Mental Health Community Residential Alternatives, 104 C.M.R. § 14.03(8) as reported in 4 *Mental Disability Law Reporter* 126, 130-131 (1980).

[126]*Id.* at § 14.03(8)(c).

[127]*Id.* at § 14.03(8)(f).

[128]*Id.* at § 14.03(f), (g), (h), (i).

[129]*Id.* at § 14.03(12)(b).

[130]*Id.* at § 14.03(12)(d).

[131]529 P. 2d 553 (Cal. 1974), *aff'd on rehearing* 131 Cal. Rptr. 14, 551 P. 2d 334 (1976).

[132]*Id.* at 345.

[133]A California court has held that this duty does not extend to relatives of a potential suicide victim since a client who threatens to commit suicide already knows of the potential danger to himself or herself. To inform others, who are not in danger, would unnecessarily breech the therapist-client privilege of confidential communications. See *Bellah v. Greenson,* 1 Civ. No. 39770 (Cal. Oct. 5, 1977) as reported in 2 *Mental Disability Law Reporter* 176 (1977).

[134]403 A. 2d 500 (N.J. Super. Ct. 1979).
[135]48 Ohio Misc. 27, 358 N.E. 2d 639 (1976).
[136]391 N.E. 2d 297 (N.Y. Ct. App. 1979).

8

RECOMMENDATIONS FOR DELIVERING APPROPRIATE TREATMENT PROGRAMS

The preceding chapter specified the major issues that should be considered in developing an appropriate treatment program for clients being served in community centers. Detailed requirements, mandated by courts and legislators, were given. The purpose of this chapter is to describe how a community center might comply with those legal requirements. It is obviously impossible to list every issue to which a program must attend or to describe every situation that might arise. Rather, a look at the reasoning or justification behind judicial and legislative mandates is provided so that community center administrators and personnel may apply that reasoning in solving individual problems that might arise. As mentioned previously, however, whenever a serious question arises that an administrator is uncertain about, an attorney should be contacted.

DEVELOPING APPROPRIATE ASSESSMENT INSTRUMENTS

Assessment should be an important part of any community center's program. In order to treat a client adequately or to provide the appropriate placement in

The recommendations found in this chapter have been developed, in large part, from years of addressing and discussing problems that arise in community programs serving developmentally disabled persons. The authors are indebted to the following individuals for their invaluable questions, answers, discussions, and recommendations provided throughout the years: James Sherman, Joseph Spradlin, Paula VanBiervliet, Karl Morris, Barbara Griggs, John Anthony, Randy Kindred, and numerous graduate students at the University of Kansas and teaching counselors at Concerned Care, Inc., in Kansas City, Missouri.

a training, rehabilitation, or vocational program, it is mandatory that the center's personnel have accurate knowledge of each client's abilities. Furthermore, without assessment instruments, it would be impossible to determine if a program was providing treatment to a client and if that client was actually making progress.

As stated in Chapter 7, all assessment instruments should be *nondiscriminatory, valid,* and *reliable.* Remember, as Schwitzgebel and Schwitzgebel (1980) point out, it is important that an assessment tool discriminate between individuals (i.e., between those who have certain skills and those who do not). The assessment tool should not, however, discriminate *against* an individual on irrelevant factors, such as one's race, heritage, or sex. Furthermore, as Martin (1978) suggests, it is probably wise to use more than one diagnostic instrument when assessing a person's strengths and weaknesses. The standardized IQ test may be of little value due to the problems discussed in Chapter 7. The same problems may arise with many of the projective tests "which often give more information about the tester's interpretations than they do about the client" (Martin, 1978, p. 8). What is most helpful is an assessment tool that gives objective and specific information about clients' behaviors and about the clients' behavioral assets and deficits (Repp, 1978; Repp & Deitz, 1978).

A community center can purchase assessment instruments or can develop its own. In either case, the instrument should contain only those items that are *program related,* i.e., those behaviors or skills that are rationally and functionally related to the reason that the person is in the program. The assessment and evaluation instruments should be complete and should address all relevant skill areas, yet at the same time, they should be designed to measure only behaviors that should be changed as determined by the program's goals. For example, a residential program serving developmentally disabled individuals may justifiably have an assessment tool that measures specific behaviors related to the grooming, housekeeping, or social skills of a client. It may be inappropriate, however, to have items on the evaluation instrument that specifically apply to job performance (e.g., rate of work or number of jobs completed), especially if performance on those items is used as a criterion for release from the program. Those items, however, may be acceptable for an evaluation tool used at a sheltered workshop. If the items are rationally related to the overall goals of the program and the purpose for the client being in the program, however, evaluation of them may be justified. Thus, in the above example, if the goals of the residential program were to teach successful community living (which some might argue includes being able to perform adequately in a job situation) and if the job-related items on the assessment or evaluation tool were *general* ones (e.g., how well did the client perform at work today—poorly, satisfactorily, or excellently?), then those items may be acceptable to include on an assessment instrument. The critical consideration is whether the behavior or skill being assessed is one that is being taught or addressed in some significant manner by the program.

The items on the assessment instrument should not unduly or unjustifiably invade the client's *right to privacy*. In determining which items might conceivably invade a client's right to privacy, the purpose of the program and the reason for the client's placement in the program should be considered. Only those personal behaviors that are related to the client's treatment program should be observed and assessed. Therefore, for example, it may be inappropriate to observe and record a client's toileting behavior at a sheltered workshop or in a community recreational program since toileting is unrelated to either the vocational or recreational program. In a residential program, however, it may be justifiable to ask to observe a client's toileting skills because teaching proper personal hygiene may be one of the program's treatment goals for a particular client.

If it is determined that the behavior is an appropriate one to observe, it is important to observe the client in a manner that protects the client's right to privacy as much as possible. Thus, personal behaviors of clients should be observed in private and by a staff member who is the same sex as the client. If it is at all possible to determine if a client has a skill in his or her repertoire by observing a final product, it is preferable to do that than to make the client perform the personal behavior in front of a staff person. If, for example, the program needs to determine if a client knows how to bathe properly, one might initially ask the client to take a bath. When the client was finished, a staff person could look at the client carefully to determine if the client appeared clean (e.g., hair wet and smelling of shampoo; face, neck, and hands clean with no dirt on them; client smelled clean). The staff could also check to determine if the bathtub had water drops in it and whether the towel was wet. This type of assessment may not give the most accurate information about the personal hygiene skills in a client's repertoire, and it may be necessary to observe the client actually engaging in the behavior. Nonetheless, the client's right to privacy should always be protected.

The items on an assessment instrument should be *sensitive to change*. This means that any item on an assessment tool should be clearly defined and broken down into small enough steps to allow the staff to conceivably note some change in the behavior in a 3- to 4- month period (if that behavior had been targeted for change). It would be inappropriate, therefore, to have only the general item "appropriate social skills" on an evaluation tool because a client could improve in many social behaviors, e.g., accepting criticism or using the phone properly, and yet not receive an improved rating on appropriate social skills because this item is so vague and encompassing and, consequently, not sensitive to change.

In order to assess a client's progress in a program accurately, it will be necessary to *observe and record the client's behavior on a regular basis*. Certain target behaviors that are specifically being treated may be assessed much more frequently (e.g., every day or several times a week); otherwise, it is a good idea to assess or evaluate a client's progress on a periodic basis of every 3 to 4 months.

When recording data on the client, it is often better to give the items a numerical rating (e.g., 0, 1, 2, 3) than merely to record the presence or absence of the behavior (Repp, 1978). A numerical rating scale is much more sensitive to change and would reflect small improvements in behavior. Thus, one may want to utilize a rating scale similar to the one developed by Morris, Kindred, Sheldon-Wildgen, and Sherman (1977). Their rating scale requires giving a client a 0 when the client does not satisfactorily perform any part of a target behavior, provided the client has had the opportunity to engage in the behavior. An example of this might involve rating a client's ability to wash his or her hair appropriately. Assuming that washing one's hair can be divided into six steps, the client would receive a 0 rating if he or she could not satisfactorily perform any of the six steps without help or supervision. A 1 rating indicates that the client performs the behavior without supervision but needs help with particular steps. In the hair washing example, it may be that the client can properly apply the shampoo, adjust the water to a suitable temperature, and appropriately wash the hair, but cannot adequately rinse or towel dry the hair; therefore, the client would receive a 1 rating. A 1 may also indicate that although the client is able to perform the behavior properly, the client needs *frequent* reminding, prompting, or instruction. For example, a client may have been observed as able to interrupt a conversation appropriately, but does not do it frequently and often has to be reminded; thus, a 1 rating would be given. A 2 rating indicates that the client can appropriately perform all of a behavior without help or supervision but needs some additional training or motivation to ensure that the client does it on a regular basis. In the hair washing example, a client would receive a 2 rating if the client usually knew when and how to wash his or her hair but *occasionally* needed to be reminded to do so or needed some help or prompting in the process. Finally, a 3 rating indicates that the client regularly performs the target behavior appropriately without prompting or supervision. Thus, for example, a client would know when it was necessary to wash his or her hair and would do it in an appropriate manner, e.g., perform all the steps correctly.

Whenever a program is assessing a client's behavior, it is necessary for the program to take *reliability* on the observer's scoring of the behavior. This type of reliability involves two or more observers simultaneously, but independently, recording the behavior. This implies that most behaviors observed be observable and be specifically defined in order that two independent observers might have a high probability of agreeing on the rating of the behavior. An assessment instrument, therefore, should reflect specific behaviors that can be observed. For example, it is better to have a list of behaviors such as "gives negative feedback to others in an appropriate and positive manner," "responds to criticism in an appropriate way," "refrains from teasing others," "does not destroy other's property," etc., than is to have the one general and vague behavior, "client is a nice person." After the observers rate the client's performance, a comparison of the observers' records can be made. To obtain a reliability score, the number of agreements can be divided by the number of agreements plus disagreements and this number can be multiplied by 100 to give a percentage of reliability obtained. If the observers are using a rating scale, e.g., a 4-point scale similar to the one previously described, the observers may want to use a sliding scale to calculate reliability. Under this type of system, if both observers gave the client the exact same rating on an item, that would be scored as total agreement and could be counted as 100% for that item. If, however, the observers disagreed by one point, e.g., one observer gave the client a 1 rating and the other gave a 2 rating, this could arbitrarily be designated as a 50% agreement. The percentages one assigns to the various distances of difference could vary according to the number of points on the rating scale. The percentage agreement for all items would be totaled and divided by the number of items rated to obtain a total percentage of agreement.

In summary, assessments of client behavior and progress should be done regularly. The instruments used should be valid, reliable, and nondiscriminatory. Items on the assessment instrument should be related to program goals and to the reason why the person is in the program. These items should be specifically stated, sensitive to change, and scored in a way that will reliably indicate a client's progress in the program. The assessment should be administered in a way that does not violate a client's right to privacy. Finally, reliability between observers should be taken periodically to ensure that the results obtained are a true measure of the client's behavior rather than a biased reflection of an individual observer.

DEVELOPING INDIVIDUALIZED TREATMENT PLANS

The development of an appropriate and individualized written treatment plan for each client is one of the most important duties of any community center. It is not a task that should be delegated to one individual nor should it address only one area of the client's life. The treatment plan should represent an integrated effort of all professionals working with a client and should attempt to coordinate all goals that these professionals would like to see the client achieve. Because the Developmentally Disabled Assistance and Bill of Rights Act mandates that states receiving federal funds under the act require all public programs serving the developmentally disabled to have habilitation plans for each client served,[1] most states will have specific requirements that must be met. Each community center should determine its own state's requirements and comply with them. Below is a comprehensive description of how treatment plans can be developed, monitored, and evaluated. Following these recommendations should ensure compliance with most state requirements, but all centers should obtain and follow their own state regulations to be legally protected.

1. *The plan must be individualized.* This is an obvious requirement since the word "individualized" appears in the name of the plan. Many programs, however, disregard this important mandate as evidenced by the fact

that client treatment plans are often mimeographed with several clients having the exact same goals and objectives. Although a community center may want to develop a standardized *form* that can be used for everyone, the individualized treatment plan, including the goals and objectives, should reflect an individual assessment of the client with consideration given to the client's assets, deficits, past performance (both appropriate and inappropriate), and past treatment. Thus, for example, if a client has a history of suicide attempts, the treatment planned should reflect this both by providing an appropriate intervention strategy and by placing the person in an environment that is not conducive to attempting suicide. Having the general objective for this client (or for other clients) of "learning to live in the community" would not be individualized enough.

2. *An interdisciplinary team should meet to develop the treatment plan.* As the court in *Brewster v. Dukakis*[2] pointed out, this team should address both the residential and the nonresidential needs of the client. Thus, the team should be broad enough to include all the professionals and other persons needed to give an accurate assessment of the client's abilities and needs. In order to develop a complete and comprehensive treatment plan, information will be needed about the client's medical and dental needs; psychological needs; social and recreational needs; residential, transportation, and daily living skill needs; education and vocational needs; and physical, occupational, or speech therapy needs.

In reality, it may not be feasible in terms of time or money to attempt to assemble all the necessary professionals who could adequately comment on each of these areas. One method of solving this problem is to have evaluations done by specialists in each of the relevant areas. Each specialist or professional would write up recommendations of what the client needed, after having evaluated the client. These recommendations would include goals for the client with short- and long-term objectives, and these objectives would be assigned priorities. The professional could send this recommendation to the interdisciplinary team meeting where that information would be considered and incorporated into the client's treatment plan. After the treatment plan had been developed, it could be circulated to each of the professionals who could evaluate it and determine if the goals and objectives appeared appropriate for the client. For example, a physician might give a client a physical examination and send a recommendation to the interdisciplinary team that the client needed to lose 30 pounds. At the team meeting, the residential teaching counselors may decide to put the client on a restricted diet. Concurrently, the recreation specialist may decide that the client should begin a regimented schedule of exercise. When the plan is circulated back to the physician, the doctor would need to determine if both of these treatment objectives are appropriate. For example, although the client may need to lose weight, if the client had a heart ailment, it may not be wise to begin the client on a strenuous exercise program. The physician would note this and specify what exercises would be appropriate. This type of a procedure would usually be less expensive than asking the physician to attend a 2–3-hour meeting, yet it would protect against a fragmented and potentially contradictory or dangerous program being developed.

There are certain people who *should attend* the interdisciplinary team meeting. These include the people who will be having daily or frequent contact with the client, such as the teaching counselors, foster parents, or aides in the residential program, and a representative staff member from the day program in which the client will participate, e.g., an educational program, a sheltered workshop or work program, or a day care or day training program. Additionally, if a community center has a programming specialist, that person should be there as well as the social or mental health worker assigned by the county or state to the client. Finally, and perhaps most importantly, the client should be a part of the team meeting, if at all possible, along with the client's guardian or representative. It is critical to have the client involved in the determination of the treatment. This is true not only because it is legally mandated but because it is the client's life that is being discussed. It will be difficult to achieve the desired type of change if the client is unwilling to participate. One of the best ways to encourage a client to participate in a treatment program is to have client involvement from the initial stages of treatment development. If the client is consulted from the beginning and encouraged to express his or her views, there is a much higher probability that the client will feel that it is truly his or her treatment plan rather than one developed strictly by others. Having a vested interest in the treatment plan because it reflects the client's feelings and ideas, the client will be more likely to work to make it succeed.

In any event, when developing the individualized treatment plan, it is mandatory to remember that the client is a complex person with varied needs. The treatment plan should, at all times, reflect this. Finally, whenever an interdisciplinary team meeting is going to be held, all necessary persons, including the client and guardian, should be given at least 2 weeks' notice.

3. *At the team meeting when developing the treatment plan, it is important to begin by listing the client's assets and capabilities.* People have a tendency to emphasize the negative and what the client cannot do. If one begins a team meeting by analyzing only the client's deficits, the client will undoubtedly be disturbed and the meeting will take on a negative air. Instead, the team should spend the first part of the meeting listing the client's capabilities and areas in which improvement has been shown.

4. *Next, all assessments and evaluations that have been done on the client should be assembled in addition to any recommendations sent by professionals who were unable to attend the meeting.* All of these should be reviewed to determine the client's capabilities and needs.

In an attempt "to maximize the client's ability to function in culturally-typical settings"[3] and to adapt successfully to living in the community, the following areas should be addressed:

Residential needs
Medical needs
Everyday living needs, including:
  Care of individual living area
  Household management
  Management, preparation, and service of meals
  Selection, purchase, and use of appropriate clothing
  Grooming and personal hygiene skills
  Preventive health and dental care
  Appropriate telephone skills
  Safety and self-preservation skills
  Use and management of money
  Basic information about legal rights and responsibilities
Psychological needs
Social and communication needs
Recreational and leisure-time needs
Transportation needs
Educational needs
Vocational needs
Physical therapy needs
Occupational therapy needs
Speech therapy needs[4]

Included in these areas are behaviors that need to be reduced, controlled, or eliminated as well as those that need to be taught.

After considering all of these goals, the team needs to decide what the general goals should be for the client while the client is in the program (this might include, for instance, general goals for the next 3 to 5 years). The goals should be relevant for the objective of the program. Thus, for example, a sheltered workshop would develop goals related to vocation while a residential program may be more concerned with daily living and social skills. Nonetheless, it is important that all of the team members meet together to determine the different goals so that the services are coordinated and everyone can work together to provide treatment in the best manner possible.

Following the determination of general goals, short- and long-term objectives should be developed. In deciding on what these objectives should be, the team should review and establish priorities for the client's enumerated needs. The objectives chosen, then, should represent the ones that are the most critical for the client in terms of health, safety, legal rights, and achieving independence. Thus, for example, a client with a serious medical problem may have as a number one priority the objective to either learn how to monitor the problem or how to take the proper medication to control the problem. After listing and assigning priorities to the most critically needed objectives, other objectives can be designated. They would be arranged by priorities and scheduled to be taught according to the client's basic needs. Additionally, many skills build on one another; thus, the simplest should be taught first followed by the more complicated. Finally, the team should decide on a reasonable number of objectives to be accomplished within a certain time period. For example, in a 3-month period, the team may have three to five objectives for each client. The number would depend on the difficulty of each objective and the amount of time needed to address each one adequately.

Some goals that undoubtedly will be selected for clients will involve providing the client with more freedom outside the center in an attempt to teach independent living skills but which likewise expose the client to some *potential risk*. Often, this places the staff in a precarious position: How do they allow clients to take normalized risks in the community without unduly exposing the center to liability? For example, when does one allow a person to take public transportation or go out on dates alone? To attempt to handle this type of problem, staff should specify all behaviors that move the clients toward independent or semi-independent living but that involve some risk taking. The staff should then specify the requisite skills needed before allowing a person to engage in these independent behaviors. Thus, a checklist of needed skills could be developed for each behavior, e.g., taking a bus, going shopping alone, going on a date, etc. When a client has demonstrated (and it has been reliably recorded) that he or she can perform all the necessary skills, the client should be gradually allowed to engage in the behaviors independently. These behaviors are, therefore, goals that are targeted to be taught by staff. The necessary behaviors should be specified and taught, and the client should be gradually faded into performing them independently before he or she is ever allowed to perform them alone. Thus, community centers should not avoid establishing goals that involve clients taking risks because only by engaging in those behaviors will they learn to live independently or semi-independently. Community centers must, however, follow the necessary procedures to ensure that clients are adequately prepared to take appropriate risks in the community.

5. *A timetable should be developed for each of the goals and objectives to be accomplished in a year.* Within this yearly timetable, target dates should be specified by which time a particular objective should have been accomplished. Although the timetable would not constitute a contract or promise to have accomplished the objective by the specified date, it should represent the team's best estimate concerning how long it will take to complete an objective. If the objective is not accomplished within the specified time period, a documented explanation should be offered.

6. *The person(s) responsible for developing and implementing a treatment plan for each objective should be specified.* Some programs have program specialists who write all treatment programs, while others depend on direct care staff to do this. Independent of who writes the actual program, the team should identify and specify which staff member(s) or consultant(s) will be

responsible for carrying out the program. Normally, the person with the most expertise in the target area would be designated to carry out the treatment objective. For example, it would appear logical to have a speech therapist conduct speech training with a client or to have a vocational workshop supervisor train job skills. Many everyday living skills can be taught by a variety of staff members. One consideration should be kept in mind, however, when teaching personal hygiene skills. To respect the dignity of a client, whenever possible, a staff member of the same sex as the client should be the person responsible for teaching personal hygiene or toileting skills. In most cases, for example, it would be inappropriate for a male staff member to teach a female client how to take a bath or vice versa. Emergency situations will come up when it is necessary for an opposite sex staff member to help a client, for example, in getting out of the bathtub. Normally, though, staff should respect the privacy and dignity of the clients as they would any other human being.

Finally, by designating a staff member who is in charge of implementing a treatment objective, responsibility can be placed on a particular person if the objective is not obtained. When objectives are established with several people identified as carrying out the treatment, no one person is responsible if the goals are not accomplished. Each person can say, "I thought someone else was working on that." To avoid this problem, the team should designate one staff member to be responsible for each objective. Several people can, in fact, work on the objective with the client, but one person still remains ultimately responsible.

7. *The responsibilities of the client, the client's family, and client's guardian should be specified, and all involved should agree on them.* As mentioned in this chapter and in Chapter 7, a client and the client's guardian and/or family should be integrally involved in the process of deciding on a treatment program. Once this plan has been developed, however, a client has a duty to participate in it to the best of his or her abilities. The client, at that point, does not have the right to refuse to participate in any treatment plan and also remain in the program.

The client's family may also have a duty to assist in the treatment process depending on the client's age and whether a member of the family is the client's legal guardian. If the client is a juvenile, the parents or guardians may be instructed to participate in the treatment program: for example, they may be requested to agree to have the juvenile come home on weekends for trial visits. If the parents or guardians refuse to agree, the court may have the authority to permanently remove the child from the parents' or guardians' custody. An adult client's family may be under no legal duty to participate in the treatment program, especially if the client is not under legal guardianship. On the other hand, if the adult client does have a legal guardian, that guardian may be required to assist in some of the treatment, for example, agreeing to home visits. A court would normally not require a legal guardian to provide explicit treatment, but the court could require the guardian to aid in the care, custody, and support of the client. Many state statutes even allow the state to collect payments from the immediate family for the treatment of a client.

8. *A description of the treatment procedure specifying how each particular objective is to be accomplished should be contained in the client's treatment plan.* This description would include a *task analysis* of the objective (e.g., listing the steps that are involved in teaching an appropriate target behavior as well as in reducing, controlling, or eliminating an inappropriate behavior). For instance, if a client were to be taught how to accept criticism, the behavioral steps involved in that skill (e.g., looking at the person, remaining calm, acknowledging what the person said, etc.) would be specified. Or, if a client were to receive articulation training, the target phonemes or sounds would be specified.

Next, the *training procedure* should be outlined. This would involve describing the method that the staff would use in teaching or reducing a behavior. For example, the following factors could be considered: Will the client receive one-to-one training or group training? Will the behavioral steps be taught one at a time and then chained together? Will the client be taught to relax everytime the client begins to get upset?

Any *motivational system* to be used with a client should also be outlined. If the client is to receive privileges, tokens, or points for participating in a training program or for responding correctly, the privileges or the number of tokens or points should be specified. If the client can lose privileges, tokens, or points, this must also be stated. Additionally, the back-up reinforcers that would be available to the client should be listed.

Finally, the number of times this treatment objective is to be worked on each week should be delineated. If special training sessions are to be held, the time of day and number of days per week should be specified. If training is to occur on a more incidental basis, some method of ensuring that the target objective will be treated must be provided.

9. *Along with describing how the treatment for each objective and goal is to be accomplished, the interdisciplinary team should specify the reason for choosing the particular form of treatment.* The team should also provide an assurance that the treatment is being provided in the *least restrictive* or *least intrusive* way possible in order to accomplish the desired goal. If the procedure is not the least intrusive one possible, the team should document that less intrusive or restrictive procedures have been attempted and have failed or that less intrusive procedures were considered but not used, and then state the reasons for not using those less restrictive procedures.

10. *The final consideration that the interdisciplinary team should address is designing a method to evaluate if the objectives and goals are being accomplished.* Chapter 7 discussed the issue of determining whether the treatment being provided is appropriate or adequate. One method of determining appropriate treatment involves looking at the results (Schwitzgebel, 1973).

Ultimate goals can be evaluated in order to determine if appropriate treatment has been provided. Thus, if the ultimate goal of a treatment program was to teach independent living skills, one could measure if the program was successful by examining the number of persons who moved out of the program and were living independently. This is only one goal, however, and it is such a long-term one that it would take several years to determine if a treatment program was successful. There are other intermediate goals and objectives. These should be specifically identified, defined, and then measured. The more of these objectives that are accomplished (assuming they are relevant and appropriate objectives), the more successful the program is, and, thus, the easier it is to say that appropriate treatment is being provided.

In determining progress, some type of written instrument should be used to record the client's advancement or lack thereof. As mentioned in the previous section, any evaluation or assessment tool used should be valid and reliable. Some methods of recording progress are described in the following section along with the other types of records that a program should keep.

RECORD-KEEPING

Although Chapter 7 quoted an expert as stating, "A sterling record says nothing about a patient's likelihood of recovery" (Schwitzgebel, 1973, p. 427), that should not be interpreted to mean that records have no place in a treatment program. Quite the contrary, records are a necessary and integral part of maintaining a good treatment program. It is true that records alone should not be relied on in order to determine whether treatment has occurred; actual observations and behavioral measures are needed. It is difficult, however, to provide an appropriate treatment program without keeping good records. This is due to a variety of reasons. First, it is necessary to have written assessments of a client's abilities and needs to which one can continually refer. It is also necessary to know what programming decisions were made by the interdisciplinary staff. Written records additionally can provide a means of keeping track of a client's progress on a treatment objective. One of the most important reasons to require that staff have good written records is so that a continuity of treatment can be provided to clients by a number of staff members. For example, often a community center will have several staff members who alternately take responsibility for different clients. It would be impossible to maintain a continuous treatment program if there was not some method of informing each of the staff what the others had done and what progress the client had made with each of them. This is also true whenever there is a turnover in staff. Maintaining good records can save the program and staff a considerable amount of time.

Many state regulations now require that community centers maintain comprehensive records.[5] Developing an orderly system of record-keeping will not only meet the legal or licensing mandate but will also help a community center to organize its treatment operation and will, in the long run, prove extremely useful in saving staff time. The following is a description of a method that can be used in record-keeping and the type of records that a community center should keep. Considerations that should be addressed in keeping client records are then discussed.

Types of Records

Perhaps the easiest way to establish a record-keeping system for clients is to keep two notebooks, that can be divided into sections, on *each* client. One notebook can contain information and progress logs that are current and that can be referred to or used daily. The second notebook can be used to place relevant, but old, information, i.e., information that should be kept on a client but that is not needed on a current daily basis. The notebooks can be divided into the following sections:

1. *Personal information.* This is often the first section in a client's notebook. It should contain all identifying information on the client, e.g., date of birth, sex, place of birth, schools attended, place of residence. The client's family history and social history can be placed in this section. The client's legal status (e.g., under guardianship) and the persons to be notified in case of an emergency should be listed here. Any prior programs, along with the entrance and release dates from those programs, that the client has been in would be appropriate to note. One may even want to place a picture of the client in this section. Generally, this part of the notebook should contain enough of the relevant personal information on a client to allow an evaluator to form a clear picture of the client's life up to this point in time. Thus, any treatment that is provided should take these personal factors into consideration.

2. *Examinations and diagnostic evaluations.* A record of all medical, dental, psychological, or other examinations given to the client should be kept in this section along with the results from those examinations. Additionally, any diagnostic evaluation or assessment that has been given to the client and the results from each evaluation would appropriately be placed here. All examinations and results should be dated. If it is possible to obtain the actual assessment instrument with the client ratings on it, that should be contained in this section rather than the results alone. Thus, for example, if a program uses a behavioral checklist to evaluate a client's performance four times a year, it would be useful to place the actual checklist with the client ratings on it in this section of the client's notebook. In any event, a descriptive, rather than interpretative, inventory of the client's assets and needs should be provided (Sheldon-Wildgen, 1976).

3. *Individualized treatment plans.* This is one of the most important sections and should summarize the interdisciplinary team's meeting on the client. It might begin by specifying the client's assets or capabilities and

outlining the major deficits or areas that need improvement, as evidenced by the evaluation results contained in the previous section. Program goals and long-term objectives for the client should be listed in addition to three to five short-term objectives with target dates for accomplishing these objectives. A separate page should be devoted to each short-term objective. The treatment plan that is designed to accomplish the objective should be listed on that page. This may include a specific description of the individual steps involved in the treatment program.

Following this explicit description of the treatment plan, the staff may want to provide a space where actual data on the progress of the client can be recorded. One method of doing this is to list each step in the sequence of behaviors that comprise the skill. These steps would be listed in ascending order of difficulty or in sequence according to how they are learned. For example, the first step in the program would be listed at the bottom of the page, one line up would be the second step, and so on. Horizontal and vertical lines could be drawn across the page to form a grid. Whether or not a particular step was performed correctly could be indicated in one of the boxes on the grid to the right of step. As the client improved, one would see vertical movement up the page (in terms of recording) as opposed to horizontal movement across the page.

All entries in this section should be dated and initialed to indicate the staff member who was responsible for the evaluation or training as well as the time and date when training took place.

4. *Educational, employment, or vocational training history.* This section of the client's notebook should contain the relevant information about the schools that the client attended and the grade-levels completed. Any vocational training should be listed as well as some measure of the client's performance to indicate what the client is qualified to do. Names, dates, and descriptions of past jobs should be included, and any current information in any of these areas should also be recorded here. Treatment plans that center around educational or vocational topics would normally be found under the major section on treatment plans.

5. *Drugs and medication.* Often, clients take many drugs to control either physiological or emotional problems. In many instances, it may be that a client is taking too many drugs. In order to protect the program and to get an accurate picture of what drugs a client actually does take, complete medication records need to be kept. All of the client's prescriptions should be recorded along with the name of the doctor who prescribed the medication, the name of the drug, the level prescribed (e.g., 5 mg) and the amount given in the total prescription (e.g., 100 tablets), the frequency with which it is to be taken (e.g., one tablet, four times a day), how long the client should continue to take the medication, and the reason for the medication. Every time the drug is dispensed, a record should be made indicating the medicine given, the dosage, the time of day and the date

given, and the initials of the person who dispensed the drug. If the client takes his or her own medicine, the client should be asked to indicate the time and date on which he or she took the drug.

6. *Use of aversive procedures.* As mentioned in Chapter 7, whenever possible, it is more desirable to use positive techniques than to employ aversive techniques. It is not always possible, however, to treat some clients adequately with positive procedures alone; thus, aversive techniques may be necessary. Whenever aversive techniques or procedures, such as seclusion or therapeutic timeout, shock, squirts of lemon juice, or restraints, are employed, their use must be documented. The time and date must be recorded along with a description of the precipitating event and the less intrusive or aversive techniques that were used in an attempt to reduce, control, or eliminate the undesirable behavior before using the aversive technique. The length of time that the technique was in use should be recorded. Whoever authorized the use should be noted as well as the person(s) who actually implemented the technique. Any unusual or extraordinary results should be noted.

7. *Log sheets.* Anecdotal log sheets should be kept to record any contacts the client has with certain people or any significant information or comments made by others in the client's life. Thus, individual sheets should be provided in the client's notebook to record contacts with and comments from the following types of people or agencies: teachers (the school), the workshop, parents, the court, the client's social worker, the client's dentist, the client's doctor, or any significiant individual in the client's life. Additionally, any accident, illness, or seizure that the client has could be recorded on a log sheet along with any immunizations that the client receives. Weekly workshop earnings could also be recorded. Finally, the staff may want to keep a daily anecdotal log on each client and note any special or unusual happenings. Depending on the particular section, whenever the information becomes outdated, it should be removed from the current notebook and filed in the client's second notebook, the one that is not used daily. Thus, the information obtained can be constantly updated with the old material still remaining available.

Confidentiality

All records kept on clients should be considered confidential. Therefore, only those individuals who are legitimately involved in the treatment of the client should have access to them or, as the Massachusetts regulations point out, only those persons who are monitoring or evaluating the quality of services being provided to the client.[6] If the client is under some disability and has a guardian, that guardian and/or the client's attorney should have access to the records. If the client is able to knowledgeably consent, the client can allow whomever he or she wants to examine the records. In any case, the client or legal guardian should always have the right to examine the records and to challenge any information contained in them. The more consistent the staff is in following a set record-keeping practice and in carefully documenting all entries, the less likely it will be that anyone will challenge the information contained in the records.

Maintaining Records That Could Be Potentially Detrimental to the Client

Some community programs work with clients who have come, or could come, into contact with the judicial system, e.g., juvenile offenders or parents of abused children. In some instances, staff members will be obtaining information that could be used against the client. For example, staff working with abusive parents may tape-record abusive encounters in the home or may actually observe and record such encounters. Although the staff would maintain the highest level of confidentiality with this information, it would still be possible for a court to subpoena the information. Another example might involve a juvenile telling his or her teaching parents that he had taken some drugs. Normally, teaching parents are not protected under the law of privileged communications[7] and are, therefore, required to divulge this information if asked to do so in a court of law. Thus, a teaching parent may be asked to reveal information about the juvenile to a judge. Whenever there appears to be a *real* threat that the staff's records may be subpoenaed or the staff may be called to testify, the staff should inform the client about this possibility before the client reveals any information. This, obviously, could have an effect on the client-therapist relationship. Since judges and courts differ on their views concerning this issue, if a community center is faced with the possibility of this type of event occurring, the center should contact either an attorney or the court and seek its opinion on a hypothetical issue.

Keeping Personal Notes Separate

In some instances, staff members make notes about clients that they do not want the client or others to see and that they do not want to become a part of the client's records. If a staff member makes a "personal note" about a client, that note should not be shown to anyone and should not be placed in the client's records, but should be placed in the individual staff member's own personal files and should only be used to refresh the staff member's memory about a particular incident. Obviously, if others find out about this information, the client or court could seek to obtain it considering it to be part of a client's records.

INFORMED CONSENT

The issue of consent arises daily in everyone's life. Usually, the consent that is given is implicit, e.g., one consents to listening to or reading the information that the media has to present by turning on a television set or purchasing a newspaper. Normally, few requirements, if any, are placed on the individuals or organizations who enter, affect, or influence people's lives. When the activities or interventions are extremely intrusive or expose a person to some potential risk or danger, however, the law often requires that explicit informed consent be obtained from the person who is to be affected. This section specifies procedures that should be considered in deciding when consent is necessary and in subsequently obtaining consent. An excellent source for those readers who want a more in-depth consideration of the subject is the *Consent Handbook* published by the American Association on Mental Deficiency. Readers may also want to examine a model form developed for use with aversive procedures (Cook, Altman, & Haavik, 1978).

Obtaining Consent

As stated in Chapter 7, there are some basic requirements that must be met and issues to be considered when obtaining consent. First, the person who is asked to give the consent must have the *capacity* to do so. This usually refers to the person being at least the age of majority (i.e., most states require the person to be 18 or older) and having the mental competence to understand what is happening to him or her and the consequence of that action. Additionally, the person should be able to engage in an objective and rational decision-making process and be capable of expressing any decision made (American Association on Mental Deficiency (AAMD), 1977).

Although this definition refers to all the appropriate considerations, how does one know if the person has the capacity to consent? Age is normally easy to determine. To be legally safe, whenever consent is needed, community centers working with clients who are minors should obtain the consent of the client's parent or guardian. That is not to imply, however, that the consent of the minor should not also be obtained. Children have rights and feelings, and if they are the target of a treatment program, they definitely should be informed about what is conceivably going to happen to them, and their consent should be solicited. If children and parents disagree on the issue of giving consent, an unbiased third party (e.g., a protective mechanism such as a human rights committee) should be consulted (this is described in more detail later).

The issue of mental competence is more difficult to determine than that of age. Other factors than intelligence alone need to be analyzed. The client's adaptive behavior, life experiences, and common sense can all affect the person's ability to consent. It is impossible to define one way in which all these items can be assessed in order to determine a client's capacity to consent, but one method used has been to test the client's understanding of the procedures to be used and the consequences (Strouse, 1980). The test can be given orally or in writing and should be constructed in such a way as to determine whether the client understands the words and terms being used in addition to understanding the procedures and consequences. Thus, a test given to a client should not allow the client to give only *yes* or *no* answers; it should require that the client give reasons or explanations for answers. This requirement is not there to place a burden on the client but rather to ensure that the client understands what he or she is saying.

A second requirement of consent is that enough information is provided to the client so that the client can make an intelligent and *informed* decision about whether or not to participate in treatment or research. It may be impossible to describe in detail every aspect of the treatment or experimental procedure; furthermore, the law does not require that that much information be given. What is basically required is that all the material and relevant facts are given including: a full explanation of the procedures to be used and the purpose of the treatment or research, a description of the potential risks or discomforts that could be involved, a description of the presumed benefits, a description of any alternative treatments (especially less intrusive ones) that are available with their potential risks and benefits, an offer to answer any questions honestly and explicitly that the client might have, and a statement explaining that the person is free to withdraw from the treatment or experimental procedure at any time without fear of negative repercussions (other than not being in the treatment program) (AAMD, 1977). Once again, a test might be given to determine the extent to which the client understands the information given.

The third requirement is that the consent be given in a *voluntary* and uncoerced manner. The issue of voluntariness often involves such things as freedom from force, freedom from coercion, or freedom from duress. More subtle considerations involve the relationship between the person asking for consent and the person from whom consent is to be given (e.g., the client). Is the client dominated by the party who is seeking consent? Are the two parties in relatively equal bargaining positions, or is the one seeking the consent in a powerful position whereby he or she can exert undue influence over the client? The AAMD *Consent Handbook* outlines some additional issues to be considered in determining the voluntariness of the consent given by clients who are retarded. These include whether the client is in an institution, in custody, involuntarily detained or committed (perhaps with expectations that consenting to a procedure will increase the likelihood of being released), or is just used to doing what people in authority tell him or her to do. Is the client overly eager to please other people? Does the client succumb to inducements or threats more easily because of his or her mental disability? Does the client have the ability and opportunity to seek independent advice (AAMD, 1977, p. 11)?

In determining the voluntariness of any consent given by a client in a residential program (where the client depends on others for the client's basic needs and for personal relationships), one should always protect against subtle forms of coercion. For example, if the client refuses to consent to a particular treatment or therapy program, an administrator should ensure that staff members do not then treat the client in a different manner, e.g., are less friendly to him or her, give less attention or less privileges, or require more work from the client. Such forms of responding to the client may, in fact, have the effect of making the client more willing to agree to a particular type of treatment or research even though the client actually would prefer not to agree.

The Formality of the Consent

The form (e.g., implied, oral, or written) that the consent needs to take as well as the formality of the process in which one should engage in obtaining the consent of a client depends on a number of factors. The AAMD *Consent Handbook* identifies various considerations that would affect the formality of the needed consent. Thus, as a client's mental incapacity, lack of information or understanding, or potential for unwilling consent increases, the effectivenes of the client's consent needs to be scrutinized more carefully. Additionally, "as the risk, intrusiveness, or irreversibility of activities or procedures increase, the effectiveness of [the client's] consent becomes subject to closer scrutiny . . ." (AAMD, 1977, p. 21). Therefore, a general principle that a community center may want to adhere to is: "the riskier, more intrusive, or more irreversible the activity, the more formal the consent process must be" (AAMD, 1977, p. 22).

The formality of the consent can range from implied consent to a form of consent where a third party (e.g., a protective mechanism such as a human rights committee) would need to evaluate the procedure and determine if the procedure can justifiably be used. Obviously, this last type of consent is the most formal and would be used in those cases where the client's ability to consent is scrutinized in addition to using procedures that are intrusive, risky, or irreversible.

A possible range of the different means of obtaining consent could include the following: 1) implying the consent from past behavior in a related type of activity, 2) obtaining the consent orally, 3) obtaining written consent and recording it in the client's notebook, 4) requiring the client to take a test to determine the client's comprehension of what is involved in the procedures and then asking for written consent and recording it, 5) requiring the client to consult with an independent third party, then obtaining written consent and recording it, and 6) allowing written consent to be effective only after the procedures have been reviewed by a protective mechanism, such as a human rights committee (AAMD, 1977).

Who Can Give Consent?

Normally, the person to whom the treatment is to be given or who is to participate in the experimental or research project is the one who should give the consent; this is often referred to as *direct consent*. This is not always possible, however, due to the client's age, mental competency, or the potentially coercive nature of the community center. In cases where it is not feasible for the client alone to give consent, what should be done?

When consent is required from the client and another person, it is referred to as *concurrent consent*. When a third party gives consent in place of and for the client, it is referred to as *substitute consent* (AAMD, 1977). Deciding who should be able to give substitute consent is not an easy task. Often, community centers, when needing substitute consent, will ask a parent, guardian, or conservator to give the consent. Although this appears to be the most likely way to proceed, it may not serve the best interests of the client. A recent case, *Bartley v. Kremens*,[8] raised the issue of allowing parents to consent to the institutionalization of their children in cases where the child did not wish to enter the institution. In such a situation, there is a conflict between the interests of the substitute decision maker and those of the client. Another fairly common example has been when parents of retarded people consent to the sterilization of their children.[9] Both institutionalization and sterilization involve extremely intrusive and often irreversible interventions into a person's life. When the client does not have the ability to make these decisions, they should not be made by people who have a potential conflict of interest.

In determining who should be the substitute decision maker, a community center should evaluate the intrusiveness, the risk, and the irreversibility of the procedure. As mentioned previously, the more serious the activity, the more need there is for the person giving consent to be totally unbiased. For example, it may be appropriate for a parent to give consent for a client to have his or her picture taken or to go on a field trip or vacation. It may not be appropriate, however, for that parent to consent to a surgical operation such as sterilization.

Whoever the community center selects as the substitute person or organization to give consent, that person must "act *on the basis of the best interest of the person for whom his or her consent is sought*" (AAMD, 1977, p. 18). This means that the substitute consent-giver must make a decision in the same manner that the substitute feels the client would do if the client were able to give consent. Finally, the substitute consent-giver must be competent, adequately informed, and free from any coercion—the same factors that are required when a client gives informed consent (AAMD, 1977). Community centers may find that the easiest way to handle the issue of substitute consent is to have an independent body, that acts as a protective mechanism, review the more serious and intrusive procedures. This independent group, such as a human rights committee, could then give or withhold consent according to what the members feel is appropriate. In any event, a community center should always check with the state statutes and regulations to determine what is required by law in the area of consent.

Consent to Release Information

In the previous section, the issue of releasing client records to other individuals was discussed. Normally, client information can be released to the client or client's guardian, to the client's representatives (e.g., the client's doctor, attorney, or advocate), to judicial agencies, to direct service providers (e.g., schools, mental health agencies, vocational rehabilitation agencies, workshops, group homes), to indirect care providers (e.g., departments of social services), to monitoring and evaluation agencies, and depending on the information sought, to researchers. The more the person requesting the information is in a direct care position or is going to provide some benefit to the client, the less formal and less scrutinized the consent procedure needs to be. The information that is released and the determination of the type of consent needed depends greatly on the nature of the information. If personally identifiable information is being released, then a more formal consent procedure should be followed. If, on the other hand, statistical, summary, or non-identifiable information is being released, the consent procedure can be less formal (AAMD, 1977).

There are instances when a community center may need to disclose information given to the staff by a client without obtaining consent from the client. Chapter 7 discussed the issue of the duty to warn third parties if a staff member, in his or her professional judgment, believes that the client may harm the third party and that the third party is in clear and imminent danger. Another area of concern involves clients who have committed or are contemplating committing a crime. Generally, disclosure of a crime, *after* the crime has been committed, is protected by statutes that give privileged communications to certain professional relationships (e.g., doctor–client, attorney–client, certified psychologist–client). If the staff members fall under one of these statutorily protected privileges, they are not required to disclose the information and can be prevented from doing so by the client. (An exception to this is in the area of child abuse where no confidentiality or privileged communication exists, and professionals are required to report any suspected cases.)

If the staff members are not professionals who are given the right of privileged communication, the issue is not as easy to decide. If a client informs the staff that he or she has committed an illegal act, the staff members must decide if the offense was serious enough to report and whether or not reporting could conceivably make them an accessory-after-the-fact. No clear-cut answer to this problem can be given. The staff should weigh several factors, including the duty to society, the duty to the client, whether restitution can be made, the need of the client for a more specialized type of treatment, the probability of the client committing this type of act again, and the actual or potential harm to others. For example, staff would probably not "turn in" a client who revealed that he or she had been speeding. If, however, the client had been shoplifting, the staff may want the client to make restitution. They therefore might require the client, accompanied by a staff member, to go to the store owner and return or pay for the item. If the client were caught smoking marijuana, the staff could call the police or could flush the marijuana down the toilet, impose some form of program punishment (e.g., loss of points if the client is on a token economy), and inform the client that if he or she were caught smoking dope again, the police would be called. If the client revealed that he had raped someone, a more serious problem is presented. At this point, the best action would be to call an attorney and, without revealing the client's name, describe the situation and ask for the attorney's advice. In fact, in any situation where the client reveals that he or she has committed an illegal act and that communication is not privileged because the staff is not statutorily recognized as being able to receive privileged communications, the staff should contact an attorney for legal advice. Remember, independent of the action taken, if staff members are not given the statutory right of privileged communications, they can be called to court and ordered to reveal anything that the client said to them.

An entirely different situation is presented when a client reveals that he or she is *planning* on committing a crime. If the community center staff actually believe that a crime is going to be committed and that someone will be placed in jeopardy, it may be necessary for the staff to contact the police. Obviously, the first step staff members should take is to attempt to talk the person out of committing the illegal act. If this does not succeed, then the staff must decide if they seriously believe the client will commit the crime. Although the *Tarasoff* case[10] indicated that a therapist was under an explicit duty to warn third parties if the therapist felt that the client presented a clear and imminent danger to the third party, case law is not as clear on what staff members should do if they feel the client will harm property rather than people. Once again, staff must balance the duty they have to their client versus their duty to society. As the crime becomes more serious, the duty to society increases. Additionally, staff members need to protect themselves from the possible charge of "aiding and abetting" in a crime or the charge of being an "accessory before the fact." These charges are especially relevant if the services of the staff have been solicited in helping the client in the commission of a crime (Schwitzgebel & Schwitzgebel, 1980).

In summary, the topic of informed consent and the need for consent to release information are similar to many other issues that community centers must consider. There is no clear-cut answer; rather, a number of factors must be weighed. The critical point is to realize that one set procedure will not work for every client and for every situation. Individual determinations must continually be made.

DEVELOPING AND MAINTAINING A HUMANE PHYSICAL AND PSYCHOLOGICAL ENVIRONMENT

This was one of the first areas to be addressed by professionals, legislatures, and judiciaries, and it will continue to be an area of concern as long as there are dependent populations who find it difficult, if not impossible, to advocate for themselves. As described in Chapter 7, conditions in facilities serving developmentally disabled individuals, mentally ill persons, or juvenile offenders were often deplorable, and because of these inhumane conditions, guidelines were promulgated and minimum standards established. Several courts and legislatures have outlined these minimum standards, and many of the minimum basic rights and conditions were listed in Chapter 7. It is impossible, however, to list every possible privilege that should be guaranteed to clients and to describe every possible exception that can be made. Independent of how long a list is provided to community center personnel, someone can always come up with an exotic example for a special client in an unusual situation. It is very difficult to make a blanket statement of approval or disapproval of certain procedures and, at the same time, ensure that appropriate treatment is provided to each individual client in the least restrictive, intrusive, or harmful way possible. Rather, a balancing procedure must continually occur with protective mechanisms developed to ensure that all procedures used are professionally warranted and humanely administered. These protective mechanisms are described in the final section of this chapter. The purpose of the present section is to educate community center administrators and staff in the basic areas that should be addressed when considering how to develop an appropriate environment for clients. With a good understanding of the considerations involved, most community center staff will be able to assess adequately whether a particular course of action would be justified. This section is divided into four main areas of concern: basic rights, involuntary servitude, the least restrictive alternative, and the use of aversive procedures.

Basic Rights

The requirement of community centers to provide basic rights to clients essentially recognizes that there are certain items that any person (but especially those persons residing in programs for dependent populations) has a right to enjoy in addition to a certain amount of freedom that all individuals should possess. Thus, for example, persons in community centers have a right to three nutritionally adequate meals a day, served in a manner that is aesthetically pleasing. Basic rights also include providing a client with the right to have seasonally appropriate clothing, a right to privacy, a right to communicate with others, a right to keep his or her own possessions, a right to participate in physical activities, a right to engage in personal activities, and a right to live in a pleasant and safe environment, to name only a few. When operating a treatment program, however, many questions come to mind. For example, what if a client does not eat a regular meal, but later wants a snack of a peanut butter and jelly sandwich or a bowl of ice cream? Does the right to communicate with others mean that a client's family can come and visit daily, especially when it has been documented that the family upsets the client and disrupts the normal flow of the program? Does the right to keep one's own possessions mean that a client can bring his or her television and stereo into the client's bedroom? Does it make a difference if the client shares the bedroom with someone else? The questions are endless, and there are no set answers. But even with no set answers, a community center must generally know how to respond.

In attempting to answer these types of questions, the first thing a community center should do is attempt to determine what the underlying justification of the guarantee of the basic right is. For example, when courts mandated that a client receive three nutritionally balanced and aesthetically pleasing meals, the courts were probably most concerned with the health of the client. The court wanted to ensure that everyone received adequate diets and that meals were served in such a way as to encourage eating. The court probably did not mean that a client should have unlimited access to food. (Courts and legislatures, however, have stressed that the client's life be structured in a normalized way, and, therefore, what "normal" families or people do should be considered.) Thus, it may make a difference whether the client was legitimately sick at dinner time and wanted to eat later when he or she was feeling better or whether the client simply did not like the dinner and was refusing to eat what everyone else did and demanding something else later. All people, at some point in their lives, do not like a particular food, so another consideration would be how frequently this type of behavior occurs. A community center should set legally justified and reasonable rules; exceptions to those rules should be examined on an individual basis with considerations given to the rationale for the basic rule and the consequences of allowing certain exceptions or deviations. Thus, for example, a residential community center should always provide at least three nutritionally adequate meals a day suitable to the clients' dietary needs and served in a pleasing manner. When a problem infrequently arises concerning this right, the center should make a rational decision, weighing the consequences to both the client and the center. If problems arise frequently, the center should present the issue to an independent protective mechanism, such as a human rights committee, and let that mechanism make the decision.

The following is a reiteration of *some* of the basic privileges listed in Chapter 7. Listed with these privileges are rationales or reasons for providing these items or activities as "basic rights." A community center should always keep the reasons for the privileges in mind when considering a modification of the basic rights in any way.

1. *The right to a normalized living environment.* This is to ensure that clients live in facilities that are as similar to what the "normal" population lives in as possible. Temperatures should not be extreme; ventilation should be adequate; daily routines should be normal and allow for individual variation. This right was mandated after courts discovered, for instance, that facilities were often bordering on the inhumane in terms of temperature, i.e., extremely cold in the winter and blisteringly hot in the summer, and thus, contributing to illness and death in the clients. Additionally, clients were treated with little individual respect. For example, in some facilities, everyone had to get up at 5:00 a.m. so that everyone could eat by 7:30. Everyone was required to shower at the same time, go to bed at the same time, be awakened to go to the bathroom at the same time. Nothing was done according to an individual's needs but rather to accommodate the staff. The rationale here is to treat clients as individuals and to allow them to live as "normally" as possible.

2. *The right to privacy.* The Supreme Court has recognized a constitutional right to privacy, with certain areas of one's life appearing more likely to be included in this right. Thus, a client should be afforded privacy in the bedroom and especially the bathroom. The client should have time to be alone, away from other clients and staff. Additionally, all correspondence that the client sends and receives should be confidential unless security or legal reasons require otherwise.

3. *The right to three nutritionally adequate meals a day served in a pleasing manner.* The basis for this right was described above and generally involves ensuring the proper nutrition for the client in order to protect the client's health.

4. *The right to religious worship.* This is another right guaranteed by the Constitution. A client should be able to choose *where* he or she wishes to worship and *when* (within a reasonable time frame) he or she wants to worship. No client should be forbidden from attending a religious service of his or her choice nor should the client be forced to attend a religious service.

5. *The right to communicate and interact with others.* There are several rationales for guaranteeing this as a basic right. First, courts believe that all individuals have the right to associate with others because this is basically guaranteed under the Constitution. Second, in an attempt to integrate clients successfully into the community, it is helpful if they have developed and/or maintained relationships with people in the community. One of the best ways to maintain these relationships is by communicating with others. Finally, if clients are not allowed to communicate with others, either in person, by phone, or in writing, the client has no way of indicating if he or she is being mistreated. By requiring that community centers allow their clients to communicate with people outside the center, the clients are being provided with a protective safeguard, i.e., being able to inform someone if something is not right.

6. *The right to physical exercise, both inside and outdoors.* This right, similar to the meals requirement, is based on health reasons.

7. *The right to have one's own clothing and storage for it.* This right is based on the desire to provide as normalized a living environment for people as possible. There is no justification for treating dependent populations as subhuman organisms who all can be treated identically with no right to personal possessions or individual desires or preferences.

8. *The right to access to public media.* Originally, courts mandated that residents in institutions had a right to access to a television set. Many people were puzzled by this right until they examined the conditions that existed in the institutions. Often, the television set was the only recreational item on the ward in addition to the residents' only means of access to knowledge about what was occurring outside the institution. People in community centers, as opposed to institutions, should have more access to recreational items and outside information since they should be out in the

community frequently. They, nonetheless, have a right (like everyone else) to obtain information about what is going on in the world. If the client can read, he or she should have access to newspapers and magazines as well as to television or radio news programs. Clients who cannot read should obviously have access to the television and radio news programs.

In considering these rights as well as the ones listed in Chapter 7 and any that might be mandated in a community center's own state, a community center should initially address the reason for the right. Next, balance that right against the need to provide appropriate and effective treatment for a client. It may, therefore, be appropriate to limit some of the basic rights if that is the only way to provide effective treatment. Whenever basic rights are being limited, however, safeguards should be provided to ensure that the justification for providing the basic right can still be attained. The safest way for a community center to proceed in instances where the staff would like to limit some of a client's basic rights in an attempt to provide effective treatment is to present the issue to an independent review committee, e.g., a human rights committee, for determination. Additionally, an individual client's right must always be balanced against the rights of the other clients. Finally, a community center should teach the clients the necessary skills so that they can utilize and benefit from their basic rights. For example, the right to communicate with others is of no use to a client if the client is unable to read or write or use the telephone. Staff should always be available (on a reasonable basis) to help a client in making a telephone call or in reading or writing a letter. Beyond that, however, teaching the client those skills so he or she can do those things independently should be high priorities.

Involuntary Servitude

Involuntary servitude refers to the practice of requiring clients or residents to perform institutional maintenance-type labor (e.g., doing the janitorial work for the entire facility such as cleaning, sweeping, mopping, painting, etc.; doing the gardening; doing the laundry; doing the cooking or serving the food, etc.) without just compensation. Also included in institutional-type labor is the requirement of caring for other clients, e.g., bathing, dressing, or feeding them. This practice was common in institutions; clients were *required* to do these things and received little, if any, compensation. Thus, the situation was similar to using slave labor, and therefore, the use of the term "freedom from involuntary servitude" was developed.

Courts were quick to prohibit this type of forced labor. The *Wyatt* court issued specific guidelines regarding work performed within an institution. First, no resident could be *required* to do labor that involved the operation or maintenance of the institution or work for which the institution was under contract with an outside organization to perform. If a resident *volunteered* to perform this type of labor, the resident had to be compensated. Second, residents could be required to engage in vocational training or therapeutic tasks, if they were part of the resident's treatment plan. In this event, there was a presumption that training would take no longer than 3 months and if the training task involved the operation and maintenance of the institution the resident had to agree voluntarily to do it and had to be compensated for it. Third, residents could be required to perform personal housekeeping chores such as making their beds. Finally, privileges or release from the institution could not be made contingent upon the performance of institutional maintenance labor.[11]

The *Wyatt* court specified that residents who did voluntarily engage in institutional maintenance-type labor should be compensated in accordance with the Fair Labor Standards Act as amended in 1966.[12] There have been various interpretations as to exactly what this order means. A federal district court addressed the issue of institutional labor and just compensation for this labor in *Souder v. Brennan*[13] and held that residents of institutions must be paid the minimum wage according to the Fair Labor Standards Act of 1966. The *Souder* decision was based on a Supreme Court decision that was subsequently reversed in *National League of Cities v. Usery*.[14] Following this latest decision, it appears that the federal minimum wage is not guaranteed to state, county, or city employees. Thus, those clients working in state or local facilities would be governed by the applicable state minimum wage.

The Fair Labor Standards Act does, however, specifically allow handicapped persons to be paid at an amount lower than minimum wage. If certain conditions are met and a certificate issued, the facility (e.g., a sheltered workshop or work activity center) can pay the handicapped persons an amount that is commensurate with what nonhandicapped workers would receive for the same amount or quality of work.[15] This provision of the Fair Labor Standards Act was designed to encourage handicapped or disabled persons to engage in work activities and to prevent a curtailment of opportunities for their employment. Thus, individuals with mental or physical handicaps should not be prevented from learning or engaging in economically useful work activities because of a financial burden on the employer.

One of the most prevalent questions in this area involves the type of work that clients can be asked to do in a residential facility without being given compensation. The *Wyatt* decision allowed only "personal housekeeping," but that decision was specifically issued for residents in a large institution. It would appear that the same guidelines would not be applicable in a community group home that operates on a family-style model and emulates a normal family environment. In such a setting, it would appear appropriate to require clients to do more housework than just their own personal housekeeping. In a "normal" family, everyone often shares responsibility for the cooking, the cleaning, the gardening, or the laundry. If one were attempting to imitate the normal family in a community-based residential facility, all clients might likewise share responsibility for those types of activities. The Massachusetts regulations appear to have acknowledged this situation. Although the regulations prohibit requiring clients "to perform labor which involves the essential operation and maintenance of the community residence or program or the regular care, treatment or supervision of other clients . . . , [c]lients may be required to perform labor involving normal housekeeping and home maintenance functions."[16] These regulations definitely seem to prohibit requiring clients to do operational or maintenance-type work in a nonresidential facility (e.g., a sheltered workshop or activity center). What *is* allowed in a residential facility is not explicitly stated, but some suggestions are given below.

If the residential facility is established on a family-style model, a community center should be justified in requiring clients to participate in household maintenance tasks which are needed for the daily operation of the home. Thus, it would not seem unreasonable to ask the clients to share in the daily cooking, in the cleaning of the common areas of the house, in the yard maintenance, and perhaps in taking care of the laundry. There are, however, certain prohibitions that should be followed. First, no client should be required to clean another client's room; each client should be responsible only for his or her own room. Second, no client should be required to perform any labor that benefits only the staff. For example, a client should not be required to clean the staff's apartment or living quarters, to take care of the staff's children, to wash the staff's car, or to do the staff's laundry or ironing. If a client volunteers to do any of these tasks, the client should be fairly compensated for them. Third, if the home's laundry is done all together, clients may be required to do this task on a rotating basis. If, however, everyone's laundry is done separately, each client should be responsible for his or her own laundry and no client should be required to do another client's laundry. Fourth, all household tasks should be performed on a rotating basis. No client should ever be consistently assigned one task. Fifth, no client should ever be forced to remain in the program because that client has become extremely proficient at certain tasks. Finally, there are some areas where it is not clear whether clients should be required to perform the task (e.g., repair work on the house or painting the house). Generally, if the work is more than what is required for the day-to-day operation of the house, or if the work will benefit the house for a longer period of time than the client's stay in the home, the client should not be required to perform the job. If the client volunteers, he or she should have the opportunity to engage in the work activity if he or she is adequately supervised and fairly compensated.

The Least Restrictive Alternative

The principle of the least restrictive alternative was defined and generally discussed in Chapter 7. It is a basic consideration that must be weighed in all treatment decisions. Whenever one considers the least restrictive alternative it should be in the context of providing appropriate and effective treatment. Thus, a balancing procedure must necessarily take place.

To illustrate this, consider the example described by Sheldon-Wildgen (1976). Assume that a client in a community center engages in a considerable amount of disruptive and aggressive behavior. The behavior may be disturbing to other clients and to staff. Additionally, this behavior may make if difficult for the staff to teach the client appropriate behaviors while the client is engaging in this aggressive and disruptive behavior. There are several treatment techniques that could be used to decrease or eliminate the inappropriate behavior. These could range from those that are fairly non-intrusive to those that are extremely intrusive; e.g., the range could include milieu therapy, group therapy, counseling, extinction, response cost, therapeutic timeout, solitary confinement, electric shock, or a lobotomy. If the only consideration is providing the least intrusive procedure, the staff may employ milieu therapy. Milieu therapy may be nonconfining and intrude very little into the client's life, yet it has a high probability of being ineffective with this particular type of behavior. Alternatively, the staff could ask that a lobotomy be performed on the client in order to rid the client of his or her aggressive behavior or, more realistically, that the client be shocked or placed in solitary confinement contingent on each disruptive or aggressive act. One of these procedures may prove to be quite successful in eliminating the inappropriate behavior, yet the procedures are extremely drastic and intrusive, especially in relation to the exhibited behavior. Sheldon-Wildgen (1976) points out what must be done to find the appropriate treatment:

> The key to effective treatment is finding the treatment procedure that successfully changes behavior and at the same time interferes the least with the person's freedom. It requires balancing treatment procedures with ethical considerations. It may also mean that treatment takes longer because the therapist should begin with the least restrictive procedure and proceed from there to determine what is effective with an individual in order to adequately rehabilitate him or her (p. 79).

It may not always be necessary to actually go through every less intrusive treatment procedure and demonstrate and document that each has failed before using more intrusive procedures, but all the less intrusive procedures should have been considered and their previous use with other similarly situated clients evaluated before moving on to the more restrictive or intrusive procedures. The staff should consistently engage in these considerations as well as seek advice from the human rights committee.

The least restrictive alternative applies not only to treatment techniques but also to treatment placement. A client should be placed in the least restrictive environment consistent with the client's needs and the client should continually be moved to less restrictive placements. This implies that communities need to develop a continuum of services including residential services, day services, recreational services, and vocational services suited to each individual's needs and designed to allow movement to less restrictive environments. This additionally implies that the goals specified for a client reflect the desire to move the client to less restrictive placements. These are concrete goals and can easily be measured by observing the degree of independence that a client has in his or her own life and the amount of freedom that the client has.

The Use of Aversive Procedures

Chapter 7 presented a discussion of several of the different aversive techniques that have been used with dependent populations in addition to specifying conditions that can be so aversive and unjustifiable as to constitute cruel and unusual punishment. Some conditions and practices to which clients have been exposed are so inhumane that no justification can be presented for their use as either treatment procedures or as part of a humane living environment. For example, randomly slapping, kicking, or beating clients is unacceptable. Tying clients to beds in a spread-eagled fashion, sexually abusing them, shaming and degrading them in front of others, providing them with inadequate nutrition, or exposing them to unsanitary living conditions all are inhumane and unacceptable. The use of procedures such as those must be strictly prohibited with criminal, civil, and professional sanctions severely imposed on those people who engage in that type of behavior and who treat clients in that fashion.

A problem is presented, however, when community centers use procedures that are potentially therapeutic but that also expose the client to some harm or detriment. The use of certain aversive techniques, e.g., physical restraints, electric shock, deprivation of basic privileges, seclusion, physical punishment, overcorrection, and response cost, can be used in a contingent and justifiable manner to decrease inappropriate behavior. Some aversive procedures (e.g., lobotomies and electroconvulsive shock treatment) are obviously more intrusive, restrictive, or damaging than others (e.g., psychotropic drugs, seclusion, or overcorrection). Nonetheless, many aversive procedures can, in certain individual cases, be justified. There are two basic problems, however, that exist with the use of aversive techniques. First, aversive techniques are less desirable to use than positive procedures because of their inherent intrusive and often painful or restrictive nature. Second, all aversive procedures are open to the possibility of misuse by the staff, with resulting harm or detriment to the client. For example, the contingent application of electric shock has proved to be successful in reducing self-destructive and other resistant inappropriate behaviors (Baer, 1971; Lovaas & Simmons, 1969). Yet, a staff member could conceivably randomly shock clients with a high voltage of electric shock. This application of shock would result in pain and discomfort to the client with no concurrent positive results. It is the inappropriate misuse of aversive procedures that has resulted in many of the legal restrictions and prohibitions on their use.

Most people would agree that if appropriate education or treatment can be provided with the use of positive procedures alone, then there is no need to even consider employing aversive techniques. Thus, community programs are urged to use the most positive and least intrusive or restrictive techniques when providing treatment to their clients. Only when these procedures have proved ineffective should more restrictive procedures be considered. In an attempt, however, to fulfill the legal mandate of providing *effective* treatment to all clients, aversive and restrictive procedures may need to be considered (Repp & Dietz, 1978).

Adhering to the requirement of using the most positive and the least intrusive treatment procedures, community centers will find that the greatest number of problems will arise with the "hard-to-treat" or severely debilitated client. To provide effective treatment for the severely debilitated client, it may be necessary to expose the client to some risk or potential harm. This is usually the case because less intrusive treatment techniques have proved unsuccessful. Often, these clients have a limited range of items or activities that can serve as reinforcers and, thus, very few things motivate them. Additionally, many of these clients engage in such disruptive, aggressive, or harmful behavior that to prohibit the use of aversive techniques may mean that they will have to be physically or mechanically restrained or allowed to cause harm to themselves or others (Baer, 1970).

When evidence indicates that the only procedure that may prove effective with a particular client is the use of an aversive technique, should a community program allow the person to remain in an essentially untreated state in order to avoid exposure to an aversive treatment technique, and can the program legally do that when a right to treatment has been mandated? Or should the community center use an aversive treatment technique in hopes of moving the person to less restrictive living conditions (in other words, providing the client with more skills so that the client has more freedom in choosing what to do)? If community centers are allowed to use aversive techniques, in the name of appropriate treatment, where do they draw the line that would allow the use of some aversive techniques but not others?

The most convenient method would be to allow community center administrators or staff to decide which techniques are appropriate for individual clients. This, however, is not the most desirable alternative in terms of providing both client and program protection because the staff has a vested interest in having the program run smoothly and operate efficiently. The staff could, therefore, advocate the use of aversive procedures for the staff's convenience rather than for the benefit of the clients. Thus, protective mechanisms need to be developed to ensure that the treatment procedures, especially those involving aversive techniques, are developed for the benefit of the clients and are ethical and humane (Griffith, 1980; May, Risley, Twardosz, Friedman, Bijou, & Wexler, et al., 1976; Sheldon-Wildgen & Risley, in press). These protective mechanisms are described in the following and final section of this chapter.

Therefore, recommendations on the use of *specific* aversive procedures are not made here.[17] Since community centers must continually balance the client's right to treatment versus the right to be free from harm, blanket statements of approval or disapproval of aversive procedures cannot be made. Rather, individual cases should be presented for discussion by the protective mechanism (e.g., a human rights committee), and that committee should decide what procedures are justified and appropriate and what restrictions or safeguards need to be provided. Community centers should, however, review any state or local laws or regulations on the use of aversive procedures and ensure that they are in compliance with them. Community center administrators and staff should also address the issues presented in Chapter 7 concerning the use of aversive techniques and should review the prohibitions placed on their use and the safeguards provided by other states' courts and legislatures. Finally, no procedure should be used that is dehumanizing or degrading, nor should any aversive procedure be used for the convenience of the staff, for retribution, or as a *substitute* for treatment. Aversive procedures that are allowed should only be used contingent on the occurrence of an inappropriate behavior.

PROTECTIVE MECHANISMS*

With the ever-increasing emphasis on accountability and protection of human rights, administrators and staff of community-based programs will constantly need to address the issue of providing appropriate treatment for each client while ensuring that each person is protected from unnecessary harm. Often programs view the establishment of protective mechanisms as safeguarding only clients' rights. When these mechanisms are developed appropriately and operate properly, however, they can provide safeguards for the staff by responding to allegations that improper treatment is being administered. Thus, protective mechanisms can serve both the clients and the staff.

Many programs have attempted to provide protection for clients by developing guidelines that address treatment considerations and ensure that clients reside in a humane environment. Often the guidelines are primarily concerned with the regulation of aversive procedures. The establishment of guidelines indicates that program personnel are aware of potential problems and are concerned about resolving them, but guidelines can also present problems. Since guidelines often address a finite number of procedures, they can give the false impression that only certain techniques need to be monitored while others need not be. This assumption is false because any procedure, either positive or aversive, is open to misuse and the client can, therefore, be exposed to harm.[18] Guidelines often allow people to forget that each case must be considered individually. Each procedure considered for use *must* be

---

*The content of this section is taken substantially from: Sheldon-Wildgen, J., & Risley, T.R. Balancing client's rights: The establishment of Human Rights and Peer Review committees. In A. Bellack, M. Hersen, & A. Kazdin (eds.), *International handbook of behavior modification.* New York: Plenum Press, in press.

examined in terms of who will carry it out and the manner in which it will be carried out, in terms of the probability of success with a particular client, and in terms of the benefits and risks to the client.

Other programs have attempted to protect clients by prohibiting the use of certain procedures, especially those involving physically painful aversive techniques or a deprivation of rights. By prohibiting the use of specified procedures, a program can ensure that those procedures will not be misused and that the client will not be exposed to harm or discomfort as a result of the use of the procedures. This type of protection may mean, however, that some clients (especially the more severely debilitated ones) are denied the right to treatment. If other less aversive techniques had been tried and had not been successful, individuals could be restricted in what progress they make and, therefore, where they live, what jobs, if any, they can hold, and what skills they can learn, all because there is not an appropriate treatment procedure that is effective and that is not proscribed. Effective treatment could be denied in the hopes of protecting these people from any type of harm or discomfort.

Guidelines regulating certain procedures or regulations prohibiting the use of specified techniques additionally do not address the issue of whether appropriate treatment is being provided. Often parents, advocates for clients, and staff are so concerned that certain procedures not be used that they forget about the critically important issue of whether effective treatment is being provided for each client. Protecting persons from harm or discomfort is important, but it should not be the only concern. Clients are usually in programs to receive treatment, and one must therefore also ensure that effective treatment is given to each client.

Thus, it appears that one cannot make a blanket statement of approval or disapproval of procedures and, at the same time, ensure that effective treatment is provided and that clients are protected from harm. Rather, each individual case must be considered on its own facts, and one must balance the need to provide effective treatment with the duty to protect an individual from harm. Protective mechanisms should be developed to ensure that when aversive techniques are advocated by staff, they are appropriate and humanely administered. These protective mechanisms can review treatment decisions and ensure that appropriate treatment is provided in the least restrictive, intrusive, and aversive manner possible (Griffith, 1980; May, Risley, Twardosz, Friedman, Bijou, & Wexler, et al., 1976, Sheldon-Wildgen & Risley, in press).

The Peer Review Committee[19]

In establishing protective mechanisms for use in programs that employ aversive, or otherwise controversial procedures, there are two separate types of concerns that need to be addressed individually. First, one must consider the professional justification of the use of any of the treatment procedures, especially those that involve aversive techniques. The critical issue here is whether the *current, relevant, published professional literature* warrants the use of a certain procedure with a particular client (Risley, 1975). To determine this, a program can establish an ongoing *peer review committee* comprised of outside, independent, and competent professionals knowledgeable in the relevant areas (e.g., the procedures used and the clients served in the program). The peer review committee could meet periodically to determine the appropriateness of the treatment procedures being utilized and to evaluate the training and supervision of the staff who are carrying out the procedures.

Members of the peer review committee should examine all aversive and controversial procedures to determine if these techniques are professionally justified, i.e., have been experimentally evaluated and have been shown to be effective as evidenced by published data in reputable journals. By examining the published data, one can determine if the procedures in use are in accord with the treatment standards found in the current relevant literature. If the procedures are not justified by the professional literature, they should not be used or should be considered experimental and, thus, appropriate procedures (e.g., obtaining informed consent) should be followed and safeguards required (e.g., review by a human rights committee). Additionally, the peer review committee can provide an educational service to the treatment program personnel by ensuring that the program administrators and staff are aware of any new procedures currently in practice in addition to providing a broader knowledge base and wider perspective of the professional literature and practices. Thus, a peer review committee can keep treatment staff up to date on new and useful procedures.

The peer review committee should meet frequently enough to examine the operation of the program and the overall effectiveness of the treatment procedures with specific clients. Members of the committee should be concerned not just about procedures in the abstract but also about individual clients, their responses to certain techniques, and their progress in the program.

Finally, committee members should be available to publicly answer any questions about the professional justification of the procedures in use or to respond to any criticisms about their use. Since the peer review committee should be an independent group, knowledgeable about *both* the program and the current, professionally justifiable procedures, with no reason to promote or support unjustifiable procedures, this committee can give assurances to parents, the community, and the public about the procedures being used and their professional justification. Normally, the peer review committee is only an advisory committee and, as such, only makes recommendations to the treatment staff; thus, the staff can then choose to comply or not. If, however, the staff continues to refuse to comply with recommendations that the committee feels are important, members of the committee should resign. Their resignation will thereby indicate that they no longer can justify to the public the procedures being used by the treatment staff.

Many community programs will find that because of their small size and the fact that they do not use controversial or aversive techniques, it is not necessary to develop and maintain a peer review committee. It is always useful and beneficial, however, to have outside, independent professional input. In cases such as these, programs may want to hire a professional consultant knowledgeable in the relevant areas or develop a relationship with professionals from a nearby college or university. The consultant could provide the needed independent expertise to determine if procedures are professionally justified as well as provide the educational function of informing staff about the most recent relevant procedures.

The Human Rights Committee[20]

The second major issue of concern is to protect clients from unnecessary intrusiveness or unpleasantness. A *human rights committee* can be established to address the issue of clients receiving humane and proper treatment or education and to ensure that due process safeguards are being provided. The human rights committee should be composed of a group of interested laypersons who do not need the professional expertise that the peer review committee members possess. In order to know what legal and ethical issues to address and what type of questions to ask, however, it is useful if human rights committee members read and become familiar with guidelines and standards, promulgated by relevant advocacy or interest groups, addressing the rights and concerns of clients and patients in treatment programs.[21] Additionally, members may find it helpful to read chapters and books on the topic of the legal and ethical issues in treatment programs (e.g., Berkler, Bible, Boles, Dietz, & Repp, 1978; Budd & Baer, 1976; Martin, 1974, 1975; Roos, 1974). Having information about the critical issues will make it easier for the members to do their job more effectively and efficiently.

A human rights committee should address both the issue of whether a client is receiving appropriate treatment and making adequate progress and the issue of ensuring that human treatment and living conditions are in existence. Often, human rights committees become preoccupied with controlling the use of controversial procedures and ensuring that all clients are treated in an ethical and humane manner and forget to consider whether a client is making any progress (i.e., learning necessary and appropriate skills). If committee members do not examine both issues, one may find that a client is allowed to exist in a pleasant, humane environment without receiving appropriate treatment.

To address the issue of receiving appropriate treatment and to operate most effectively, the human rights committee should establish a *formal* review process to evaluate and assess independently the treatment and progress of each individual client on a regular basis. It may prove most effective to assign one committee member to review and report on several clients' cases during the year. When reviewing each client's treatment, the committee member should not rely on a statement from the staff that the treatment is appropriate but rather should question the appropriateness of the staff's decision. This should not necessarily be done in an adversarial manner but rather in such a way to require the staff to justify the goals that have been established, the procedure in use, and the progress obtained. Only by critically examining these issues can the committee determine that appropriate and humane treatment has been provided. In reviewing each client, records should not be relied on solely; actual observations and interactions with the client are necessary. This committee should ensure that effective treatment is being provided for each client rather than allowing a client to merely exist in a pleasant environment where there are no controversial or aversive procedures in effect but where there is also no treatment given.

The primary purpose of a human rights committee is to provide sufficient and adequate safeguards for the clients "to insure against inhumane or improper treatment [while], at the same time, ensure that appropriate treatment is accomplished with the greatest speed possible in the least restrictive manner" (Sheldon-Wildgen & Risley, in press). When considering controversial or aversive procedures, it is the duty of the human rights committee to determine if the procedures are, indeed, objectionable if considered in the totality of the circumstances. Thus, for example the committee may not find it objectionable to shock clients who are engaging in serious self-destructive behavior that threatens their health and welfare. The committee should also determine if effective treatment could be obtained by some less intrusive or restrictive procedure. Thus, for example, although the peer review committee may have stated that a procedure is professionally justified, the human rights committee may prohibit its use in an individual case because the committee feels it is not ethical or humane to employ that procedure with a certain client. Or, the committee may allow the use of the procedure with a particular client but place severe restrictions and requirements on the staff in terms of the implementation, monitoring, and evaluation of its use.

The human rights committee must always engage in a *balancing* procedure: balancing the client's right to be free from aversive and intrusive procedures against the right to obtain effective treatment in a manner where all reasonable and less intensive treatment techniques have been considered. One might easily find that a human rights committee represents society's conscience, and in acting as society's conscience, the members must ensure that the most humane, yet effective treatment is provided for each and every client.

As with the peer review committee, some community programs may find that due to their size and the fact that they do not use any controversial or aversive procedures, it is not necessary to form a separate human rights committee if they have an interested board of directors. The board, or a subcommittee, can perform the functions of a human rights committee. In this case, the primary function would be to ensure that each client was being provided with appropriate and effective treatment in addition to a humane living environment. Finally, whether the committee's functions are served by a board of directors or a human rights committee, the members must operate and act independent of the staff in order to be a credible protective mechanism.

The establishment of credible human rights and peer review committees can protect both community programs and the clients these programs serve. By using these two protective mechanisms, no client should ever be denied the right to effective treatment, nor should any client experience abuse or unnecessary unpleasantness. These protective mechanisms will essentially allow a wider variety of techniques and procedures to be used, if approved and monitored. Thus, clients who previously may have been unable to receive appropriate and effective treatment can now do so because programs may feel more able, and may be more willing, to serve the "hard-to-treat" client. Finally, programs that establish independent, credible human rights and peer review committees and who follow these committees' recommendations will be more immune from liability than those programs that neither receive nor follow outside, independent recommendations, or input. For many programs, especially those using controversial or aversive procedures, the establishment of these committees may mean the difference between continued existence and forced closing because of the public's displeasure.

POINTS TO REMEMBER

1. Appropriate assessment instruments should be used for both the placement and evaluation of client progress. The assessment tools should be designed to give specific information about clients' behavioral assets and deficits.

2. Items on an assessment instrument should be related to the reason the person is in the program.

3. Items on the assessment instrument should not unduly invade a client's right to privacy nor should the assessment be administered in a way that invades a client's right to privacy.

4. The assessment instrument should contain items that are sensitive to change, and a rating scale that is also sensitive to change should be used when recording client behavior.

5. Reliability between observers should be taken periodically to ensure that the results obtained during an assessment are a true measure of the client's behavior.

6. Each client in a community center should have a written, individualized treatment plan.

7. The treatment plan should be developed by an interdisciplinary team so that all of the client's needs can be considered at one time. The client, if possible, should be a part of this team.

8. In developing a treatment plan, the client's assets and needs should be delineated. Following this, short- and long-term objectives should be developed and assigned priorities.

9. Goals that involve risk taking should be included (when appropriate) along with procedures to specify how the client will be taught the skills needed to be allowed to engage in risk-taking behaviors.

10. A timetable for accomplishing the goals should be specified with a statement of who is responsible for teaching each objective.

11. A description of the treatment procedure to be used to teach each skill, together with a reason for choosing this procedure, should be developed.

12. A method for evaluating whether objectives and goals have been accomplished should be provided.

13. Written records should be kept on each client. These records should include the following type of information: personal information; examination and diagnostic evaluations; individualized treatment plans; educational, employment, or vocational training history; drugs or medication prescribed and taken; use of aversive procedures; and daily log sheets.

14. All client records should be considered confidential.

15. Whenever treatment procedures expose clients to some risk or discomfort or intrude substantially into their lives, informed consent must be obtained.

16. Informed consent requires that the person consenting have the capacity to consent and that the consent is uncoerced and voluntary with full knowledge of the risks, benefits, and alternative treatments that are available. Clients should be able to withdraw their consent at any time without fear of negative repercussions.

17. Client information should not be disclosed to others who are not involved in the client's education and treatment without the consent of the client.

18. There may be instances where information is released to third parties (in order to protect them) without the consent of the client.

19. Community centers should provide a humane physical and psychological environment for the clients.

20. There are certain basic rights, including the right to a normalized living environment, the right to privacy, the right to three nutritionally adequate meals per day, the right to freedom of worship, the right to communicate and interact with others, the right to physical exercise, the right to one's own personal belongings, and the right to access to public media, that community centers should provide for all clients. In the interest of providing appropriate treatment, some of these rights may be denied, but this should only be done with the approval of a protective mechanism such as a human rights committee.

21. Clients have a right to be free from involuntary servitude, i.e., the forced and uncompensated duty to engage in institutional maintenance-type labor.

22. The least restrictive alternative should be considered in all treatment decisions.

23. Clients should be free from unnecessary aversive procedures or exposure to cruel and unusual punishment.

24. Protective mechanisms, such as human rights and peer review committees should be developed to ensure that effective treatment is provided in the least restrictive or intrusive way possible.

REFERENCES

American Association on Mental Deficiency. *Consent handbook.* Washington, DC: AAMD, 1977.

Baer, D. A case for the selective reinforcement of punishment. In C. Neuringer & J.S. Michael (eds.), *Behavior modification in clinical psychology.* New York: Appleton-Century-Crofts, 1970.

Baer, D. Let's take another look at punishment. *Psychology Today,* 1971, October, 31.

Berkler, M.S., Bible, G.H., Boles, S.M., Deitz, D.E., Repp, A.C. (eds.). *Current trends for the developmentally disabled.* Baltimore: University Park Press, 1978.

Budd, K.S., & Baer, D.M. Behavior modification and the law: Implications of recent judicial decisions. *The Journal of Psychiatry and Law,* 1976, Summer, 171–244.

Cook, J.W., Altman, D., & Haavik, S. Consent for aversive treatment: A model form. *Mental Retardation,* 1978, *16,* 47–51.

Griffith, R. An administrative perspective on guidelines for behavior modification: The creation of a legally safe environment. *the Behavior Therapist,* 1980, *3,* 5–7.

Lovaas, O.I., & Simmons, J.Q. Manipulation of self-destruction in retarded children. *Journal of Applied Behavior Analysis,* 1969, *2,* 143–157.

Martin, R. *Behavior modification: Human rights and legal responsibilities.* Champaign, IL: Research Press, 1974.

Martin, R. *Legal challenges to behavior modification.* Champaign, IL: Research Press, 1975.

Martin, R. Legal regulation of services to the developmentally disabled. In M. Berkler, G. Bible, S. Boles, D. Deitz, & A. Repp (eds.), *Current trends for the developmentally disabled.* Baltimore: University Park Press, 1978.

May, J.G., Risley, T.R., Twardosz, S., Friedman, P., Bijou, S.W., & Wexler, D., et al. *Guidelines for the use of behavioral procedures in state programs for retarded persons.* Arlington, TX: National Association for Retarded Citizens, 1976.

Morris, K.N., Kindred, R., Sheldon-Wildgen, J., & Sherman, J. Performance Assessment Scale (PAS). Lawrence: University of Kansas, 1977.

Repp, A.C. On the ethical responsibilities of institutions providing services for mentally retarded people. *Mental Retardation,* 1978, *16,* 153–156.

Repp, A., & Deitz, D. Ethical responsibilities in reductive programs for the retarded. In M. Berkler, G. Bible, S. Boles, D. Deitz, & A. Repp (eds.), *Current trends for the developmentally disabled.* Baltimore: University Park Press, 1978.

Repp, A., & Deitz, D. On the selective use of punishment—Suggested guidelines for administrators. *Mental Retardation,* 1978, *16,* 250–254.

Risley, T.R. Certify procedures not people. In W.S. Wood (ed.), *Issues in evaluating behavior modification.* Champaign, IL: Research Press, 1975.

Roos, P. Human rights and behavior modification. *Mental Retardation,* 1974, *12,* 3–6.

Schwitzgebel, R. K. Right to treatment for the mentally disabled: The need for realistic standards and objective criteria. *Harvard Civil Rights–Civil Liberties Law Review,* 1973, *8,* 513–535.

Schwitzgebel, R.L., & Schwitzgebel, R.K. *Law and psychological practice.* New York: John Wiley & Sons, 1980.

Sheldon-Wildgen, J. Rights of institutionalized mental patients: Issues, implications, and proposed guidelines. *Kansas Law Review,* 1976, *25,* 63–85.

Sheldon-Wildgen, J., & Risley, T.R. Balancing clients' rights: The establishment of Human Rights and Peer Review Committees. In A. Bellack, M. Hersen, & A. Kazdin (eds.), *International handbook of behavior modification.* New York: Plenum Press, in press.

Strouse, M. Client evaluation of teaching-counselors. Lawrence: University of Kansas, 1980.

ENDNOTES

[1]42 U.S.C. § 6011.

[2]C.A. No. 76-4423-F (E.D. Mass. Dec. 16, 1978) as reported in 3 *Mental Disability Law Reporter* 45 (1979).

[3]Massachusetts Department of Mental Health, Mental Health Community Residential Alternatives, 104 C.M.R. § 14.04(4)(e) as reported in 4 *Mental Disability Law Reporter* 126, 134 (1980).

[4]*See, e.g., id.;* Wuori v. Zitnay, No. 75-80-SD (D. Maine July 14, 1978) as reported in 2 *Mental Disability Law Reporter* 729, 732–733 (1978).

[5]*See, e.g.,* Massachusetts Department of Mental Health, Mental Health Community Residential Alternatives, 104 C.M.R. § 1403(8) as reported in 4 *Mental Disability Law Reporter* 126, 130–131 (1980).

[6]*Id.* at § 1403(8)(c)(4).

[7]*Privileged communications* is a concept that is similar to confidentiality. Confidentiality, which is usually a professional and ethical concern, protects confidences from being unethically and unprofessionally given to third parties. Privileged communications, on the other hand, legally prohibits information from being forced to be revealed in a court of law. The assumption upon which privileged communications is based is that in order for certain relationships to prosper, such as physician–patient, communications made in the course of that relationship must be free from disclosure in court. "As with confidentiality, it is feared that the threat of disclosure would unduly hamper the free-flow of communications which is essential for the relationship to exist" (Blee, B., & Sheldon-Wildgen, J. *Legal rights: A Kansas guide to developmental disabilities law,* pp. 98–99, Kansas City: University of Kansas Medical Center Printing Service, 1979). Privileged communications are usually recognized and identified by state statute. Normally, for there to be a privilege, a recognized professional relationship must exist, e.g., attorney–client, physician–patient, penitential, social worker–client, certified psychologist–client. The exception is in the case of the marital privilege.

[8]402 F. Supp. 1039 (E.D. Pa. 1975), *rev'd* 431 U.S. 119 (1977).

[9]*See, e.g.,* Stump v. Sparkman, 435 U.S. 349 (1978).

[10]Tarasoff v. Regents of the University of California, 529 P. 2d 553 (Cal. 1974), *aff'd on rehearing* 131 Cal. Rptr. 14, 551 P. 2d 334 (1976).

[11]Wyatt v. Stickney, 344 F. Supp. 373, 381; 344 F. Supp. 387, 402 (M.D. Ala. 1972).

[12]Fair Labor Standards Amendments of 1966, P.L. 89-601, 80 stat. 830 *amending* 29 U.S.C. § § 201–219 (1964) [codified at 29 U.S.C. § § 203, 206–207, 213–214, 216, 218, 225 (1970)].

[13]367 F. Supp. 808 (D.D.C. 1973), *aff'd* 494 F. 2d 100 (8th Cir. 1974).

[14]426 U.S. 833 (1976).

[15]29 U.S.C. § 214 (1970).

[16]Massachusetts Department of Mental Health, Mental Health Community Residential Alternatives, 104 C.M.R. § 14.03(7)(a)(1) as reported in 4 *Mental Disability Law Reporter* 126, 130 (1980).

[17]Although specific aversive procedures are not discussed in detail in this book, community center staff should acquaint themselves with the different behavior reduction techniques that are available for use. There are several different techniques that have been described elsewhere in detail and that are used extensively. The following is a brief list of behavior reduction techniques, ranging generally from the least aversive to the most (although this depends on the manner in which the procedure is administered and each client's individual response to the procedure):

a. Reinforcement of an appropriate behavior; reinforcement of an incompatible behavior; differential reinforcement of an other behavior (DRO)
b. Extinction (i.e., ignoring the behavior)
c. Giving verbal negative feedback (e.g., saying "No" or giving descriptive negative feedback)
d. Response cost (e.g., losing points, losing tokens, or having fines imposed)
e. Timeout (for brief periods of time)
f. Overcorrection, including restitutional overcorrection and positive practice
g. Application of a physical aversive stimulus (e.g., spanking)

[18]For example, ignoring an inappropriate behavior may seem to be a fairly benign type of a procedure. If the inappropriate behavior was banging one's head or banging the head of another child, however, one might not consider that ignoring the behavior would be the best type of procedure to decrease the behavior. In this example, ignoring the behavior could expose the child or others to harm. Consider, also, positive procedures, for example, reinforcing a behavior. If the behavior to be reinforced, however, is the aggressive play of a male child who presently enjoys playing with dolls, there may be some questions. Additionally, one could not argue that the procedure did not expose the child to some type of harm, especially if after being reinforced for being more aggressive, the child started to demonstrate delinquent behaviors. In both of these cases, either because the procedure was an inappropriate one to use with a particular behavior or because the goals of the program were inappropriately chosen, the client could experience negative or aversive results.

[19]For an in-depth discussion of the functions of a peer review committee and the procedure to follow to establish one see, Sheldon-Wildgen, J., & Risley, T.R. Balancing clients' rights: The establishment of Human Rights and Peer Review Committees. In A. Bellack, M. Hersen, & A. Kazdin (eds.), *International handbook of behavior modification.* New York: Plenum Press, in press.

[20]For detailed procedures to follow in establishing a human rights committee with explicit instructions on the procedures the committee can use to operate most effectively see, Sheldon-Wildgen, J., & Risley, T.R. Balancing clients' rights: The establishment of Human Rights and Peer Review Committees. In A. Bellack, M. Hersen, & A. Kazdin (eds.), *International handbook of behavior modification.* New York: Plenum Press, in press.

[21]*See, e.g.*: National Society for Autistic Children. *White paper on behavior modification with autistic children.* NSAC, 1975; May, J.G., Risley, T.R., Twardosz, S., Friedman, P., Bijuo, S.W., & Wexler, D., et al. *Guidelines for the use of behavioral procedures in state programs for retarded persons.* Arlington, TX: NARC, 1976; Joint Commission on Accreditation of Hospitals. *Standards for services for developmentally disabled individuals.* Chicago, IL: JCAH, 1978; National Teaching-Family Association. *Standards of ethical conduct.* Boys Town, NE: NaTFA, 1979.

9

CONCLUDING
RECOMMENDATIONS

Currently, there exist considerable social, political, judicial, and professional pressures to provide services for disabled individuals, troubled juveniles, and other dependent populations in small community-based service agencies rather than in large remote institutions. Increasing numbers of professionals and paraprofessionals, with various educational backgrounds and skill competencies, are becoming involved with the development and maintenance of community centers. In order to help ensure the success of these new service agencies, extra care must be taken in the planning and development stages. The proponents and planners of a community center must view their work with sufficient detachment and objectivity to permit the recognition of potential problem areas and to introduce the necessary modifications.

This book has been written to alert community center developers and administrators to the legal responsibility that the community center owes its clients, staff, and the general public to protect them from unnecessary harm. In the preceding chapters, the legal principles surrounding damage lawsuits were explained, several potentially hazardous situations were discussed, examples of lawsuits were illustrated, and numerous recommendations, designed to ensure that appropriate treatment is provided and to help prevent injuries and reduce the degree of damage resulting from an accident, were presented. Of course, these recommendations may need to be modified before they will be suitable for adoption by a particular community center. Some of the factors that should be considered when developing modifications are the size of the community center, the activities in which the center is engaging, the abilities and limitations of the clients and staff, the financial resources of the center, and the kinds and availability of resources within the community at large.

Independent of how careful and safe a community program is, there is always the possibility of lawsuits being brought with potential liability imposed. The risk of this liability can be minimized by following the recommendations outlined in this book. Additionally, there is one final recommendation that, if followed, could reduce the risk of liability. This recommendation involves developing a policies and procedures manual for each community center and ensuring that staff comply with these policies and procedures. The manual should address *all* the issues covered in this book including safety policies, client and staff personnel policies, and treatment procedures. Under each topic, the administrators should state what the community center's policy is on the subject and exactly what the staff should do to be in compliance with these policies.

Having these policies and procedures establishes an explicit standard of care for the center. In lawsuits, courts usually attempt to determine what the ordinary standard of care for similarly situated programs would be. Thus, the more the policies and procedures follow a standard that is normally used in community centers, the higher the probability is that a court will find that the standard of care established in these policies and procedures is appropriate. (Keep in mind, however, that a negligent standard of care used by all, or most, community centers will not protect any of the centers from liability.)

If a lawsuit is brought against a community center and the center has developed a policies and procedures manual, the court will attempt to determine two things: was the standard of care established by these policies and procedures an appropriate standard and were the staff members following these policies and procedures when the claim, leading to the lawsuit, arose. The issue of the standard of care has been addressed in the previous paragraph. The issue of whether the staff members were following the policies and procedures at the time when the claim arose is a factual question on which the court will hear evidence. The court may find that the behavior of the staff was not in compliance with the policies and procedures and that the administration, although using appropriate methods to monitor staff behavior, did not know that the staff was in noncompliance. Finding these facts, the court may hold that a staff member was negligent for not complying with the policies and procedures and was acting outside the scope of his or her employment. Thus, liability may be imposed on the staff member individually but not on the community center. If the staff member was acting outside the specified allowable procedures but did so with the knowledge and implicit approval of the administration, liability can additionally be imposed on the community center. If the staff members were in compliance with the policies and procedures but the standard of care found in the policies was too low, liability can be imposed on the community center. Finally, the best protection is offered to community centers whose staff comply with policies and procedures that set a reasonable and appropriate standard of care. As previously outlined, there is no certain way that a community center can avoid the possibility of lawsuits and legal involvement. Following these recommendations and keeping abreast of legal mandates, however, should offer a great amount of protection.

One of the purposes of this book has been to present some of the essential information that should be known by individuals involved with the development and maintenance of community centers. It is hoped that the administrators and the planners of community centers who read this book will use the information in a constructive manner to shape a more effective overall program to meet their clients' needs. No guarantee can be made, however, that all of the measures necessary for creating a safe, successful community center are contained within this book (or any other publication), or that additional measures may not be required under particular or exceptional circumstances. It is hoped, however, that the described general guidelines, which were developed after a careful examination of available resources on the issues, will help community center administrators and planners develop additional measures to meet their center's particular needs. Readers must also remember that the statutes, administrative regulations, and case law that govern the operation of the various community centers are dynamic in nature, changing (although sometimes quite slowly) to meet the demands of society. One of the most effective ways that those persons concerned with community centers can help to guide the policymakers is to develop and implement reasoned professional policies through a continuous reassessment of those professional policies in light of changing conditions.

Appendix A

Understanding the Law and Using Legal References

In order to understand fully the impact of the judicial decisions and legislative mandates described in this book, it may be useful to become familiar with the sources of law and the effect that these laws have in different jurisdictions.

SOURCES OF LAW

There are two primary sources of law. The first is based on the doctrine of *stare decisis,* which essentially means that when a *"court* has once laid down a principle of law as applicable to a certain state of facts, it will adhere to that principle, and apply it to all future cases where facts are substantially the same"[1] (emphasis added). Thus, the doctrine allows for the use of court decisions as precedents for other courts addressing the same or similar questions of law (Jacobstein & Mersky, 1973). This type of law is often referred to as common law or "unwritten" law and is found in law or court reports which publish the decisions of courts. The primary lawmakers in *case law* are judges. Case law should be distinguished from a codified body of law which can be found in legislative enactments.

The second source of law, therefore, involves the written law of legislatures. The acts of legislatures, which either command or prohibit certain things, can be found in statutes, and the primary lawmakers of *codified law* are legislators. In addition to statutes, there are also such things as ordinances and administrative regulations which are promulgated by regulatory agencies, bureaus, or departments that have received authority from legislatures or judges to enact administrative law.

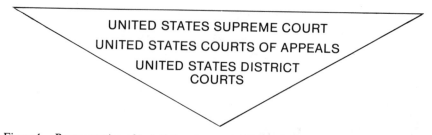

Figure 1. Representation of jurisdictional power within the federal court system.

THE POWER OF THE LAW

Laws, whether they come from court reports or from statutes, govern only those residents within the territory over which the court or legislative body has jurisdiction or power. Thus, it is important to know, generally, the hierarchy within the legal systems.

Case Law

With respect to case law, there are two court systems: the federal system and the state or local system. Figure 1 illustrates the descending amount of jurisdiction or power that different courts have within the federal system. The United States Supreme Court issues decisions that are law for the entire United States. The United States Supreme Court is considered the ultimate court of last resort because all decisions are binding and no appeals can be made from this Court. Below the Supreme Court of the United States are the United States Courts of Appeals. The United States is divided into ten geographic areas, or circuits, plus the District of Columbia. For each circuit, which encompasses several states, there is a United States Court of Appeals, and the judges in each circuit hear appeals of cases only from the states within their circuit. Any decision from one of the United States Courts of Appeals is law for all those within the particular circuit, unless appealed and reversed by the United States Supreme Court. Below the United States Courts of Appeals are the United States District Courts. These are the trial courts within the federal system.[2]

A trial court is the forum where parties actually meet in court for the first time in an attempt to resolve their differences. In a trial court, witnesses are called to testify and evidence is presented in an attempt to make a determination on the *facts* of the case. Once a final decision has been reached in a trial court, it may be allowed to be appealed to an appellate court (e.g., in the federal system, to one of the United States Courts of Appeals and then to the United States Supreme Court). When a case is heard at the appellate level, the actual parties are usually not present nor are witnesses normally called to testify. Rather, the attorneys involved in the case submit briefs detailing any question of the law that has been appealed. Appellate court judges make their decisions based on these briefs and the presentations that the attorneys make.

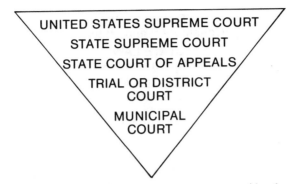

UNITED STATES SUPREME COURT
STATE SUPREME COURT
STATE COURT OF APPEALS
TRIAL OR DISTRICT
COURT
MUNICIPAL
COURT

Figure 2.   An example of the hierarchy within a state court system. Also shown is the ultimate jurisdictional power of the Supreme Court of the United States.

State court systems are parallel to the federal system, with the United States Supreme Court being the ultimate court of last resort. Different states have various names for the different courts within the hierarchy; an example of a state hierarchy is found in Figure 2. All states have a state court of last resort. This court may be referred to as the State Supreme Court or the State Court of Appeals. This state court of last resort normally hears appeals from lower court decisions and issues law that governs all residents within the state; law from this court is final law unless appealed to and reversed by the Supreme Court of the United States. Beneath the highest court in the state, there may be lower appellate courts, such as a State Court of Appeals. These courts hear appeals from trial courts, and any decisions coming from these appellate courts are law for all people within the state unless appealed to and reversed by the highest appellate court, the court of last resort, within the state. Below these appellate courts are trial courts where initial proceedings are usually brought. Decisions from these trial courts have the effect of law only for those persons living within the trial district, e.g., the city, county, or part thereof. There may be even lower courts, such as municipal, juvenile, or traffic courts.

Codified Law

With respect to codified law, that is, law enacted by legislatures, Figure 3 illustrates the descending amount of jurisdictional power given to various constitutions and statutes. The United States Constitution is the governing document and the supreme law of the United States. It provides the authority from which federal and state laws can be enacted. Federal laws passed by Congress provide laws governing all people within the United States unless specifically exempted. State constitutions provide the law of the land for a particular state, so long as it does not conflict with the federal Constitution. State statutes passed by state legislatures govern the people within a state. Finally, there are local charters that allow cities and municipalities to exist as governmental bodies with the ability to enact local ordinances governing only people within the particular municipality or city.[3]

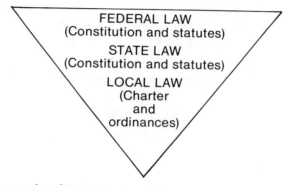

Figure 3. Representation of jurisdictional power given to various constitutions and statutes.

FINDING THE LAW

Many people, unfamiliar with legal research, may believe that finding the law, in case reports or in statutes, is a difficult task. It need not be if one understands the legal sytem of reporting cases and statutory law. The following generally describes where cases and codified law can be found.

Case Law

When one cites a particular case, one always gives the name of the court report where the case is published; the name of this reporter is often given in initials. Preceding the initials is the number of the volume of the reporter where the case can be found. Sometimes a numeral, such as 2d, follows the initials; this indicates an additional series, such as a second series, in that reporter system. Immediately following the initials is the page number where the text of the case begins in the reporter. Depending on the reporting system, additional information may follow, such as additional reporters where the case may be found. In parentheses, there may be further information identifying the court where the case was heard in addition to the year in which the case was held. Thus, for example, 344 F. Supp. 373 (M.D. Ala. 1972) refers to the 344th volume of *The Federal Supplement,* page 373. This case was heard in the United States District Court in the Middle District in Alabama in 1972. The cite 503 F.2d 1305 (5th Cir. 1974), for example, refers to page 1305 of the 503rd volume of *The Federal Reporter.* This case was heard in the Fifth Circuit United States Court of Appeals in 1974.

Listed below are common sources for federal case law.

Cases	Reporter Series	Abbreviation
Supreme Court	Supreme Court Reporter	U.S.
U.S. Courts of Appeals	The Federal Reporter	F.
	(Second Series)	(F. 2d)
U.S. District Courts	The Federal Supplement	F. Supp.

State cases are often reported by a reporter system within the state, such as the Kansas Reports. A cite to those reports, for example, would look like this: 157 Kan. 125 (1943). State cases are also reported by a larger national reporting system, which divides the United States into regions. Several states may be included in one regional reporter. The regional reporters include the following:

Reporter Series	Abbreviation
Atlantic	A.
California	Cal.
New York Supplement	N.Y.S.
Northeastern	N.E.
Northwestern	N.W.
Pacific	P.
Southern	S.
Southeastern	S.E.
Southwestern	S.W.

As with the federal reporter series, a numeral, such as 2d, that follows the abbreviation indicates an additional series, such as a second series, in that particular system.

There are also specialized abstracting services and reporters that publish summaries of legal developments in different areas such as mental health law. Often, these reporters will give summaries (or in some cases, the entire text) of lower trial court decisions that are not published in the standard reporter systems. One such reporting system, which is an excellent source for legal developments in the mental health area is a publication by the American Bar Association, the Commission on the Mentally Disabled, entitled *The Mental Disability Law Reporter*. The authors found this reporter quite useful, and it can be obtained by writing to: Mental Disability Law Reporter, American Bar Association, 1800 M Street, N.W., Washington, D.C. 20036.

Codified Law

Codified federal laws can be found in the United States Constitution (U.S. Const.) or in the statutes of the United States, the United States Code (U.S.C.). Codified state laws can be found in the state constitutions (e.g., Kan. Const.) and in the state laws (e.g., Kansas Statutes Annotated, Kan. Stat. Ann.). Federal regulations can be found in the Federal Register (Fed. Reg.) or the Code of Federal Regulations (C.F.R.). Regulations promulgated at the state level can be found in each state's published regulations, for example, the Code of Massachusetts Regulations.

Those interested in obtaining more information about legal research may want to read J.M. Jacobstein and R.M. Mersky's *Pollack's Fundamentals of Legal Research* (4th Ed.) (The Foundation Press), M.O. Price and H. Bitner's *Effective Legal Research* (Little, Brown & Co.), M. Cohen's *Legal Research in a Nutshell* (West Publishing Co.), or *West's Law Finder* (West Publishing Co.).

REFERENCE

Jacobstein, J.M., & Mersky, R.M. *Pollack's fundamentals of legal research* (4th ed.). Mineola, NY: The Foundation Press, Inc., 1973.

ENDNOTES

[1]Moore v. City of Albany, 98 N.Y. 396, 410 (1895).

[2]There are other lower courts in the federal judicial system, such as the United States Court of Claims, the United States Court of Customs and Patent Appeals, and the United States Court of Customs. For the purposes of this book, it is not necessary to go into their jurisdictional powers.

[3]Regulations, promulgated by regulatory agencies, can be enacted at the federal, state, and local level.

APPENDIX B

SAFETY CHECKLISTS

National Commission on Safety Education. *Checklist on safety education in your school* and *School safety checklist: Administration, instruction, prevention.* National Education Association, 1201 Sixteenth St., N.W., Washington, D.C.

OSHA inspection survey guide and survey report. Management Research and Development Institute, 321 E. William Street, Wichita, KS 67202.

Building safety checklist. In D. C. Seaton, H. J. Stack, & B. I. Loft. *Administration and supervision of safety education.* New York: The Macmillan Company, 1969, pp. 70–73.

The following checklists are available from the National Safety Council, 425 North Michigan Avenue, Chicago, IL 60611:

School inspection short checklist of the National Fire Protection Association

National standard student resident fire safety checklist (with National Fire Protection Association)

Inventory of safety check points in business machine classrooms and offices (with American Vocational Association)

National standard school shop inspections checklist (with American Vocational Association)

National standard checklist for teaching home safety (with American Vocational Association)

Food service safety checklist to locate hazards

INDEX